IMAGES
*of America*

# PROGRESO

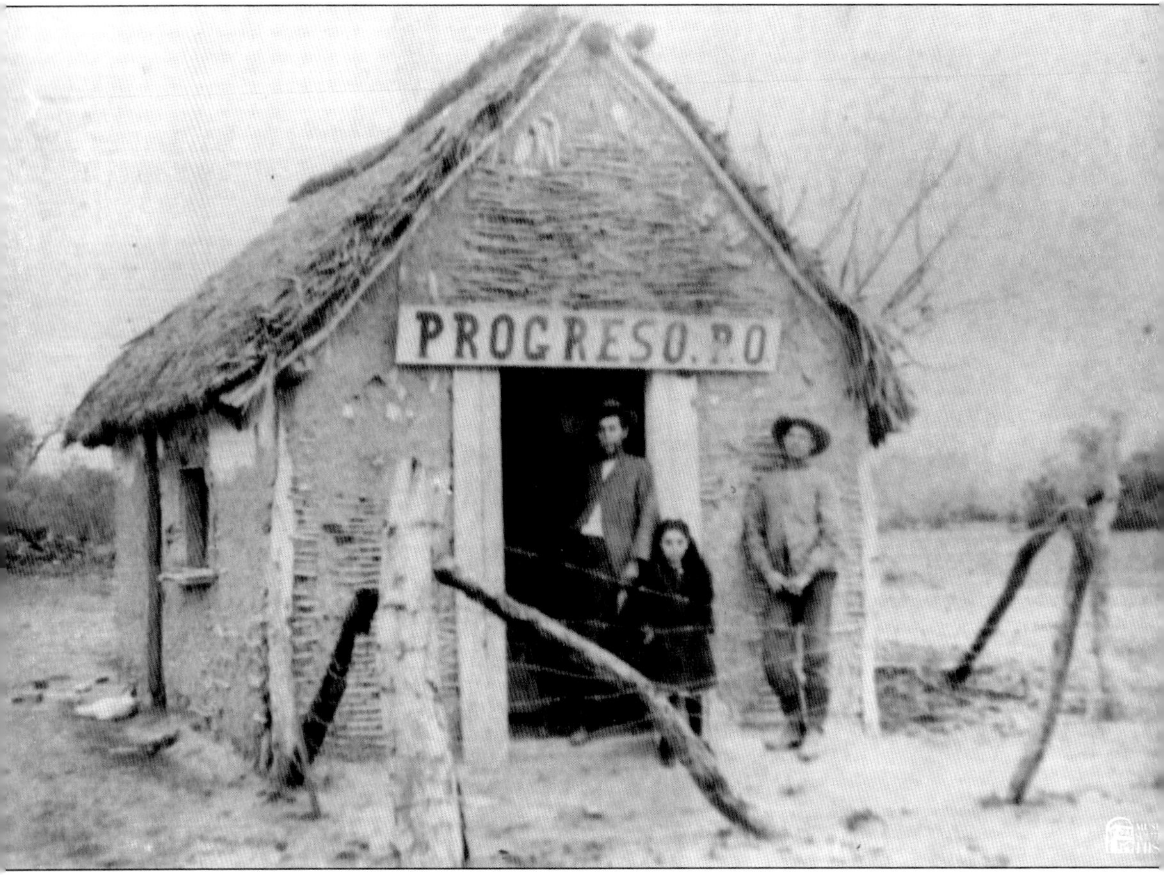


Built in 1905, Progreso's first post office was a small adobe building with a dirt floor and a roof thatched with cattails. This 1906 photograph shows the town's first postmaster, Abraham Neumann Smith, his son Matthew Curry Smith (right), and his niece Irene Zamora Watkins. At the time, mail was received by stagecoach or steamship, and Smith distributed the correspondence on horseback. (Courtesy Museum of South Texas History.)

**On the Cover:** This area along the Rio Grande has been highly contested by both Mexico and the United States, with the border shifting throughout history. Today the dividing line sits somewhere in the middle of the moving waters of the Rio Grande, perhaps a symbol of the inseparable Mexican American culture found in Progreso and the Lower Rio Grande Valley. This photograph captures that international flavor and the character of the people who have called this area home for generations. But most importantly, it introduces a man who helped shape the history of the town. According to William C. Cain family records, Al Cain (left) negotiated a 99-year land lease with the owners of Toluca Ranch for the establishment of the Progreso International Bridge. It is believed that without that land lease, the plans to build a bridge at Progreso would have been less likely. Without that bridge crossing, Progreso would not attract hundreds of thousands of tourists every year; instead it would simply be another town north of the Rio Grande. Also in this photograph are two unidentified men (center and right). (Courtesy William C. Cain family.)

IMAGES
*of America*

# PROGRESO

Rosa Flores Dee

ARCADIA
PUBLISHING

ISBN 978-0-7385-7947-4

Published by Arcadia Publishing
Charleston, South Carolina

Printed in the United States of America

Library of Congress Control Number: 2010928649

For all general information, please contact Arcadia Publishing:
Telephone 843-853-2070
Fax 843-853-0044
E-mail sales@arcadiapublishing.com
For customer service and orders:
Toll-Free 1-888-313-2665

Visit us on the Internet at www.arcadiapublishing.com

*To my parents, Juan and Rosa Flores, for climbing levees with me in search of Progreso's history; and to my husband, Nicholas Dee, for supporting my many projects.*

# Contents

# ACKNOWLEDGMENTS

Working on this book has been an adventure. I climbed levees in search of clues and visited the homes of Progreso natives in search of historical photographs.

Very warm and special thanks go to Soledad G. Rodriguez for giving me complete access to a collection of scrapbooks she inherited from Dorothy Thompson, one of Progreso's pioneer teachers. The history recorded within those pages came to life with the stories Soledad shared with me in her living room.

Very special thanks to Patricia Fernandez Mayers and Melba Ayala; both committed their personal time to the promotion of this book. Patricia also shared her collection of Toluca Ranch photographs, which make up most of the Toluca Ranch chapter of this book.

My mother and I spent hours at the archives of the University of Texas-Pan American library. I found an important clue leading to one of Progreso's most famous investors, Capt. James A. Baker, from the law firm Baker Botts. After that, I visited the archives at Rice University in Houston, but I couldn't find any reference to Progreso within the collection. So I requested the articles of incorporation from the Texas secretary of state and verified Captain Baker was indeed one of investors of the Progreso Development Company and part of the rich history of my hometown.

From there, Tootie Madden, the Weslaco Museum, Jack Holcomb, Jay Madden, Martha Marquez, Barbara Stokes, Esteban Lomas, Buddy and Gretchen Hovda, the Museum of South Texas History, Gloria C. Garcia, Hidalgo and Cameron Counties Irrigation District No. 9, Mary Angela Freeman, Archie Miles, Lala Galvan, Judy Beall, Olga and Pancho Galvan, Martha E. Ramos, and Dale Roberts helped me gather the fabulous photographs in this book.

But a history book can not be called such without the knowledge and understanding of Progreso's past. So a very, very special thanks to Frances Isbell for having an incalculable passion for the history of the Rio Grande Valley and for fact-checking the text of this book.

I also want to thank Arcadia Publishing for this opportunity—especially Kristie Kelly and Hannah Carney for being such amazing resources.

Unless otherwise noted, the introduction portion of this book is from the following sources: *Progreso, Hidalgo County, Toluca Ranch, Florencio Saenz Homestead, Spiderweb Railroad, El Horcon Tract,* and *Rio Rico*, Library Archives and Special Collections, The University of Texas-Pan American.

# INTRODUCTION

On July 4, 1776, when the United States declared its independence, Reynosa chief justice Capt. Juan Jose Hinojosa asked the Spanish crown for 53,141 acres of land that included present-day Progreso, Texas.

Hinojosa and other members of his family worked most of the land under Spanish and then Mexican rule until it became Texas territory after the Mexican-American War. According to Fernandez family records, Don Antonio Cano, a Spaniard, purchased thousands of acres of land, which included present-day Progreso, from Hinojosa's heirs. In 1830, Cano established the Campacuas Ranch on his land and married Doña Mauricia Fernandez. Cano died in 1877 and his widow hired Florencio Saenz, a direct descendant of Hinojosa, to help her manage the ranch. Saenz fell in love with one of the Cano daughters, Sostenes, and the couple got married in 1879. Florencio and Sostenes Saenz founded the Toluca Ranch the following year, 1880. The ranch is just south of Old Military Highway, a road established after the Civil War. Seanz erected St. Joseph's Church in 1899, built a Spanish-style hacienda in 1903, and established a public school in 1906.

In 1896, Saenz requested a U.S. Post Office with the name Toluca; the Post Office Department, however, assigned the name Progreso to the site. Also in 1896, Pedro Solis Champion established the San Pedro Cemetery, according to family members. It is located just west of Farm to Market Road (FM) No. 88 and south of Military Highway. A year later, Pedro and Gumecinda Champion moved to the San Pedro Ranch. The Champions sold the property to the American Rio Grande Land and Irrigation Company in 1902.

Under the name Progreso, which is Spanish for "progress," the town received mail by stagecoach or steamship, and its postmaster distributed the correspondence on horseback. During this time, traveling to and from Mexico was unrestricted, and the Mexican peso was the established local currency.

Subtropical weather and cheap land attracted sugar plantation developers, including W. P. Withers. His Llano Grande Plantation hauled sugarcane by wagon over unpaved roads 7 miles north to Llano Grande (now Weslaco), a stop on the St. Louis, Brownsville, and Mexico Railway.

From 1913 to 1916, at the time of World War I, Mexicans hoping to regain territory lost during the Mexican-American War raided the area of Progreso. To preserve the peace, the 6th U.S. Cavalry occupied Toluca Ranch for over a year.

Progreso experienced a boom in 1926, when the San Benito and Rio Grande Valley Railway added Progreso to its system. The Missouri Pacific Railroad bought out the San Benito and Rio Grande Valley Railway in 1924. The new depot gave farmers assurance that crops would make it to market quickly.

The Progreso Independent School District was established in 1928. The school's coach, teacher, and superintendent, Dorothy Thompson, gave the softball team its mascot, the Mighty Red Ants. The first school building was named after Bonnie George Kramer, a teacher who commuted by buggy to Progreso from Mercedes. Shortly after a disastrous freeze, the Llano Grande Plantation sold its property to the newly formed Progreso Development Company. The company was created in 1927 by Capt. James A. Baker, senior partner of the powerful Houston law firm Baker, Botts, Parker, and Garwood (presently Baker Botts); C. M. Malone; C. O. Miles; Ennis Cargil; and R. B. Creager. Their goal was to sell land lots.

Locals say that the Progreso Development Company entertained buyers from as far north as Chicago by taking them to Rio Rico, Mexico, just 5 miles downriver. The small Mexican village offered dog races, dance halls, cantinas, and entertainment not available in Texas during Prohibition. The rumor is that infamous gangster Al Capone had an interest in Rio Rico. After northern investors realized that land was cheap, that Mexico was fun, and that the area had mild winters, they lined up to buy property in Progreso. However, the market crash of 1929, the closing of the so-called Spiderweb Railroad depot in 1931, and the disastrous hurricane of 1933 took the Progreso Development Company into bankruptcy.

At about the time of World War II, the citrus industry in Progreso was booming. With the cost of land at an all-time low, farmers like Jack Holcomb purchased 20 acres of land at $20 an acre. But two devastating freezes—one in 1949 and another in 1951—killed the citrus industry. Holcomb said area farmers stopped growing citrus and instead grew vegetables and cotton with the help of Mexicans working under the Bracero Program, an agreement between the United States and Mexico that allowed Mexican workers to take agricultural jobs in America. At the peak of the harvest season, Holcomb alone hired between 1,500 and 1,800 people. In the 1950s, Arthur Beckwith established Beckwith Farms and purchased the Progreso depot from the Missouri Pacific Railroad; he turned it into office space.

According to the William C. Cain family, the B and P Bridge Company sold stock to finance construction of the Progreso International Bridge in 1953. Before that, the Cains built the iconic Rio Rico Bridge in 1928 that connected Thayer, near Mercedes, to Rio Rico. But the flood of 1941 destroyed the foundation of the suspension bridge and washed it away. About a decade later, the Cains built the Progreso International Bridge that connects Progreso, Texas, to Nuevo Progreso, a suburb of Rio Bravo, Tamaulipas, Mexico. The area on the Mexican side of the river was not developed, so the board of the B and P Bridge Company came up with $25,000 and convinced Arturo Arredondo, a former Rio Rico store owner, to establish the first restaurant on the Mexican side of the bridge. After Arturo's Restaurant opened, business in Nuevo Progreso started booming. Today the area, also known as Las Flores, Spanish for "The Flowers," attracts hundreds of thousands of tourists every year. The town holds Tourist Day annually in honor of winter Texans, tourists who migrate to Texas from cold northern states for the mild South Texas winter.

In 1968, Progreso farmers created the Progreso Co-op Gin, Inc. Today about 28 farmers make up the co-op and grow vegetables, cotton, sugarcane, sorghum, corn, and grain in Progreso and other parts of the Rio Grande Valley.

Progreso and Progreso Lakes had an inseparable history until the two communities incorporated in 1991 and 1979, respectively. Progreso Lakes has remained a residential and agricultural community. Lion Lake was named after a dead mountain lion that was found on the site. Moon Lake was named for its crescent moon shape. Most Progreso Development Company investors owned homes in Progreso Lakes.

In the 1980s, the Progreso International Bridge was expanded to make more room for customs authorities. Progreso High School students attended Weslaco and Mercedes High Schools until construction of the first Progreso High School in 1985.

On November 5, 1991, the City of Progreso incorporated. In 2000, the total population was 3,205, and the majority of its citizens were Mexican American. Today the town has several churches, a post office, grocery stores, restaurants, laundromats, and agribusinesses. And while Progreso has come a long way, the flavors of the Mexican American traditions that have surrounded this border town have never changed. The images within the pages of this book document that rich history.

# *One*

# Toluca Ranch

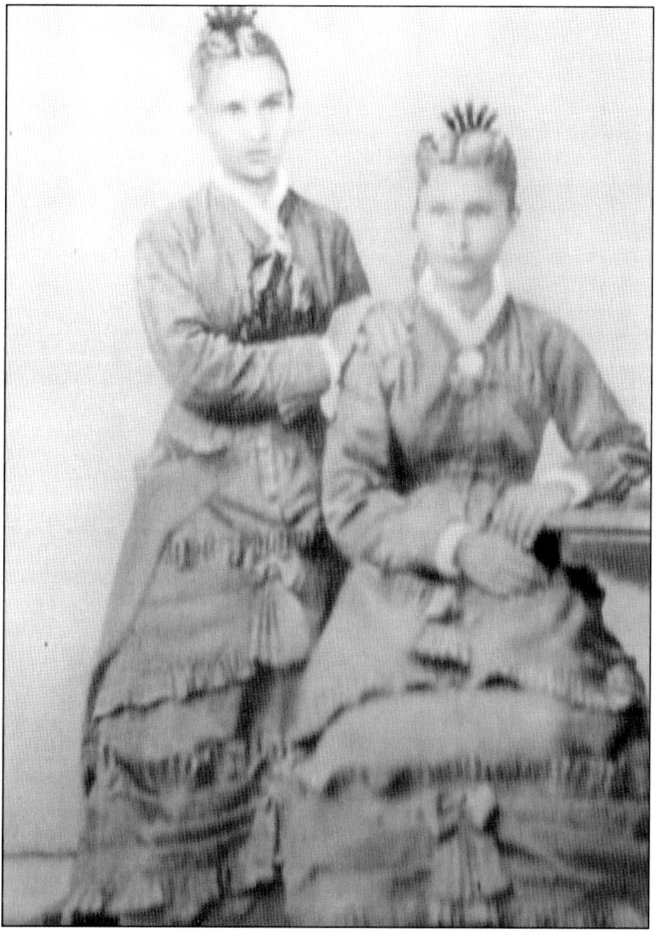

This is a photograph of young Sostenes Cano (sitting) and her sister Gumecinda Cano (standing). Gumecinda Cano is the mother of Manuela Champion, the young girl Florencio Saenz and Sostenes Cano adopted in 1883 after establishing the iconic Toluca Ranch. Manuela later married Amador Fernandez. The Fernandez family is the present-day owner of Toluca Ranch. (Courtesy Patricia Fernandez Mayers.)

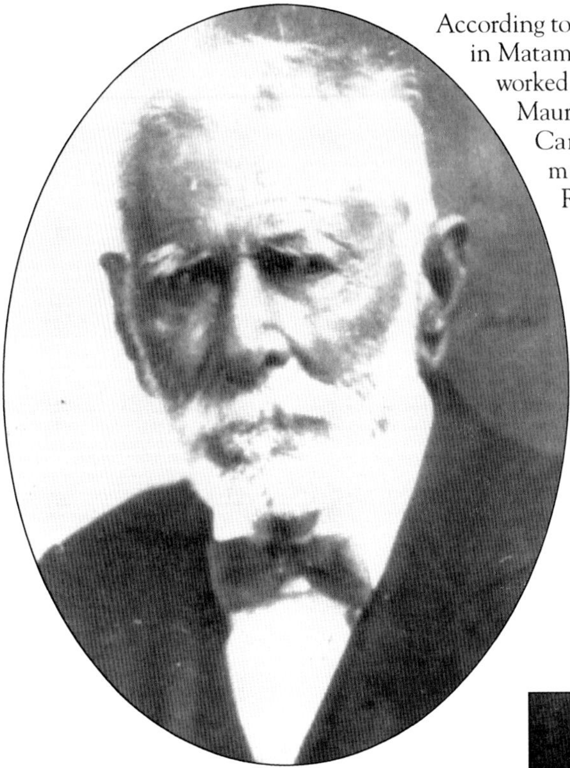

According to family records, Florencio Saenz was born in Matamoros, Mexico, on October 7, 1836. Saenz worked for the owner of Campacuas Ranch, Doña Mauricia Cano, and fell in love with Sostenes Cano, one of her daughters. The couple married in 1879 and established Toluca Ranch in 1880. Saenz became a prominent merchant and a pioneer farmer. He died on December 27, 1927, in Mercedes. Don Florencio, as he was called, liked to travel to Europe and spoke French fluently. (Courtesy Patricia Fernandez Mayers.)

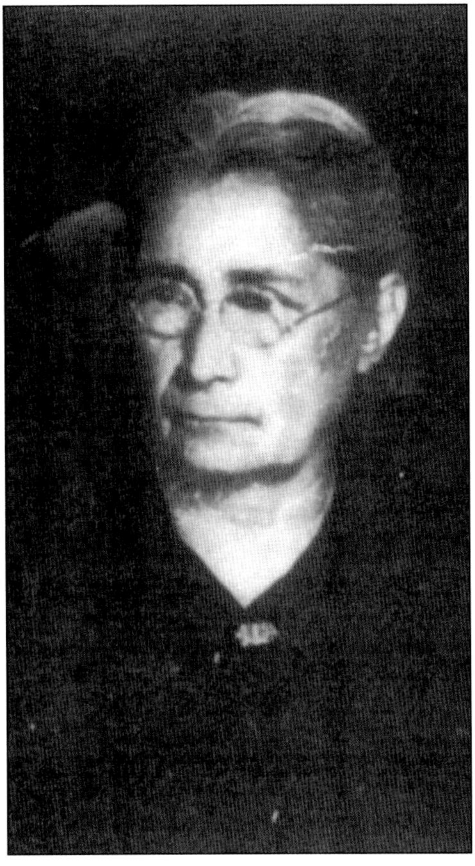

Sostenes Cano was the daughter of Don Antonio and Doña Mauricia Cano of Campacuas Ranch. She married Florencio Saenz in 1879. They produced no children but adopted their three-month-old niece, Manuela Champion, in January 1883. Doña Sostenes, as she was called, was born at Campacuas Ranch on October 7, 1858. She died on August 15, 1944, in Mercedes. The Saenz couple is buried in the family cemetery on Campacuas Ranch. (Courtesy Patricia Fernandez Mayers.)

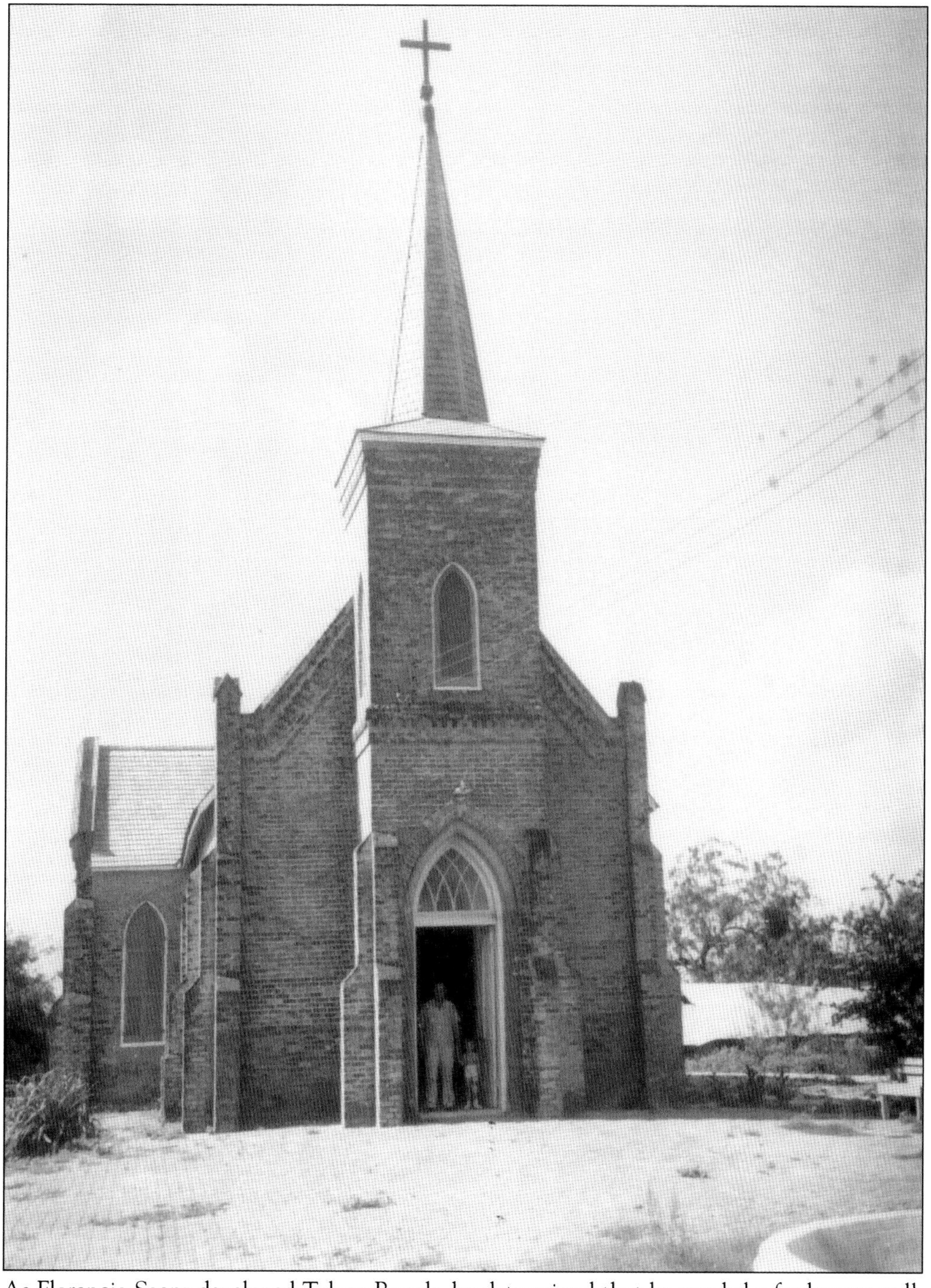

As Florencio Saenz developed Toluca Ranch, he determined that he needed a freshwater well. As his efforts to find water went sour, he promised to build a chapel if he found freshwater at Toluca Ranch. His prayers were answered in 1899, and Saenz erected St. Joseph's Church that same year. His grandson Jimmy Fernandez and his great-granddaughter Florence are seen in this 1951 photograph, standing in the doorway of the church. St. Joseph's Church was designated a Texas Historical Landmark in 1965. (Courtesy Museum of South Texas History.)

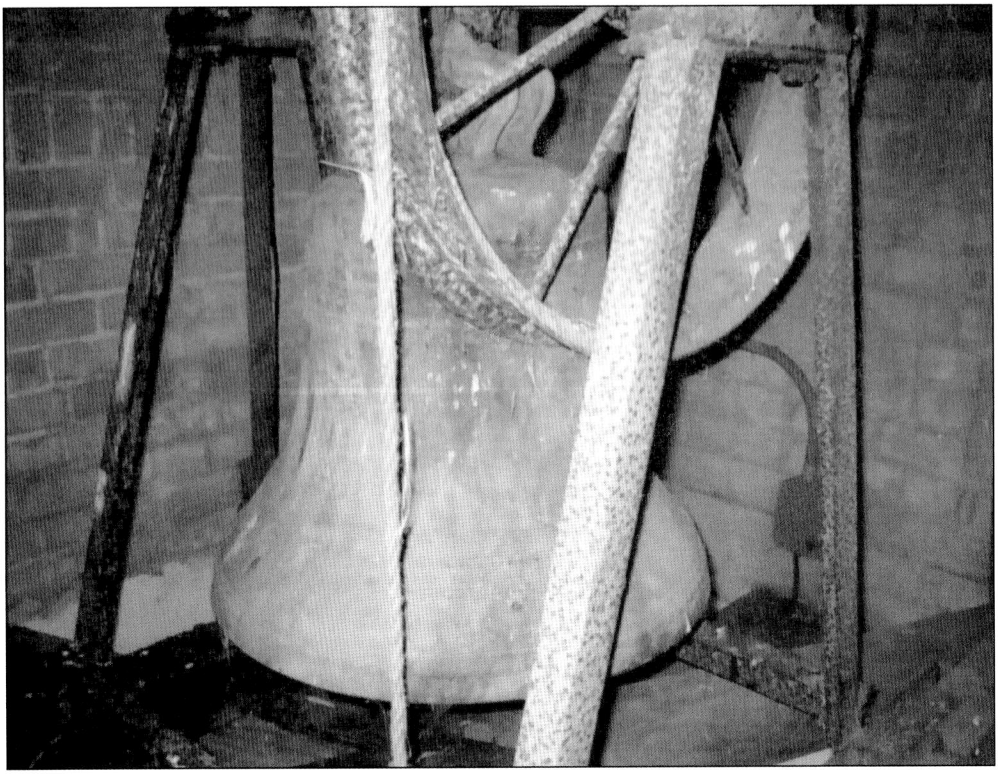

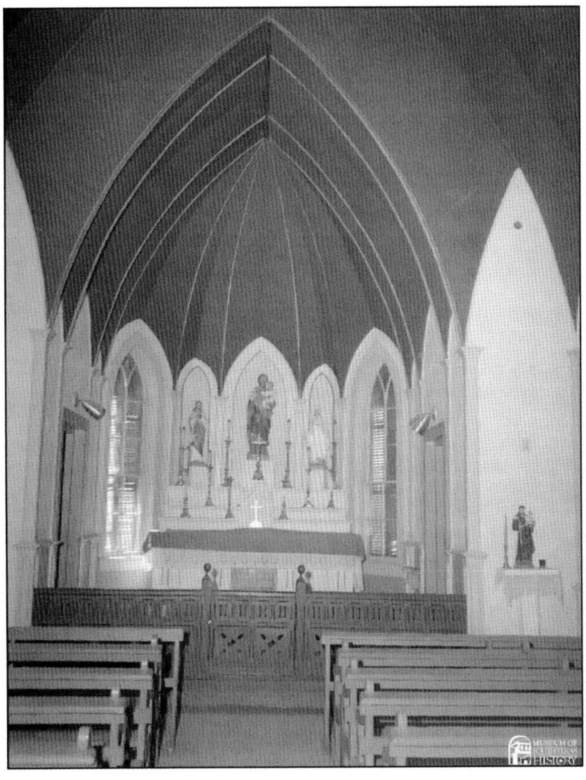

Family records show that Florencio Saenz purchased this silver-lined bell at the World Exposition in Paris, France. The bell sparked his interest after it won a second-place honor for its resonance. So Saenz imported the bell and placed it inside St. Joseph's Church. It was later moved to Our Lady of Mercy Catholic Church in Mercedes. (Courtesy Patricia Fernandez Mayers.)

Good taste meets creativity inside St. Joseph's Church. The walls are made of brick, and the altar is made of imported Spanish wood. Canvas sails, salvaged from Port Isabel, were stretched from the corners of the church to the center to create a magnificent ceiling. The chapel was dedicated and placed under the patronage of San Jose, the patron saint of laborers. (Courtesy Museum of South Texas History.)

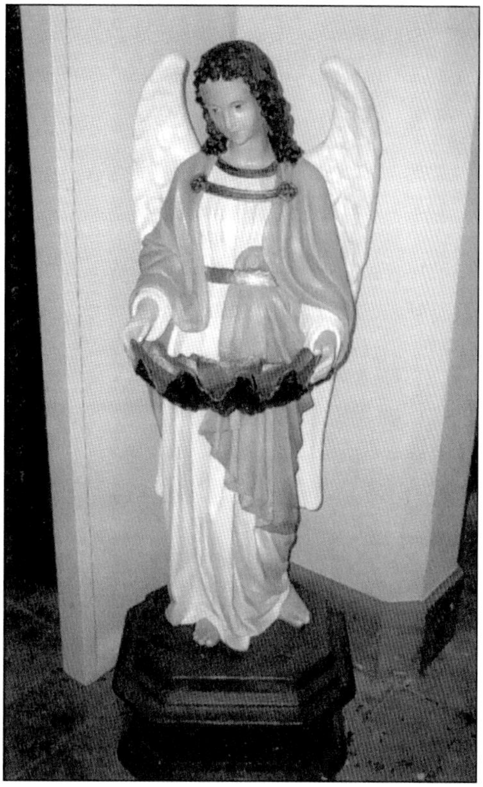

During religious ceremonies, the shells of these two angel statues are filled with holy water. The angels stand at the entrance of St. Joseph's Church and greet visitors, who typically dip their hands in the water before and after religious services. The church was built in 1899, but the statues were restored by the Fernandez family in recent years. (Both, courtesy Patricia Fernandez Mayers.)

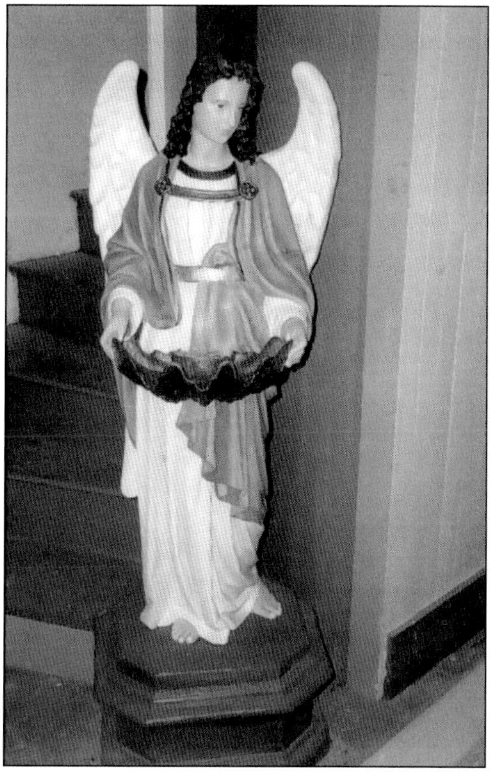

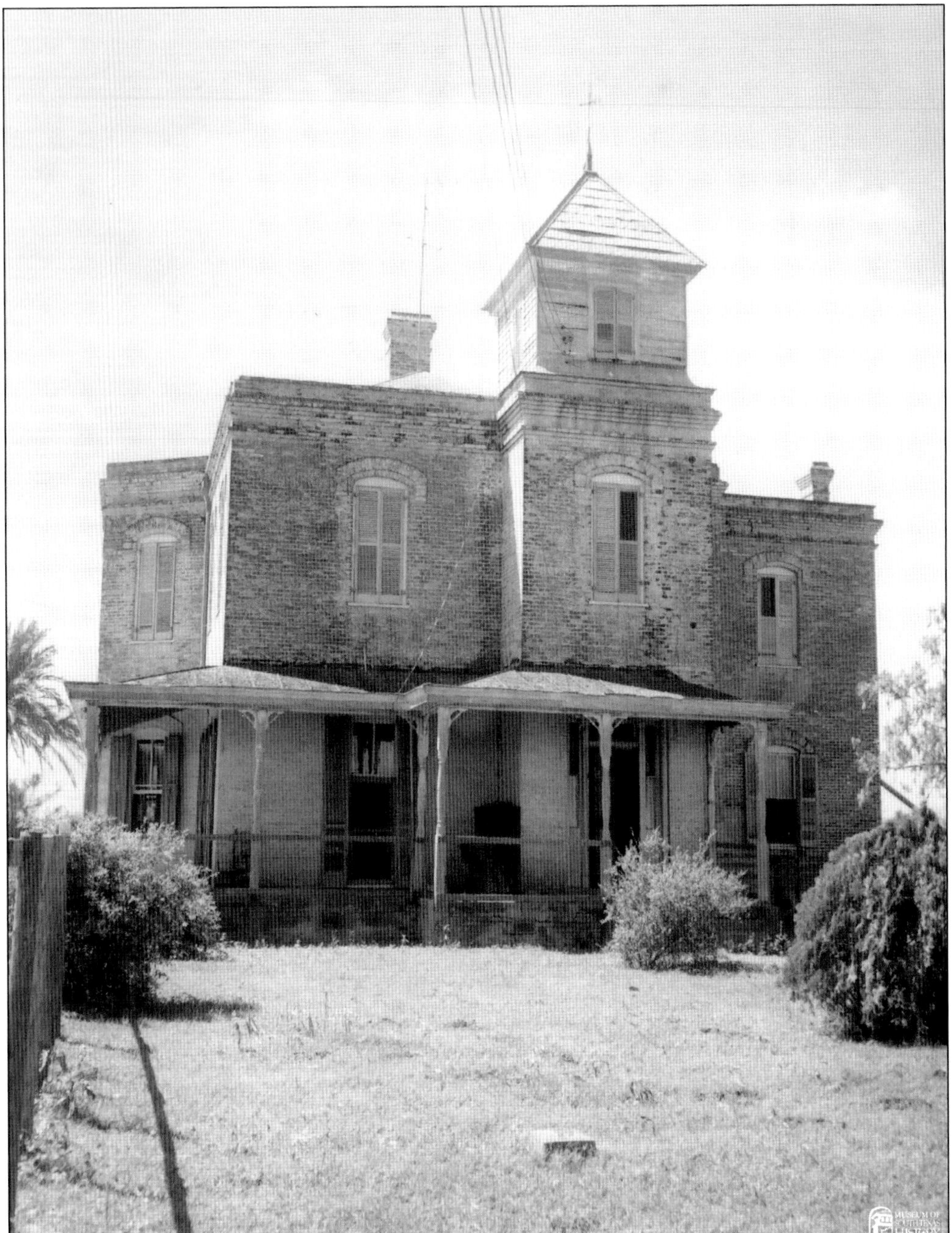

This Italianate ranch house was erected in 1903. Its nine rooms, 12-foot ceilings, attic, and tower (used for lookout purposes) served as the grand house of the iconic Toluca Ranch for many years. In the basement, the Saenz-Cano family kept barrels of wine and nonperishable food. This residence eventually became the Fernandez family home and was made a Texas Historical Landmark in 1967. (Courtesy Museum of South Texas History.)

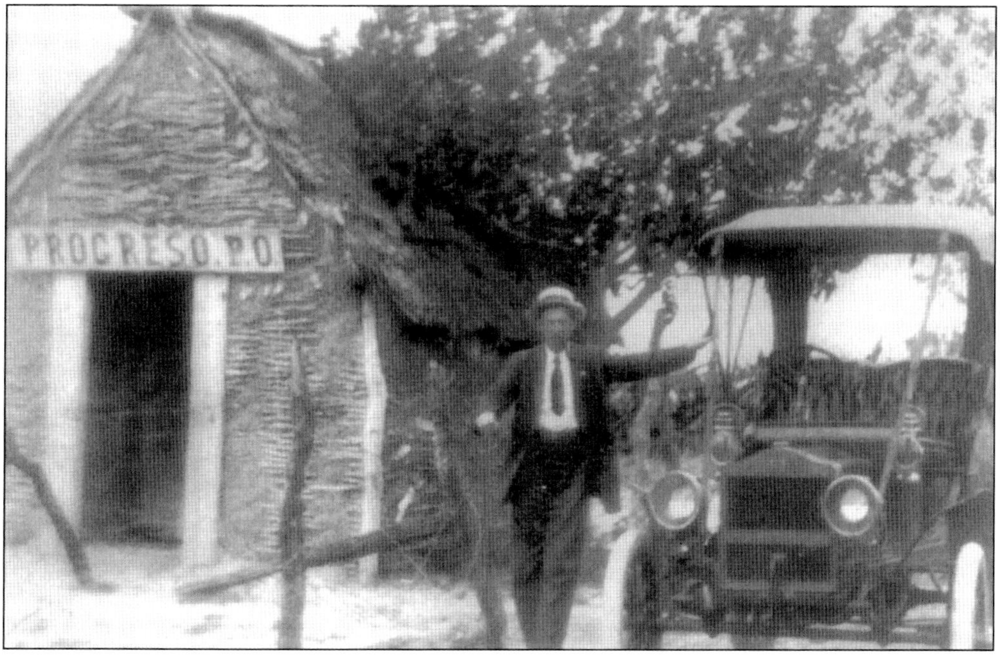


Built in 1905, Progreso's first post office was a small adobe building with a dirt floor and a roof thatched with cattails. This photograph shows the town's first postmaster, Abraham Neumann Smith, standing by a car of the time. (Courtesy Weslaco Museum.)

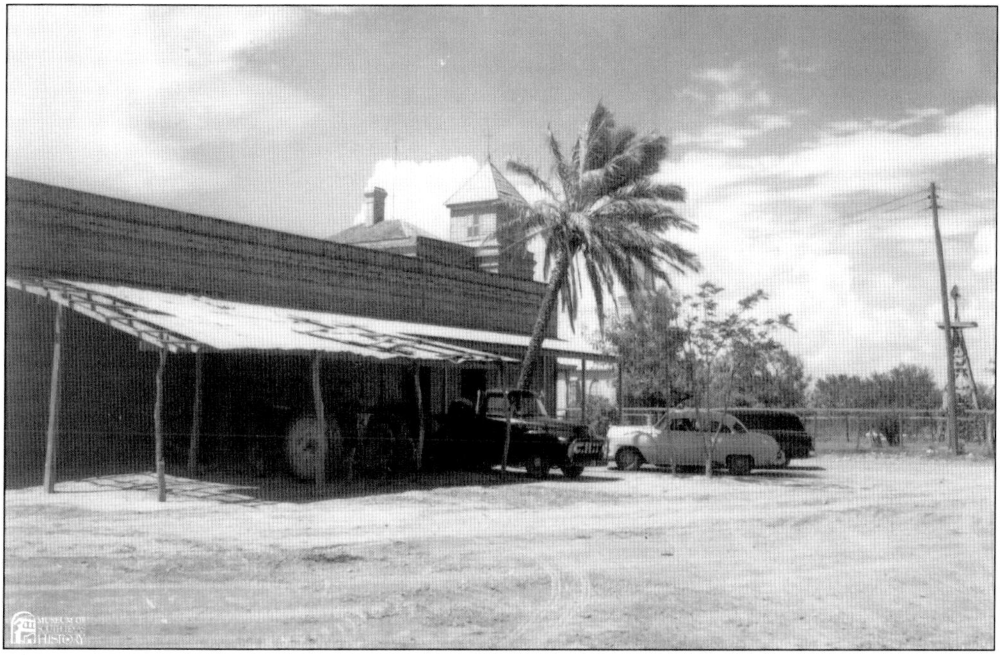

This general merchandise store was built in 1908 and sits east of the grand ranch house at Toluca Ranch. The store maintained a large inventory of groceries, furniture, clothing, hats, shoes, and farming equipment. Most of the items were brought in from Brownsville by steamboat. The store did a lot of business with people from both Mexico and the United States. (Courtesy Museum of South Texas History.)

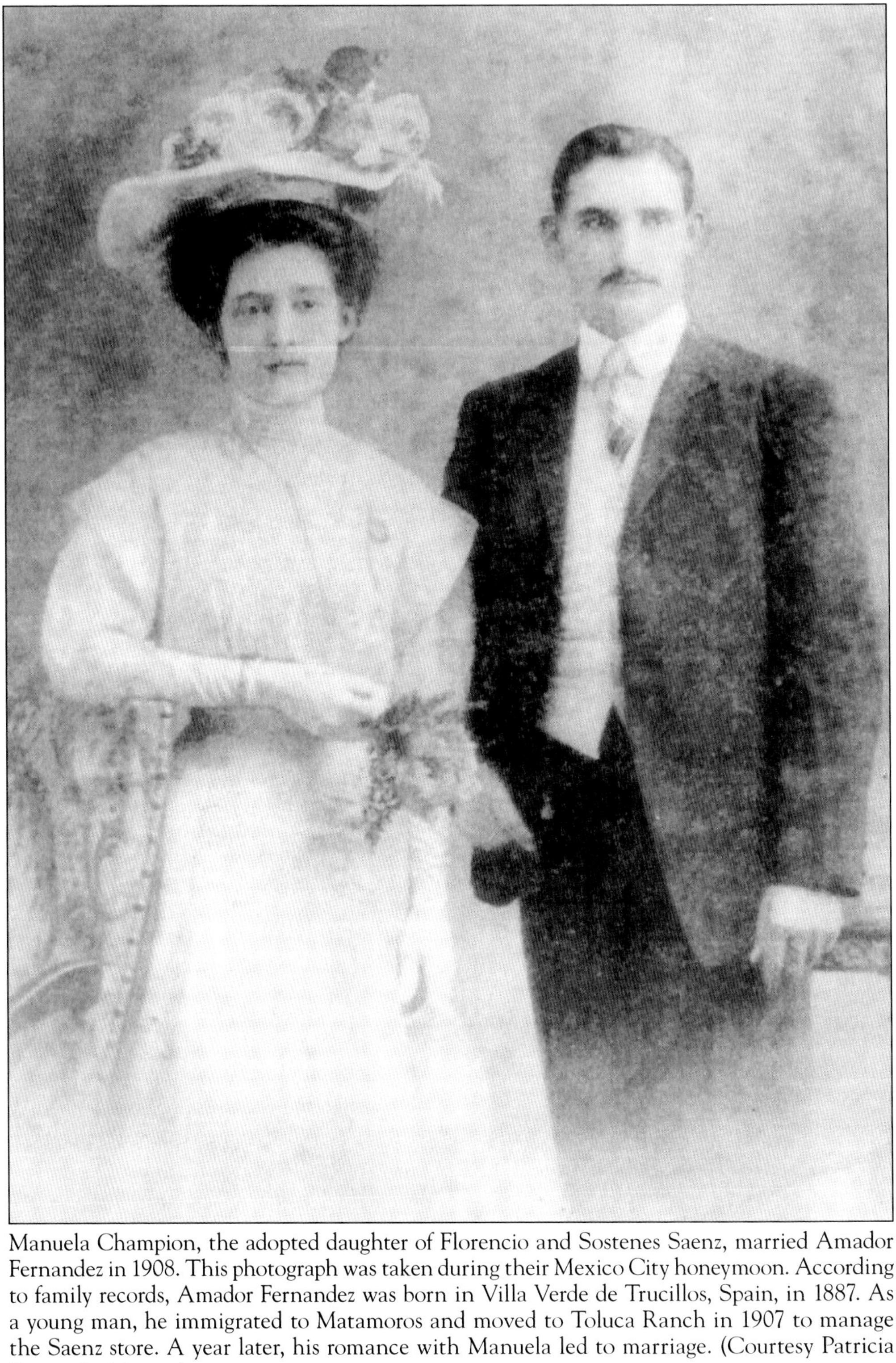

Manuela Champion, the adopted daughter of Florencio and Sostenes Saenz, married Amador Fernandez in 1908. This photograph was taken during their Mexico City honeymoon. According to family records, Amador Fernandez was born in Villa Verde de Trucillos, Spain, in 1887. As a young man, he immigrated to Matamoros and moved to Toluca Ranch in 1907 to manage the Saenz store. A year later, his romance with Manuela led to marriage. (Courtesy Patricia Fernandez Mayers.)

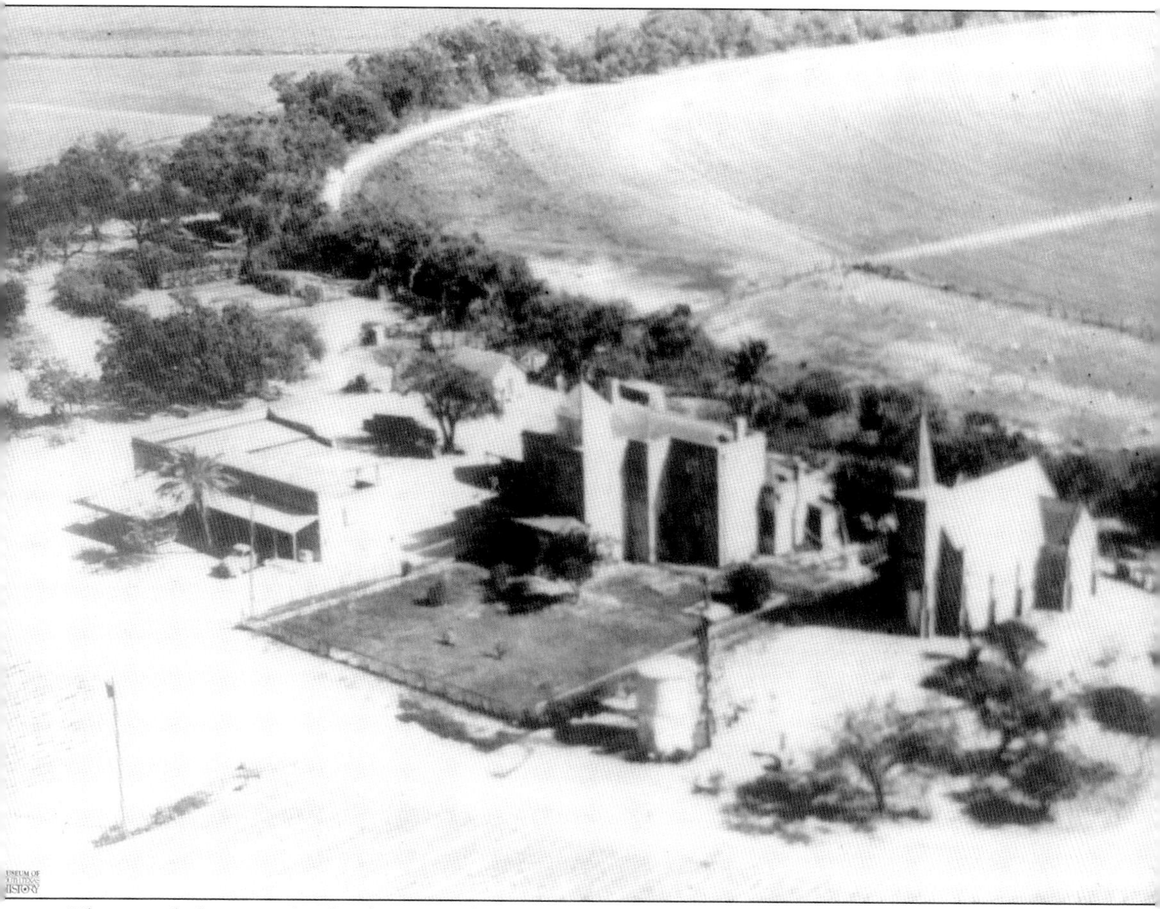

This aerial photograph of Toluca Ranch was taken in 1940 or 1950. The general store (left), the grand house (center), and St. Joseph's Church (right) still exist today. Toluca is one of the few ranches in the Rio Grande Valley that has three historical buildings still standing. (Courtesy Museum of South Texas History.)

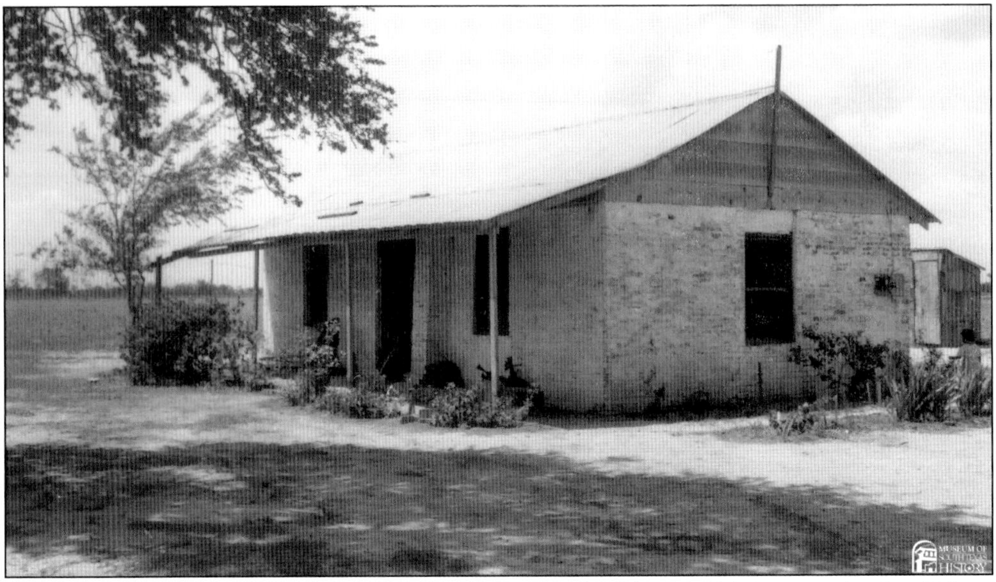

Family records show Amador Fernandez had little schooling, but establishing a school at Toluca Ranch was important to him. Unbeknownst to Fernandez, he established the first education system in the area when he convinced his father-in-law, Florencio Saenz, to build a school at Toluca Ranch. This building operated as a school until 1911 and was then turned to a rental home and leased out to Progreso families. (Courtesy Museum of South Texas History.)

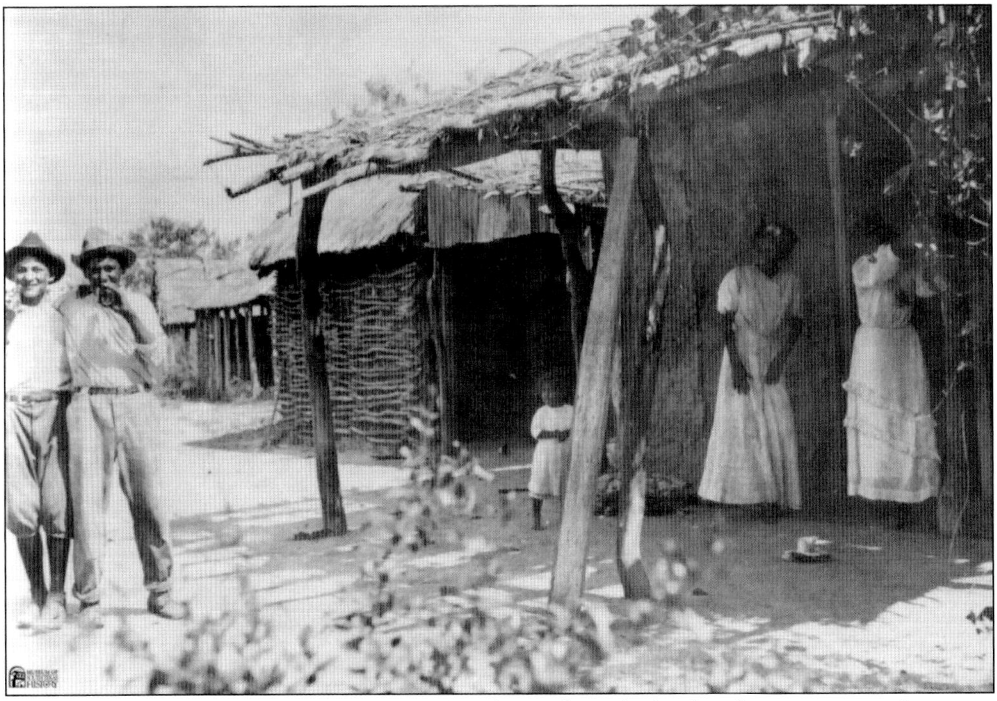

As a pioneer ranch, Toluca employed many families to farm the land and run a masonry business. The bricks made at Toluca Ranch were used to erect buildings in nearby cities like Mercedes and Progreso. This 1900 or 1916 photograph shows a tenant family in front of homes made out of mud and wood. (Courtesy Museum of South Texas History.)

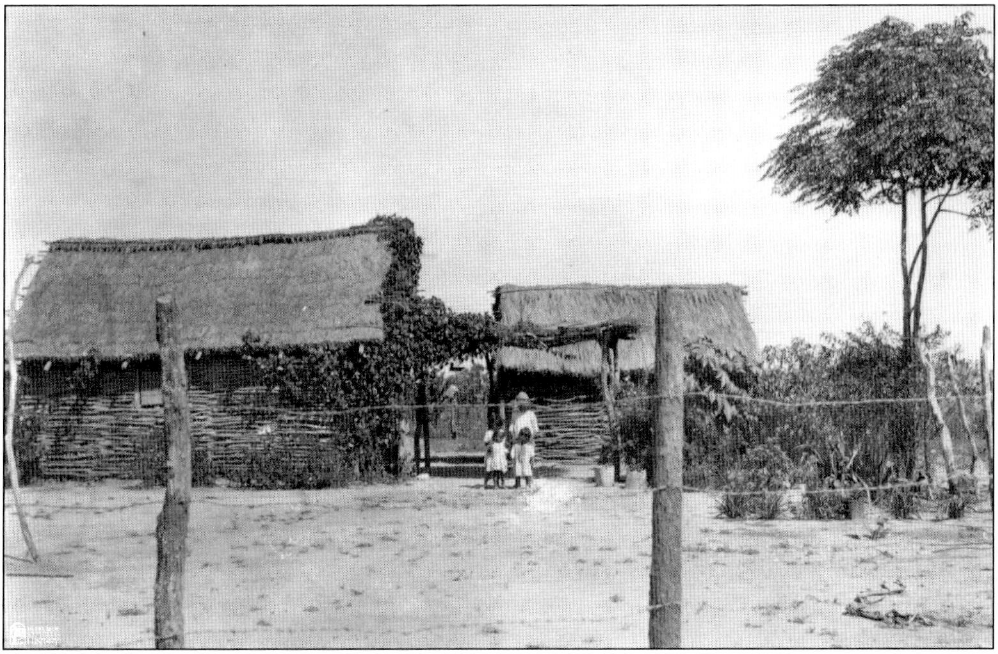

A tenant family stands outside a thatched-roof home at Toluca Ranch in 1916. Like many other Toluca Ranch photographs that have survived the test of time, this one was taken by an unidentified person, who perhaps unknowingly documented history. (Courtesy Museum of South Texas History.)

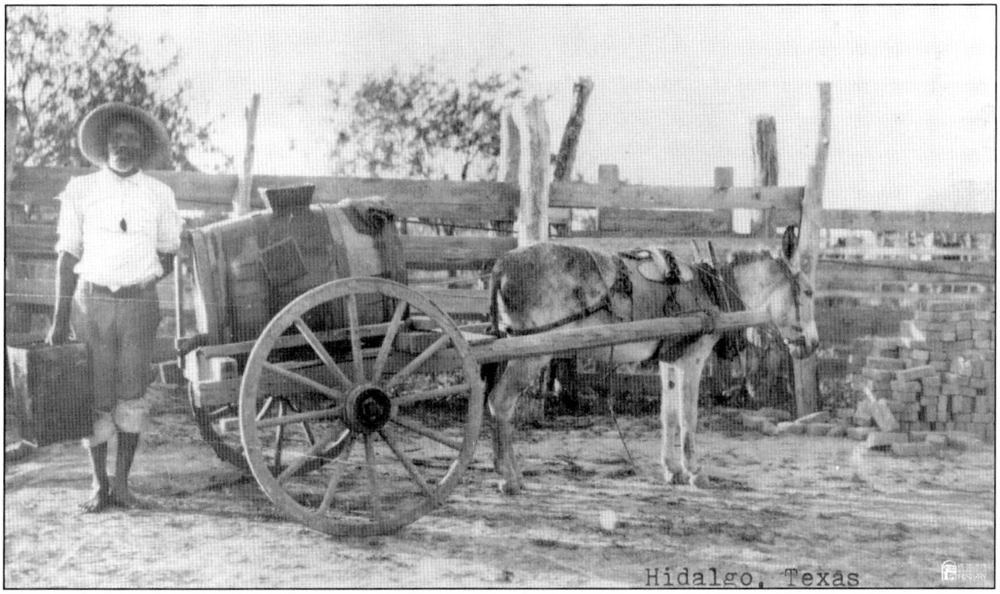


This photograph was taken at Toluca Ranch in 1916 by an unidentified soldier. This carrier delivers water barrels by donkey. (Courtesy Museum of South Texas History.)

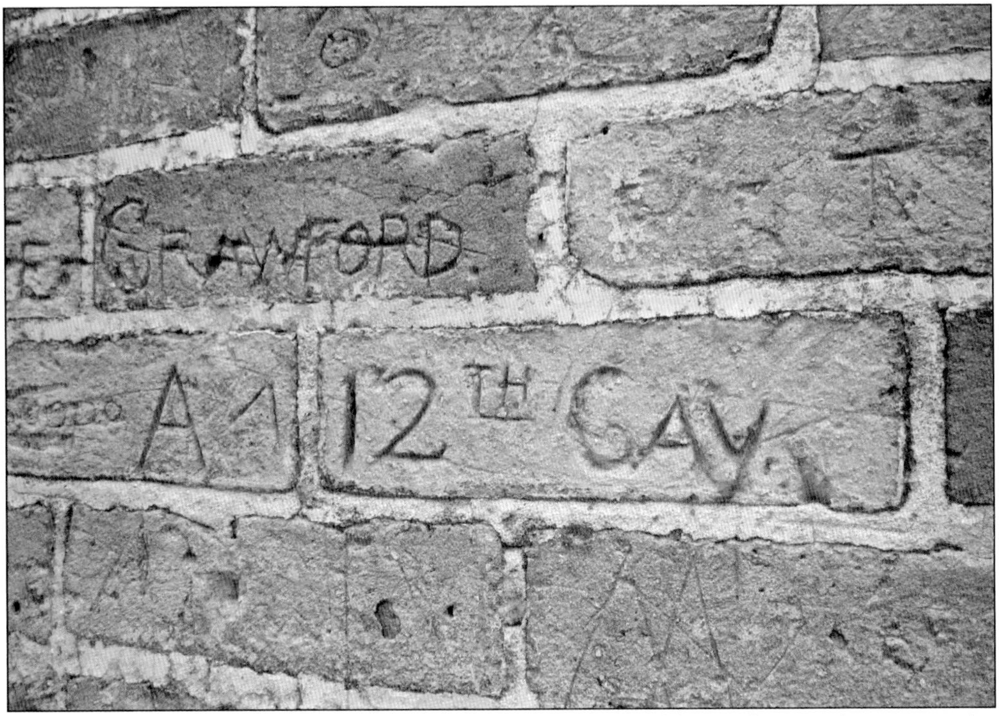


The east wall of the Toluca Ranch general store was engraved by inadvertent historians who perhaps never thought their writings would help tell the story of Toluca Ranch. These four photographs show carvings made by soldiers of the 12th U.S. Cavalry in 1916. (Both, courtesy Patricia Fernandez Mayers.)

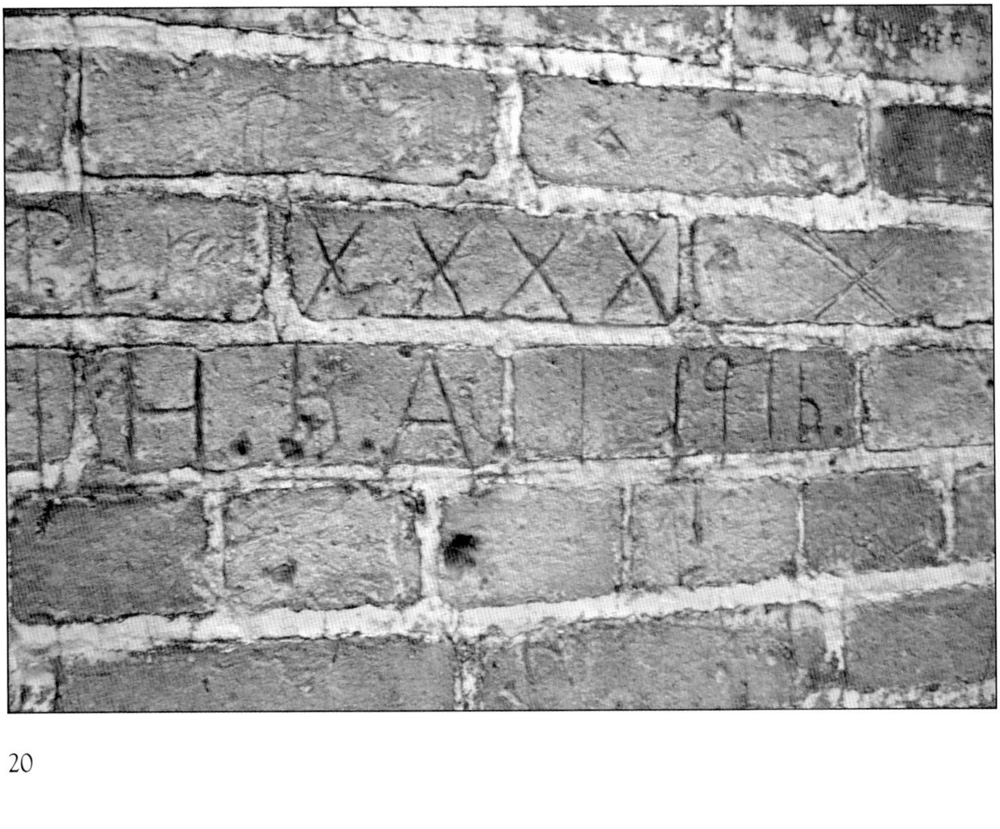

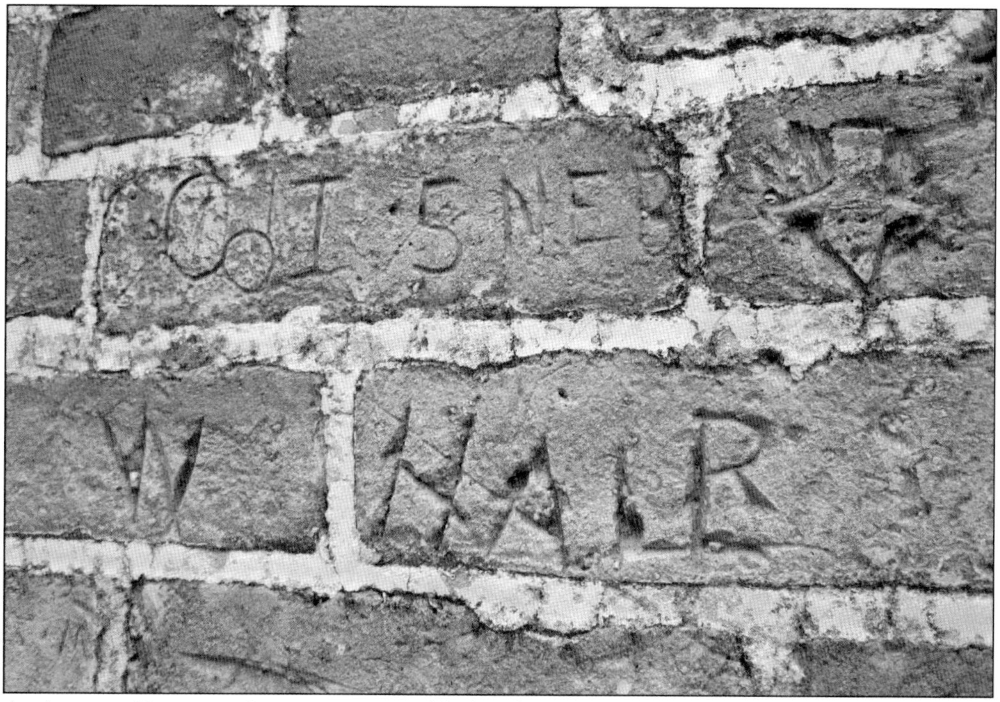

At the time, Texas ranchers were targeted by bandits, and soldiers occupied the ranch to protect it. Bullet holes and blood stains are also visible in other parts of the building. (Both, courtesy Patricia Fernandez Mayers.)

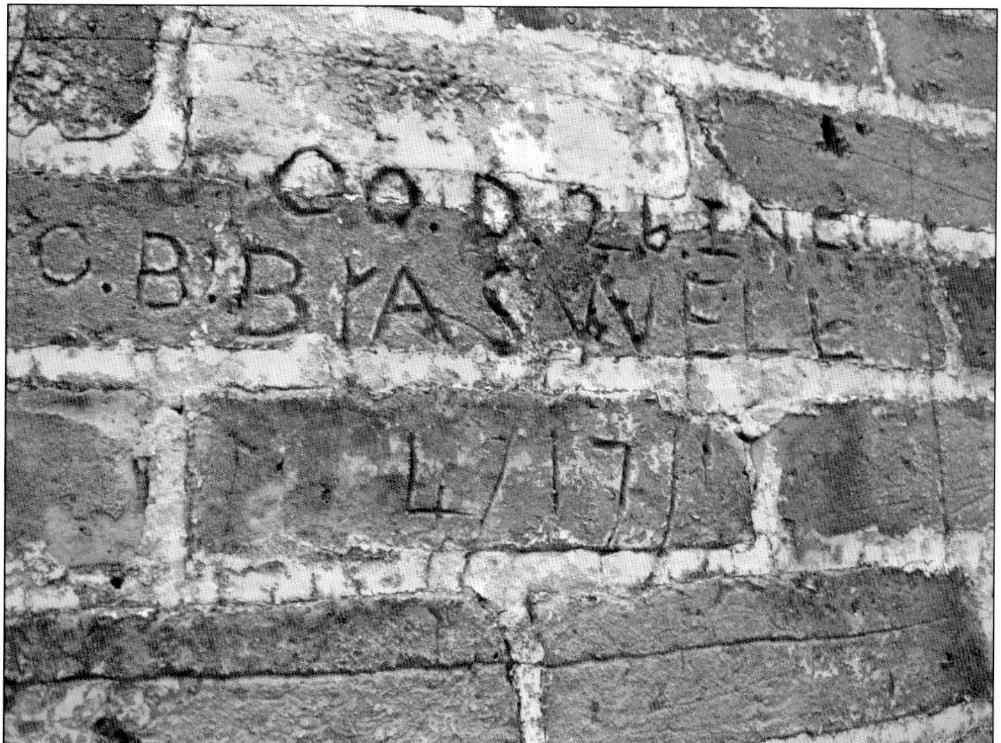

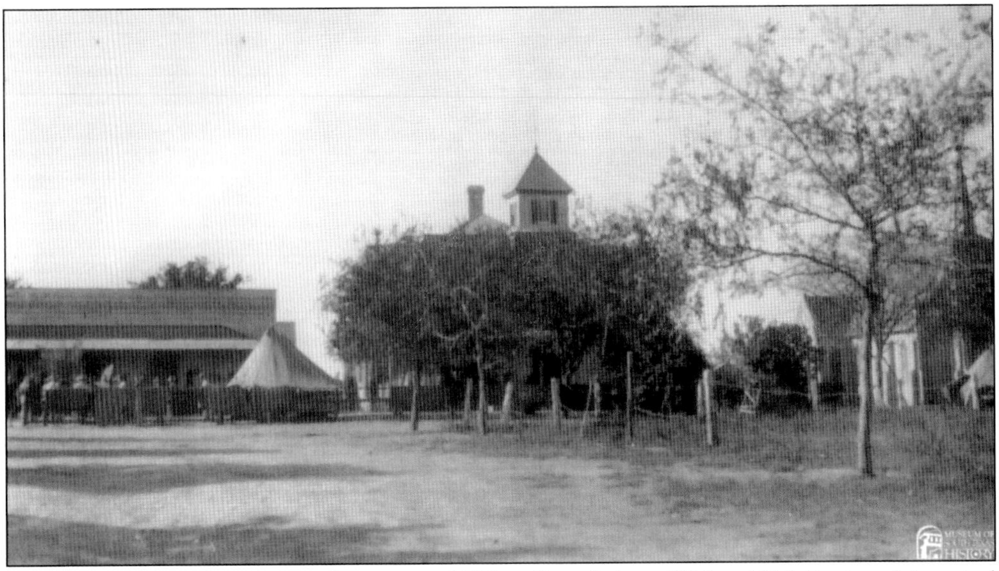

Soldiers from the 6th U.S. Cavalry occupied Toluca Ranch from 1915 to 1916. During this period of unrest along the border, local ranchers were targeted for the property they owned, which at one point was Mexican territory. Many area ranchers moved temporarily to nearby cities, like Mercedes and Weslaco, until the government authorized reentry into their homes. (Courtesy Museum of South Texas History.)

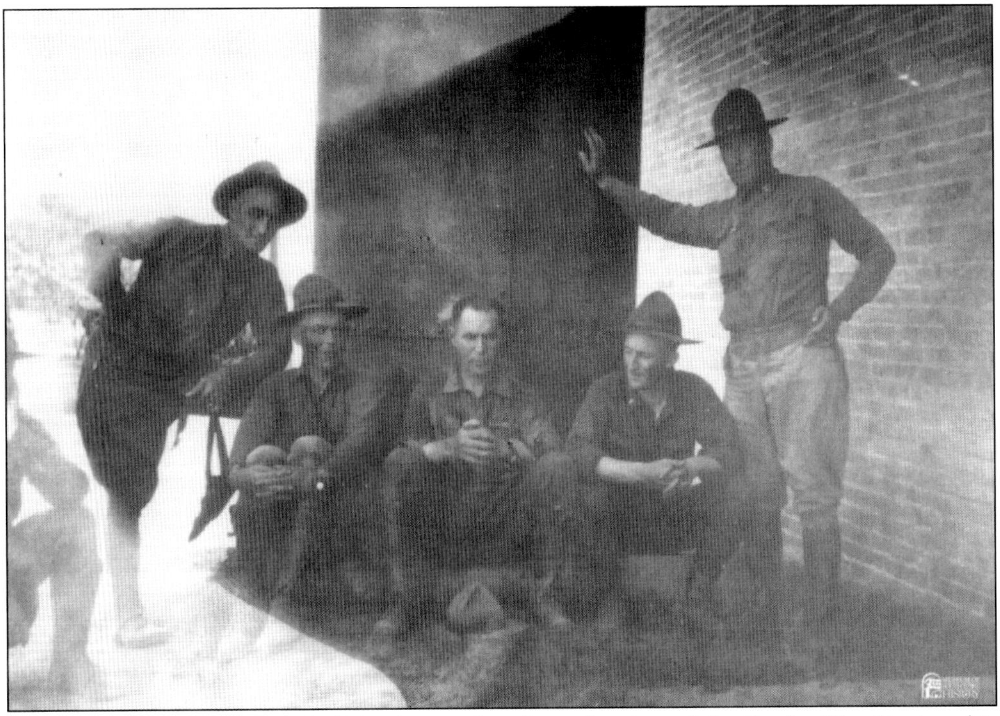

The period between 1913 and 1916 is known locally as the time of the Border War. During this time, thousands of national guardsmen were stationed in the Rio Grande Valley to protect this prized U.S. territory. The 6th U.S. Cavalry camped at Toluca Ranch until peace was restored. (Courtesy Museum of South Texas History.)

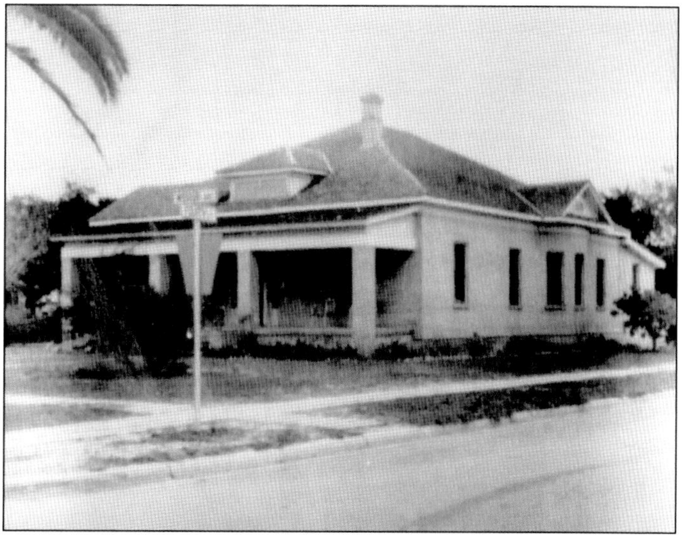

The Fernandez-Saenz family built this house in 1916 on the corner of Fourth Street and Missouri Avenue in Mercedes to escape the unrest at Toluca Ranch. Family reports indicate that the bishop of Corpus Christi enjoyed visiting the family and stopped at this house frequently. (Courtesy Patricia Fernandez Mayers.)

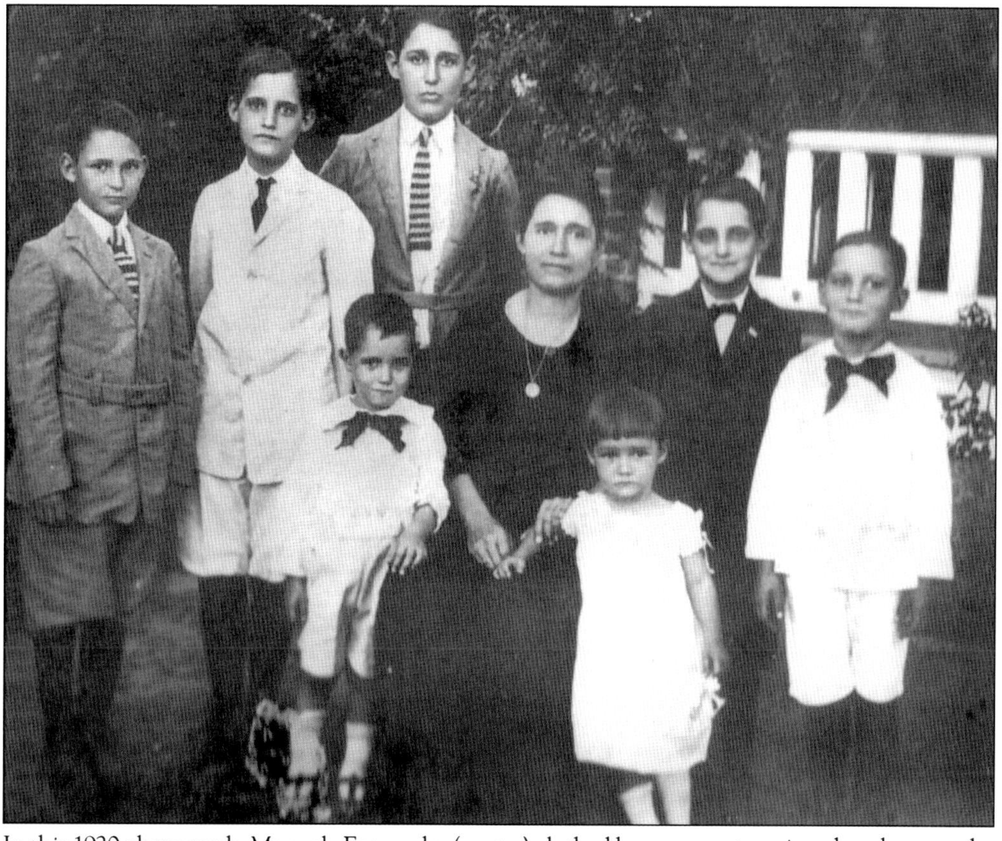

In this 1920 photograph, Manuela Fernandez (center) clothed her youngest son in a dress because she did not have daughters at the time. From left to right are (first row) Ernesto Monico and Santiago "Jimmy"; (second row) Jose Agustin, Amador Tomas, Jose Florencio, Guadalupe Anastacio, and Joaquin Jorge. The Fernandez moved to Mercedes to escape the violence along the border that came to be known as the Border War and later moved back to Toluca Ranch. (Courtesy Patricia Fernandez Mayers.)

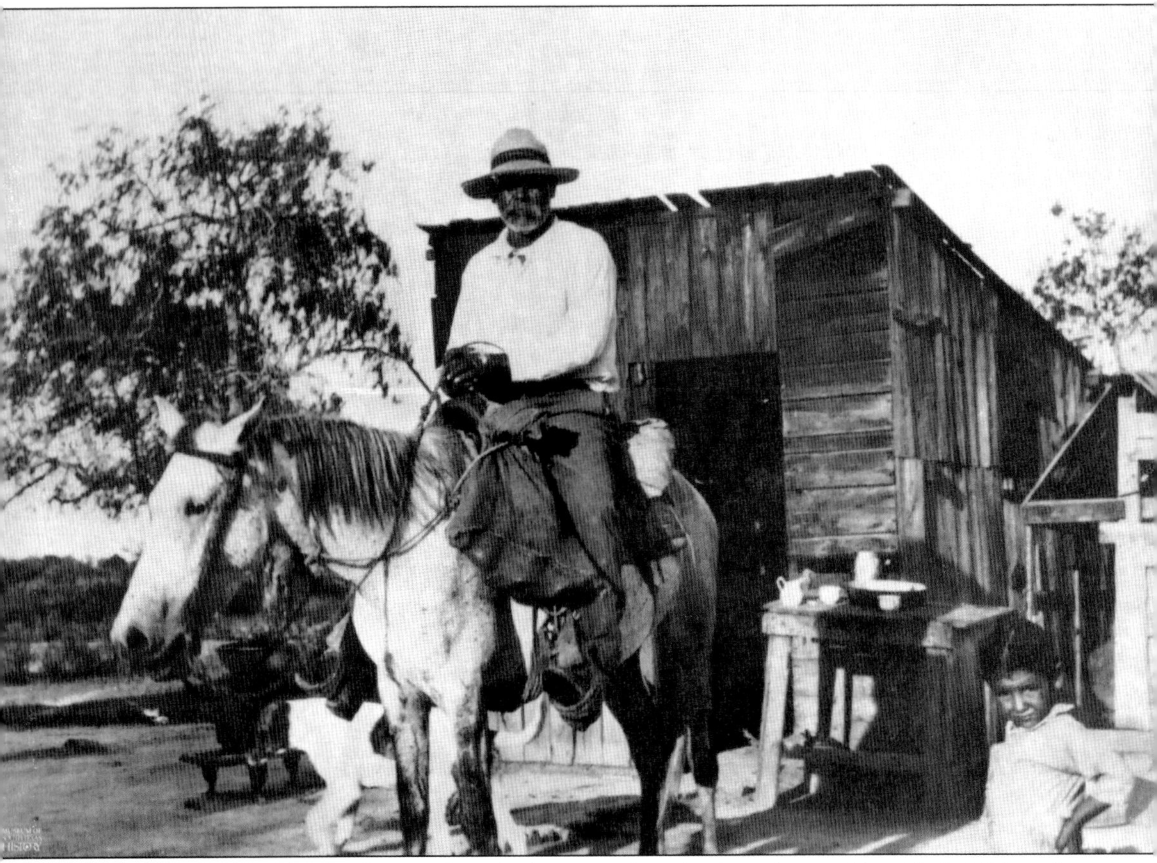

This 1920s photograph of an unidentified man on horseback and an unidentified child on foot shows another type of house built for workers at Toluca Ranch. The handmade shed appears to be constructed entirely of wood. Records indicate that at one point homes were also made of mud and wood. (Courtesy Museum of South Texas History.)

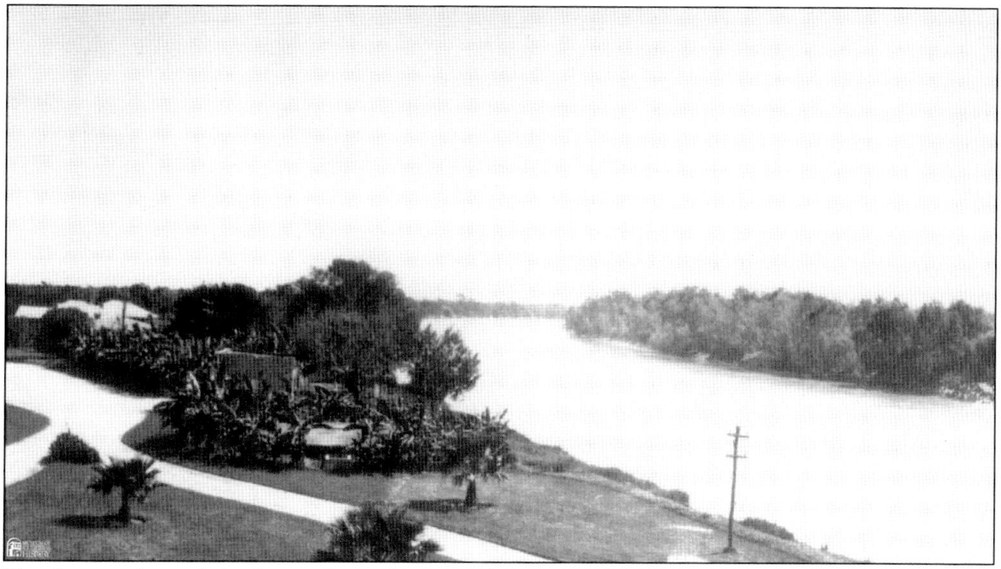

Floods complicated the lives of people along the Rio Grande—so much so that entire families moved to temporary homes on higher ground during the rainy season. The Rio Grande overflowed its banks in 1916, and this photograph shows the severity of the floodwaters at Toluca Ranch. (Courtesy Museum of South Texas History.)

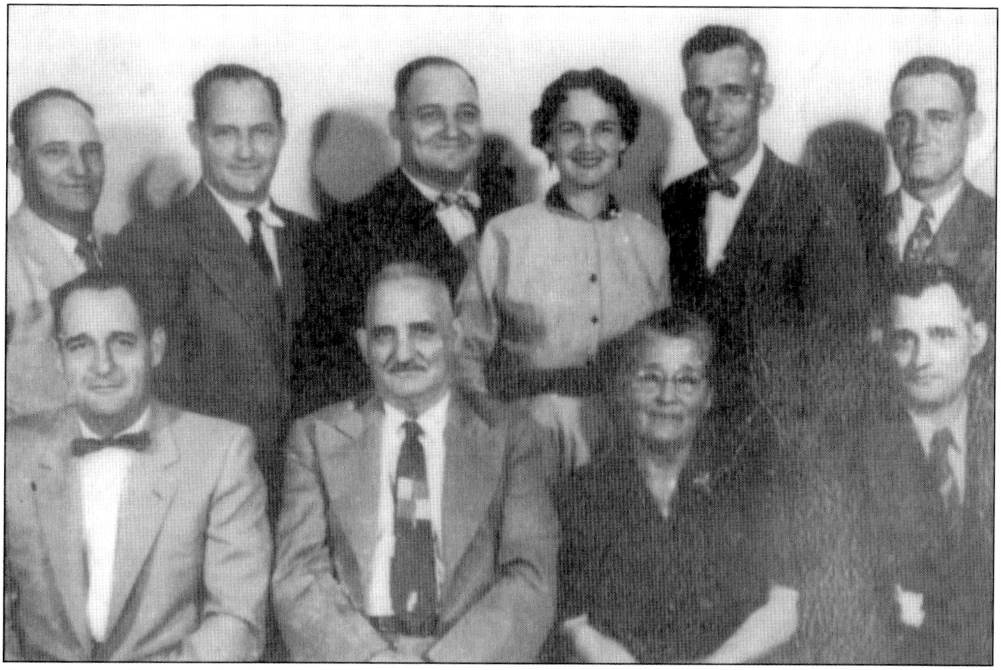

Amador and Manuela Fernandez gave Florencio and Sostenes Saenz eight grandchildren. This family photograph shows the Fernandez couple and their children. From left to right are (first row) Jose Florencio, Amador, Manuela, and Amador Tomas; (second row) Jose Agustin, Guadalupe Anastasio, Joaquin Jorge, Manuela Lourdes, Ernesto Monico, and Santiago "Jimmy". (Courtesy Patricia Fernandez Mayers.)

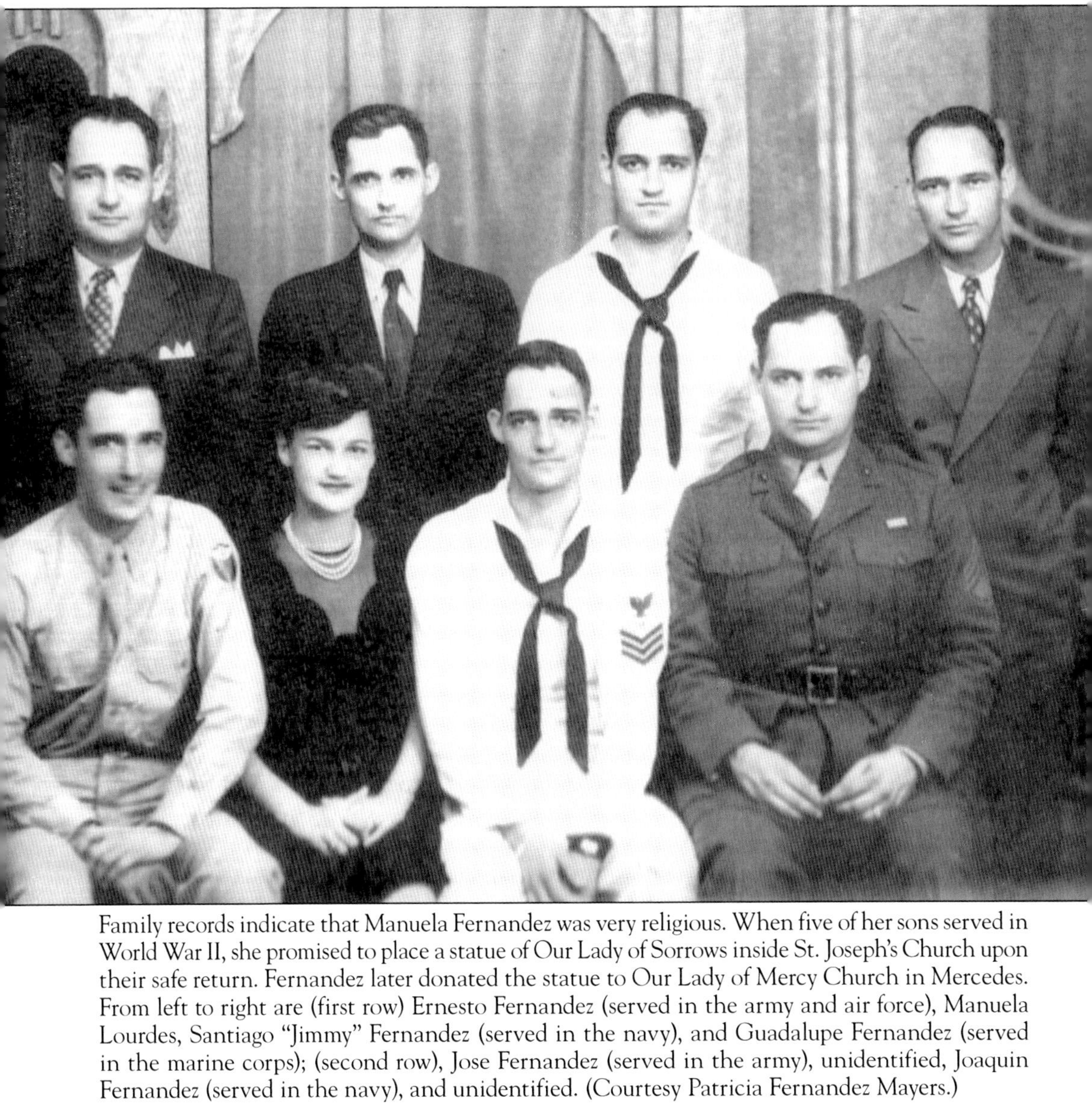

Family records indicate that Manuela Fernandez was very religious. When five of her sons served in World War II, she promised to place a statue of Our Lady of Sorrows inside St. Joseph's Church upon their safe return. Fernandez later donated the statue to Our Lady of Mercy Church in Mercedes. From left to right are (first row) Ernesto Fernandez (served in the army and air force), Manuela Lourdes, Santiago "Jimmy" Fernandez (served in the navy), and Guadalupe Fernandez (served in the marine corps); (second row), Jose Fernandez (served in the army), unidentified, Joaquin Fernandez (served in the navy), and unidentified. (Courtesy Patricia Fernandez Mayers.)

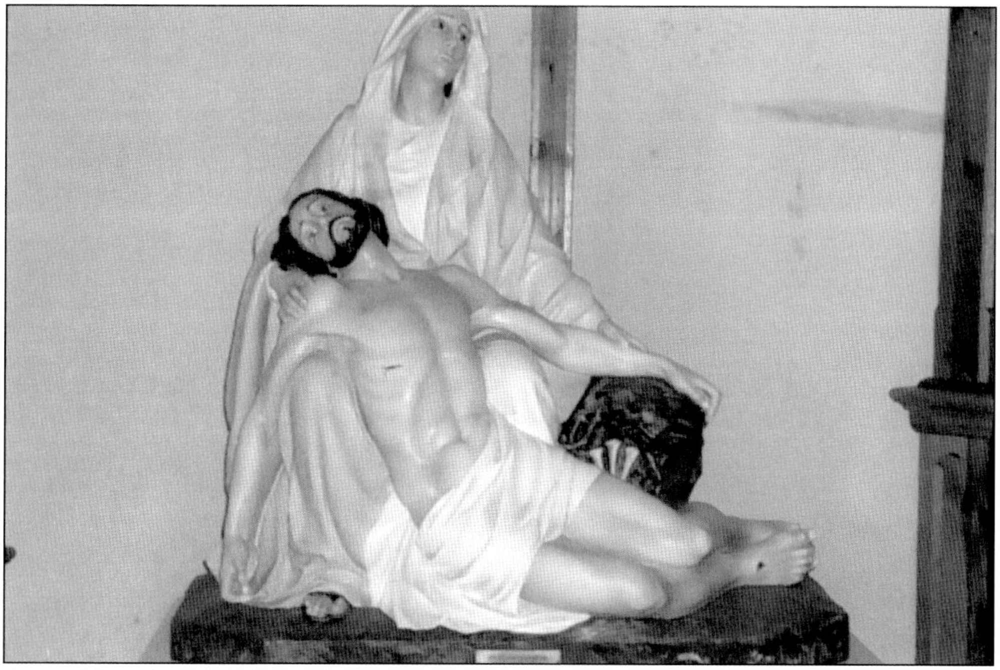

*Sorrowful Mother* (above) was donated to St. Joseph's Church by Manuela Fernandez in 1945, after five of her sons returned safely from World War II. *St. Joseph* (right) stands on the altar, next to the *Sacred Heart of Jesus* and the *Blessed Mother*. (Both, courtesy Patricia Fernandez Mayers.)

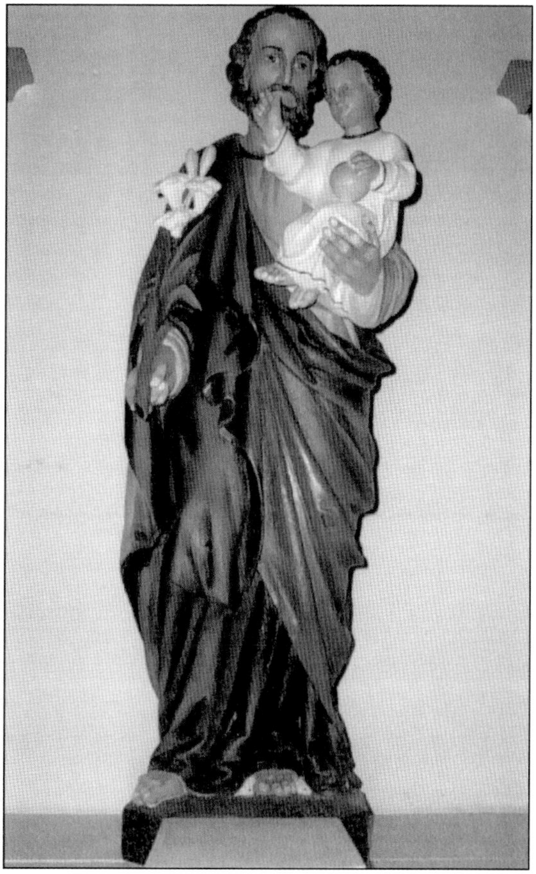

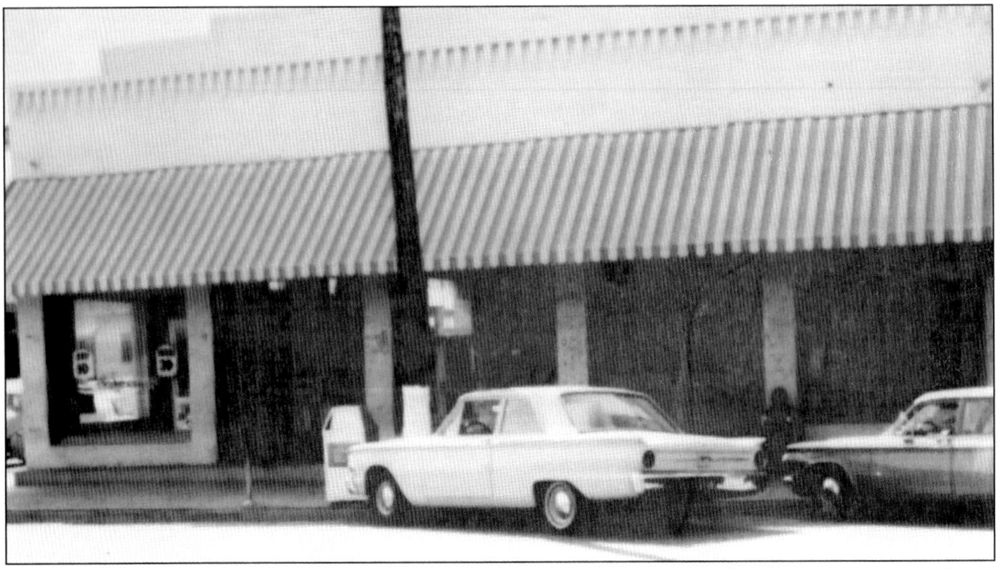

Like many other buildings in Progreso and Mercedes, the F. Saenz and Company store was built with bricks made at Toluca Ranch. The establishment was located at the corner of Fourth Street and Texas Avenue in Mercedes. During periods of unrest along the Rio Grande, the Saenz family moved to Mercedes temporarily. This photograph was taken in 1964. (Courtesy Patricia Fernandez Mayers.)

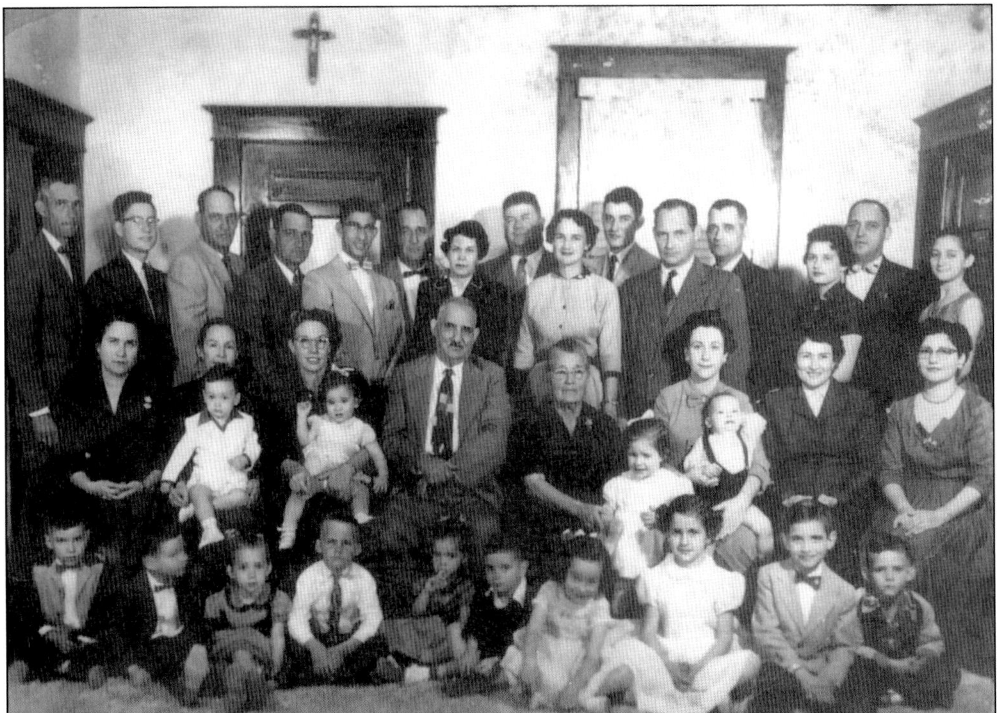

Amador and Manuela Fernandez had eight children and 22 grandchildren. This photograph shows the size of the family and the new owners of the Toluca Ranch. Amador Fernandez died on May 31, 1955. Manuela Fernandez died on March 29, 1971. (Courtesy Patricia Fernandez Mayers.)

# *Two*

# San Pedro Ranch

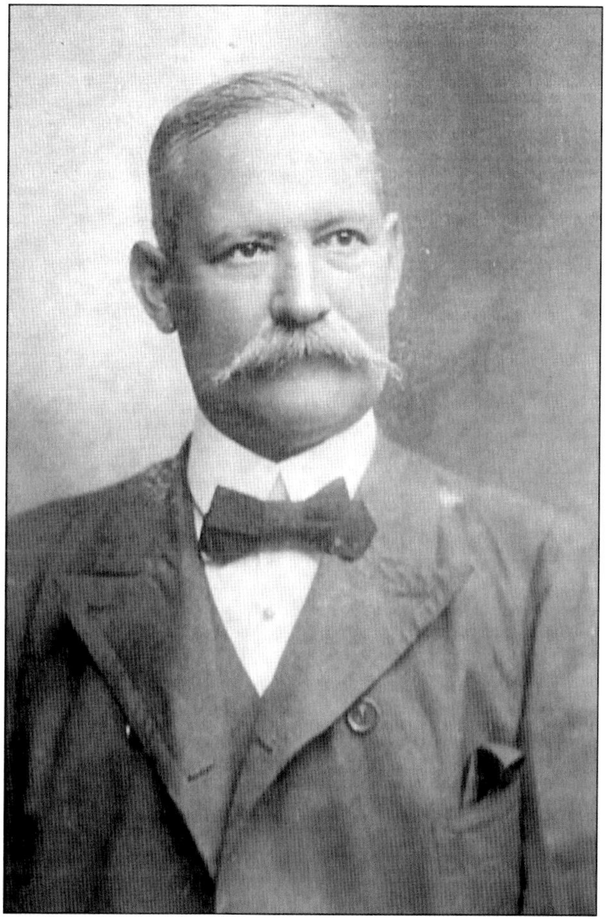

Pedro S. Champion, from the prominent Italian family that settled in Point Isabel and Brownsville in the mid-1800s, is the biological father of Manuela Champion, the young girl Florencio and Sostenes Saenz adopted in 1883. According to family records, Pedro Champion's father, Pietro Campeoni, was born in 1818 in an Italian province that is in present-day Croatia. Pedro S. Champion and Gumecinda Cano, daughter of Campacuas Ranch owners Antonio and Mauricia Cano, married in 1897, and Gumecinda's mother deeded a large piece of land to her. Pedro and Gumecinda Champion established a ranch on that land and named it after Pedro's patron saint, San Pedro. (Courtesy Patricia Fernandez Mayers.)

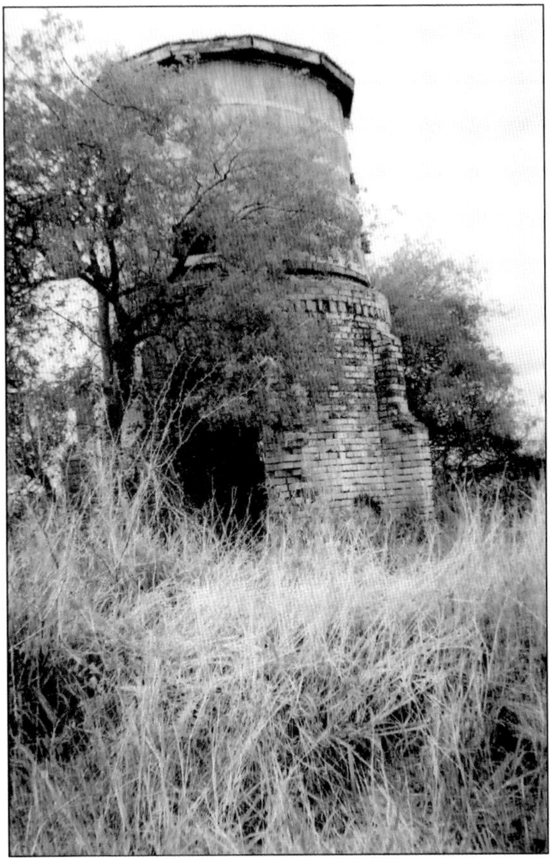

Few photographs of the San Pedro Ranch of the late 1800s have survived the test of time. In fact, this water tank is the only ranch building standing today. It is considered a relic by descendants of the Champion family. The circular wall is 8 feet high and is set on a concrete slab. (Courtesy Gloria C. Garcia.)

The San Pedro Ranch Cemetery was established by Pedro S. Champion in 1896, but the earliest burial is dated 1912. It is located just east of FM 88 and south of Military Highway. Five years after San Pedro Ranch was established, the Champions sold the land to the American Rio Grande Land and Irrigation Company of Mercedes. (Courtesy Gloria C. Garcia.)

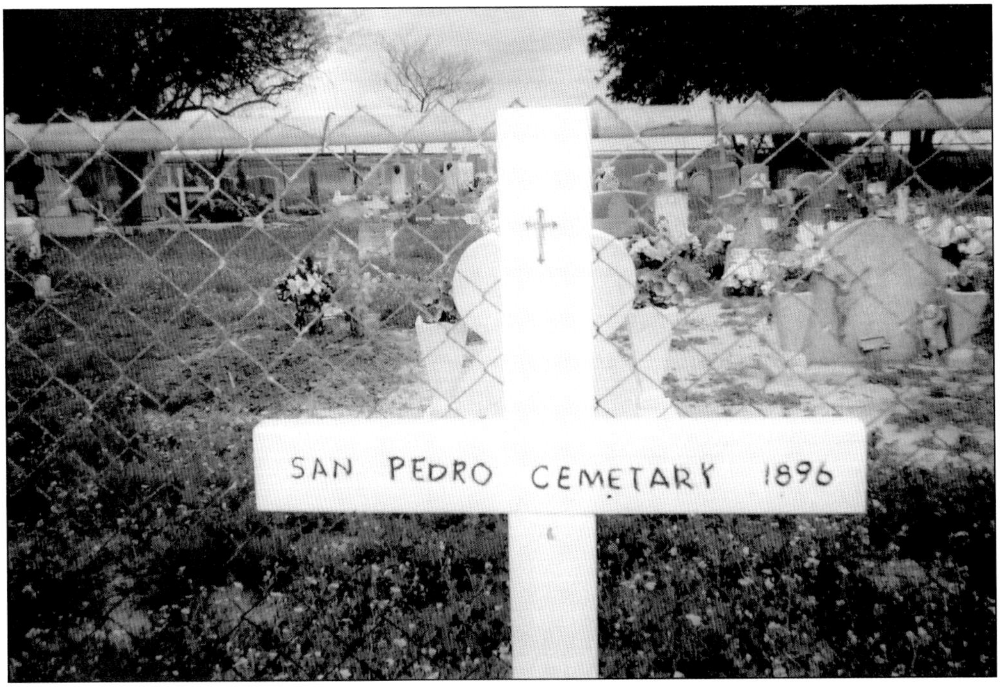

This photograph of Pedro Cleto Champion and Josefina Muñoz was taken in 1944. Pedro is the son of Pedro S. Champion, the original owner of San Pedro Ranch. The Champion-Muñoz family lived in Progreso most of their lives. Their home was on Camino Real Road near Highway 281. (Courtesy Gloria C. Garcia.)

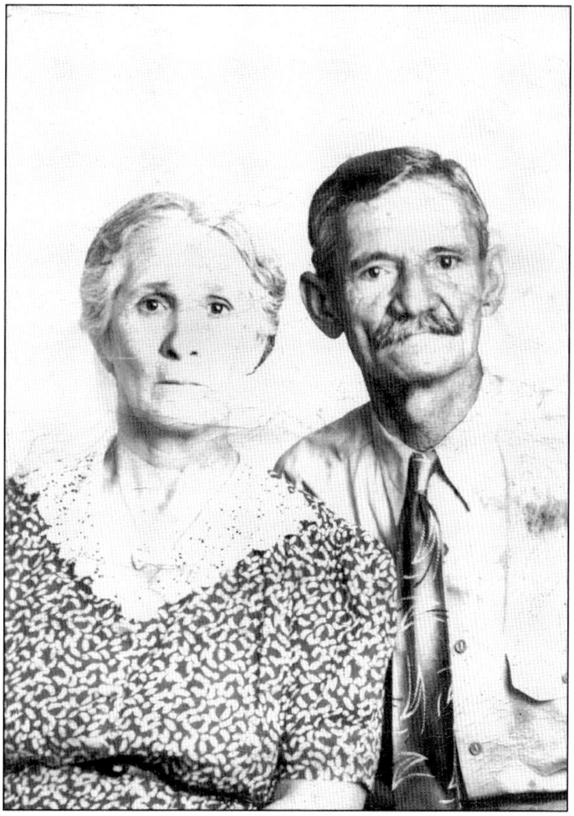

This 1936 photograph of Roberto Cleto Champion shows him riding a horse and holding a .45-caliber handgun near the family pier on Lion Lake. Family records show Roberto courted his wife-to-be, Santitos Treviño of Mercedes, on horseback, as did other men of the time. (Courtesy Gloria C. Garcia.)

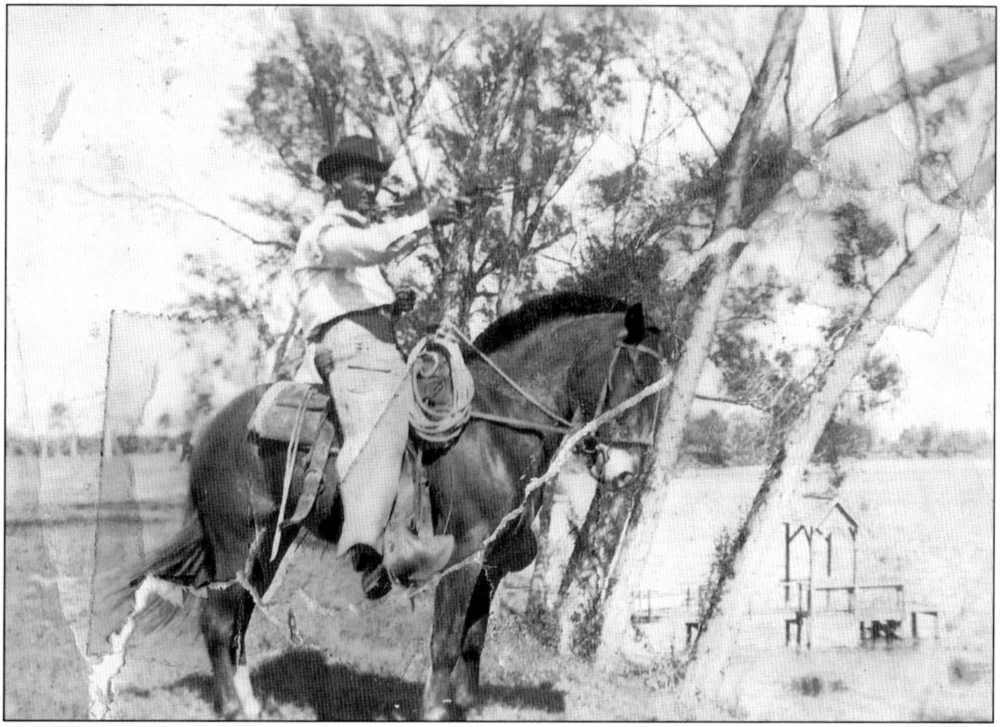

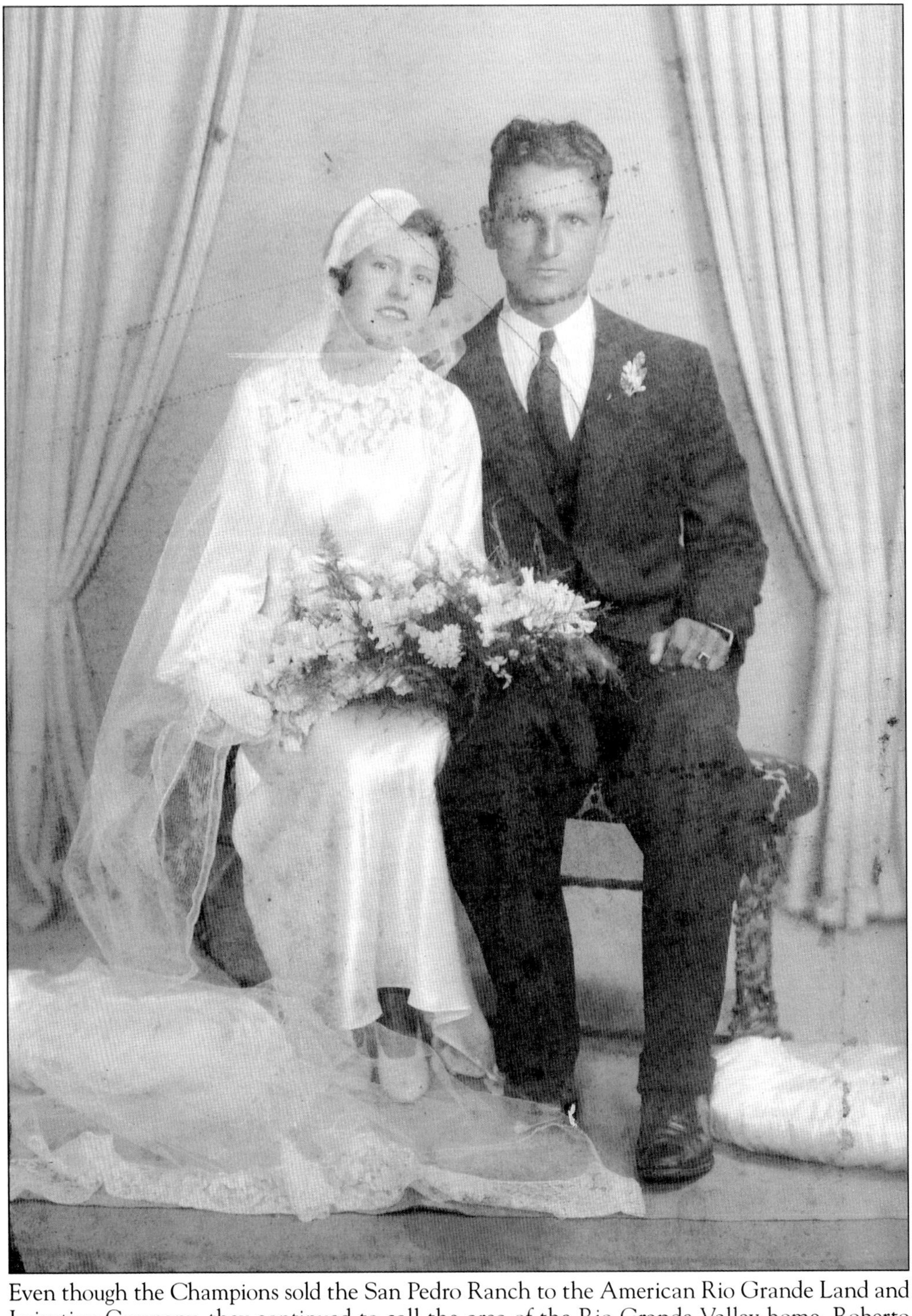

Even though the Champions sold the San Pedro Ranch to the American Rio Grande Land and Irrigation Company, they continued to call the area of the Rio Grande Valley home. Roberto Cleto Champion and Santitos Treviño married on January 26, 1936, at Our Lady of Mercy Church in Mercedes. Roberto is the son of Pedro Cleto Champion and grandson of the original owner of the San Pedro Ranch. (Courtesy Gloria C. Garcia.)

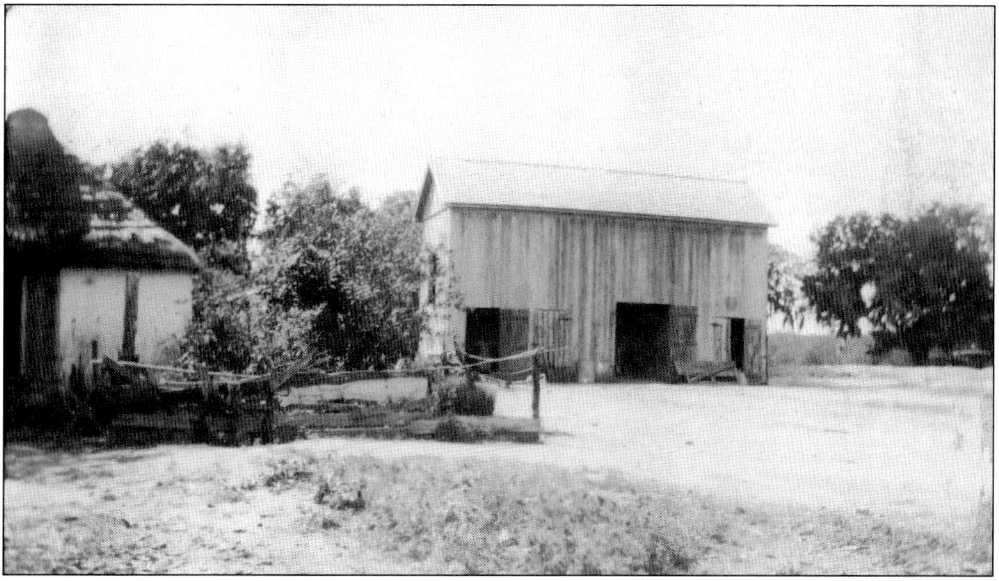

Few photographs remain of the original San Pedro Ranch, like these taken before the 1920s, when all the buildings were demolished except for one, a circular water tank that still stands today. These two photographs are perhaps some of the only images of a ranch house (left) and a barn (right) at San Pedro Ranch. (Both, courtesy Buddy and Gretchen Hovda.)

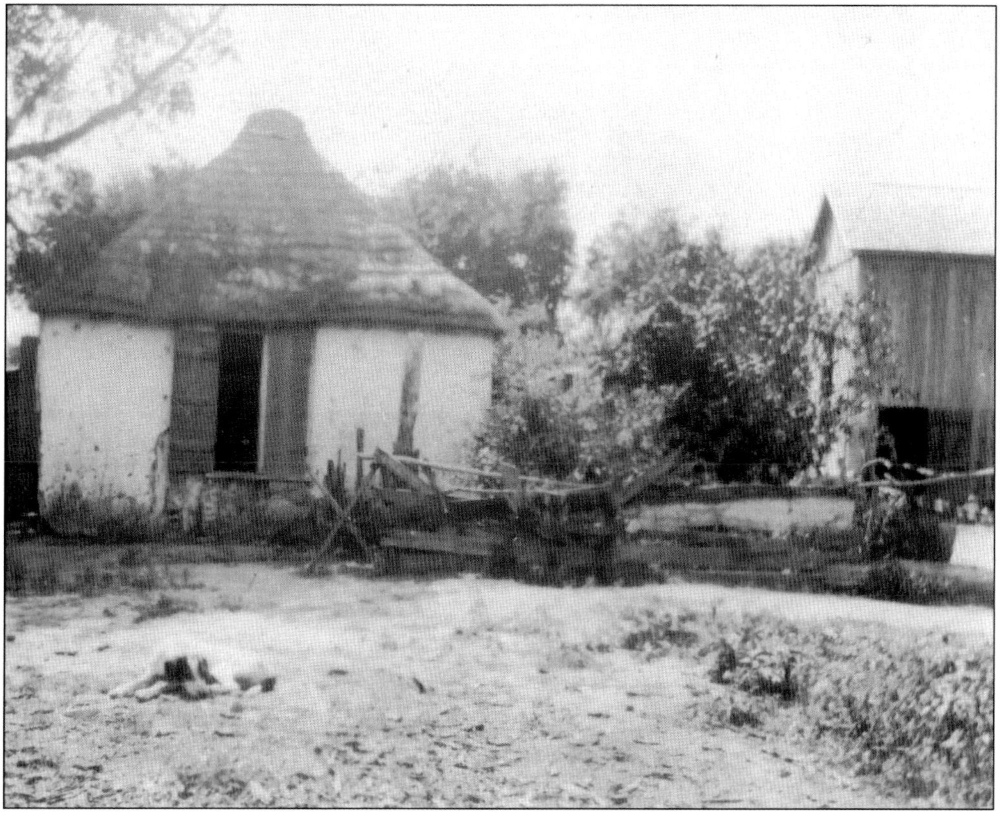

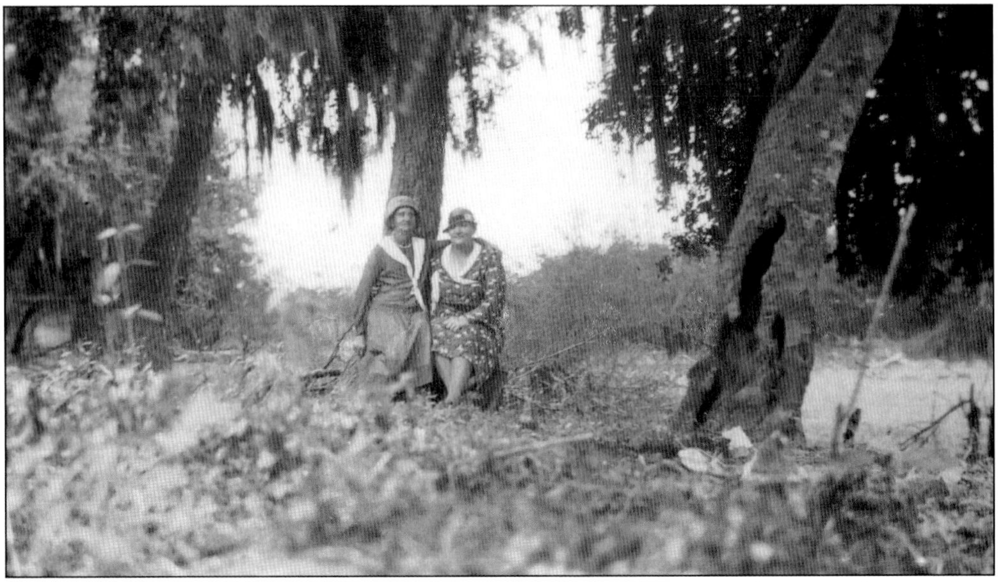

Timeless and magical, this 1920s photograph of Hannah Theimer and Mrs. Karle was taken along the banks of the Rio Grande while the Theimer family shopped for real estate. Ben and Hannah Theimer fell in love with the area and paid about $26 an acre for land that continued to be known as San Pedro Ranch. (Courtesy Buddy and Gretchen Hovda.)

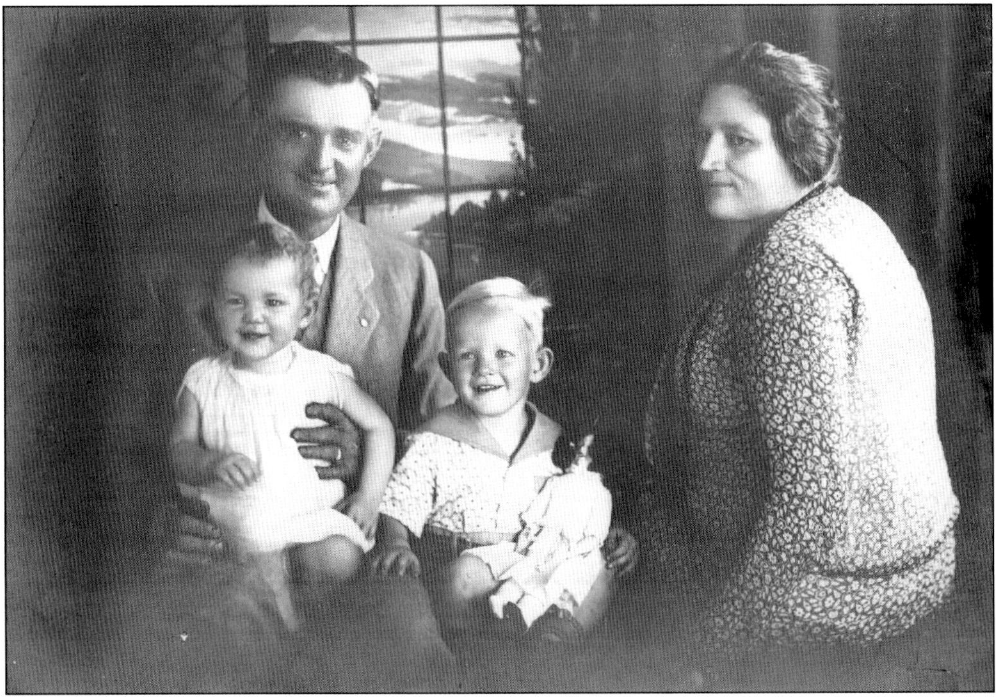

Ben and Hannah Theimer purchased the San Pedro Ranch around 1929, but it took the couple about three years to clear the title to the property. They believe the much-contested boundary of the United States and Mexico complicated the purchase. Ben Theimer (left) is holding daughter Gretchen (later Gretchen Hovda), son Benjamin sits in the center, and Hannah is at right. (Courtesy Buddy and Gretchen Hovda.)

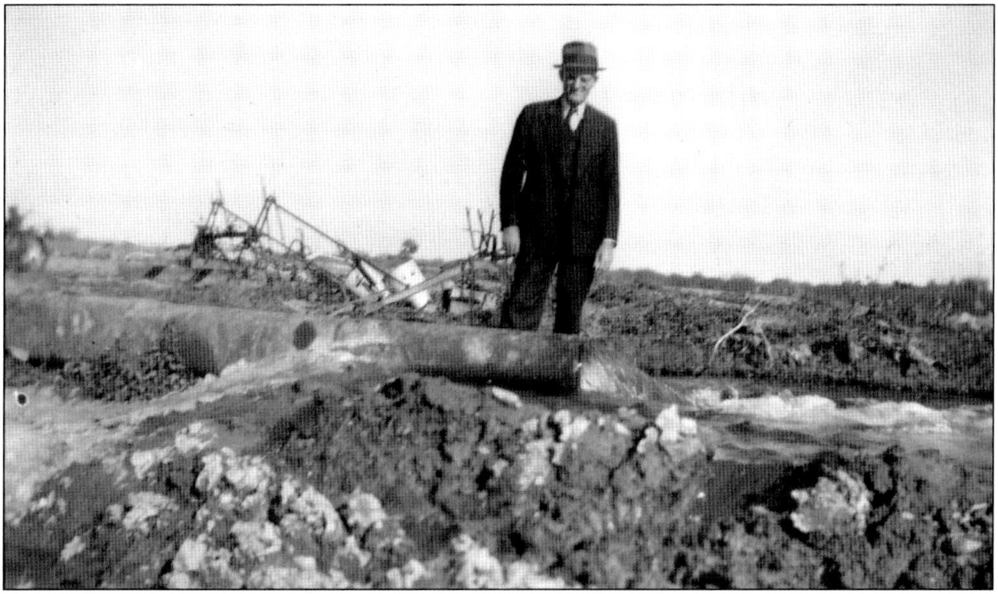

To farm in San Pedro, Ben Theimer discovered he needed irrigation wells. In this 1926 or 1929 photograph, Theimer is shown standing above his San Pedro Ranch irrigation system. The method proved fruitful in a short period of time. (Courtesy Buddy and Gretchen Hovda.)

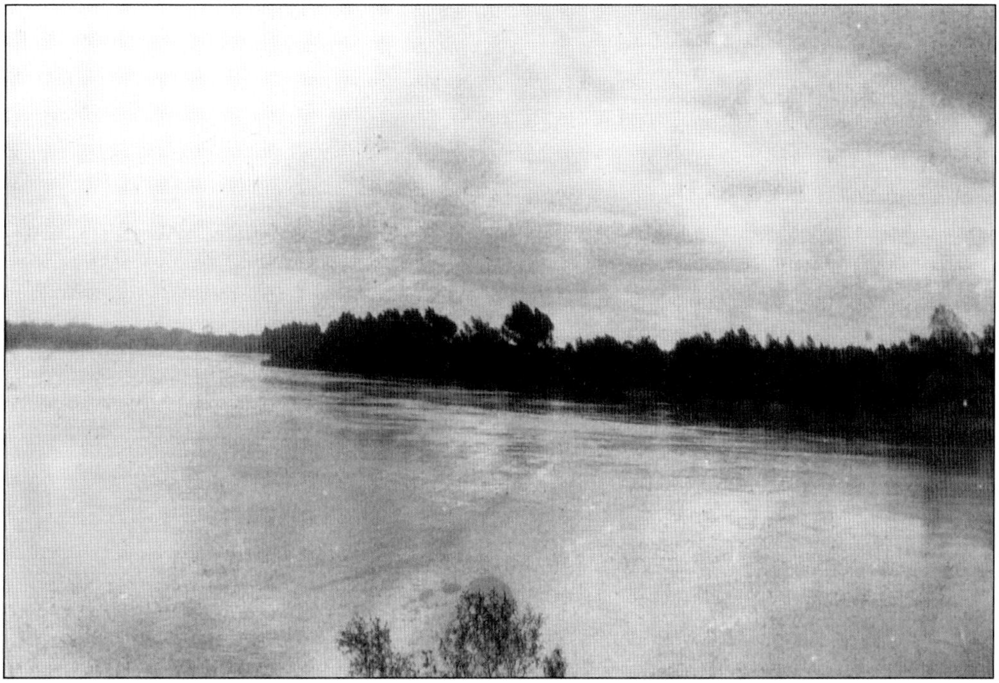

The Rio Grande is the southern boundary of the San Pedro Ranch and the international boundary of the United States and Mexico. When the river spilled over its banks, the San Pedro Ranch experienced serious flooding. This photograph was taken in 1967 after Hurricane Beulah. (Courtesy Buddy and Gretchen Hovda.)

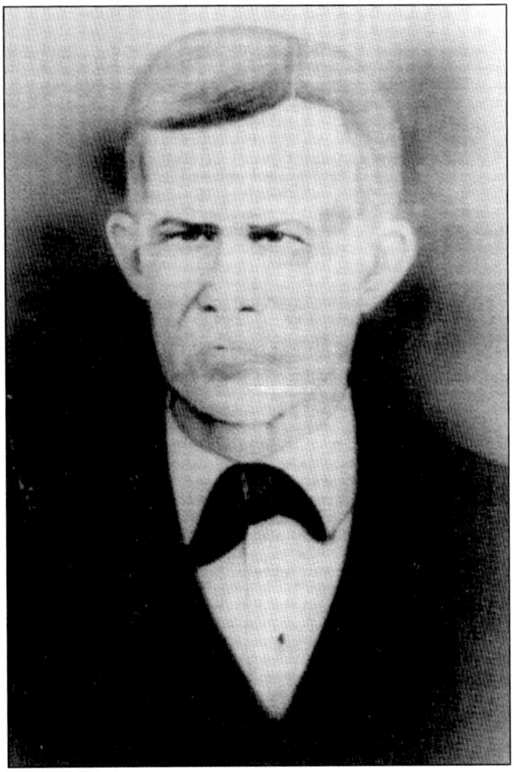

Adam Jacob Krummel, of German descent, was born in 1844 and died in 1907. Gerarda Solis Krummel was born on October 3, 1867, and died on December 29, 1938. The couple met in the Rio Grande Valley and lived in Parajitos Ranch for many years. Parajitos, Spanish for "little stopping places" and named for campsites of Confederate patrols along the river, was located just west of present-day Progreso. The couple eventually moved to Progreso, where many of their descendants still live today. (Both, courtesy Lala Galvan.)

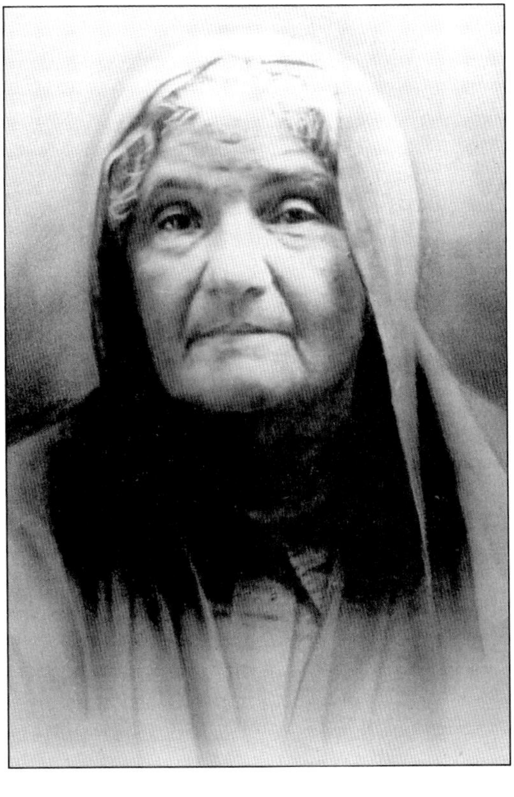

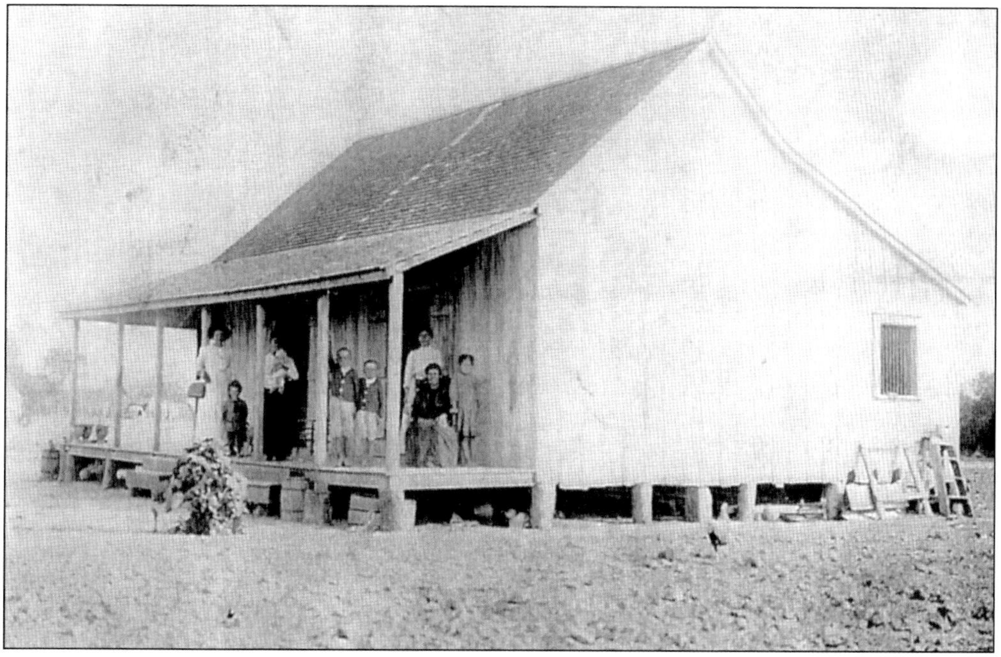

This is a 1906 photograph of Adam and Gerarda Krummel's home at Parajitos Ranch. Parajitos was located just west of present-day Progreso and just east of Runn, south of Donna. This is a typical ranch home of the time. Many of the Parajitos residents eventually moved to other towns in the Rio Grande Valley, including Progreso. (Courtesy Lala Galvan.)

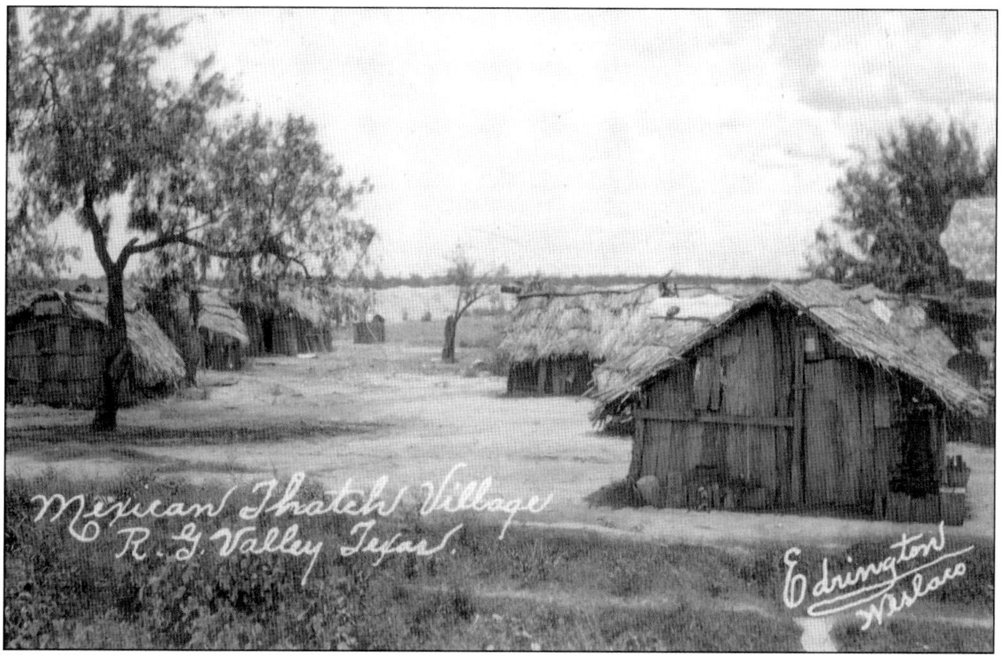


For many years, the boundary of the United States changed with the dynamic flow of the Rio Grande. This 1910 or 1920 postcard shows a "Mexican Thatch Village" in the Rio Grande Valley and the homes people inhabited along the Rio Grande, including in Progreso. (Courtesy Weslaco Museum.)

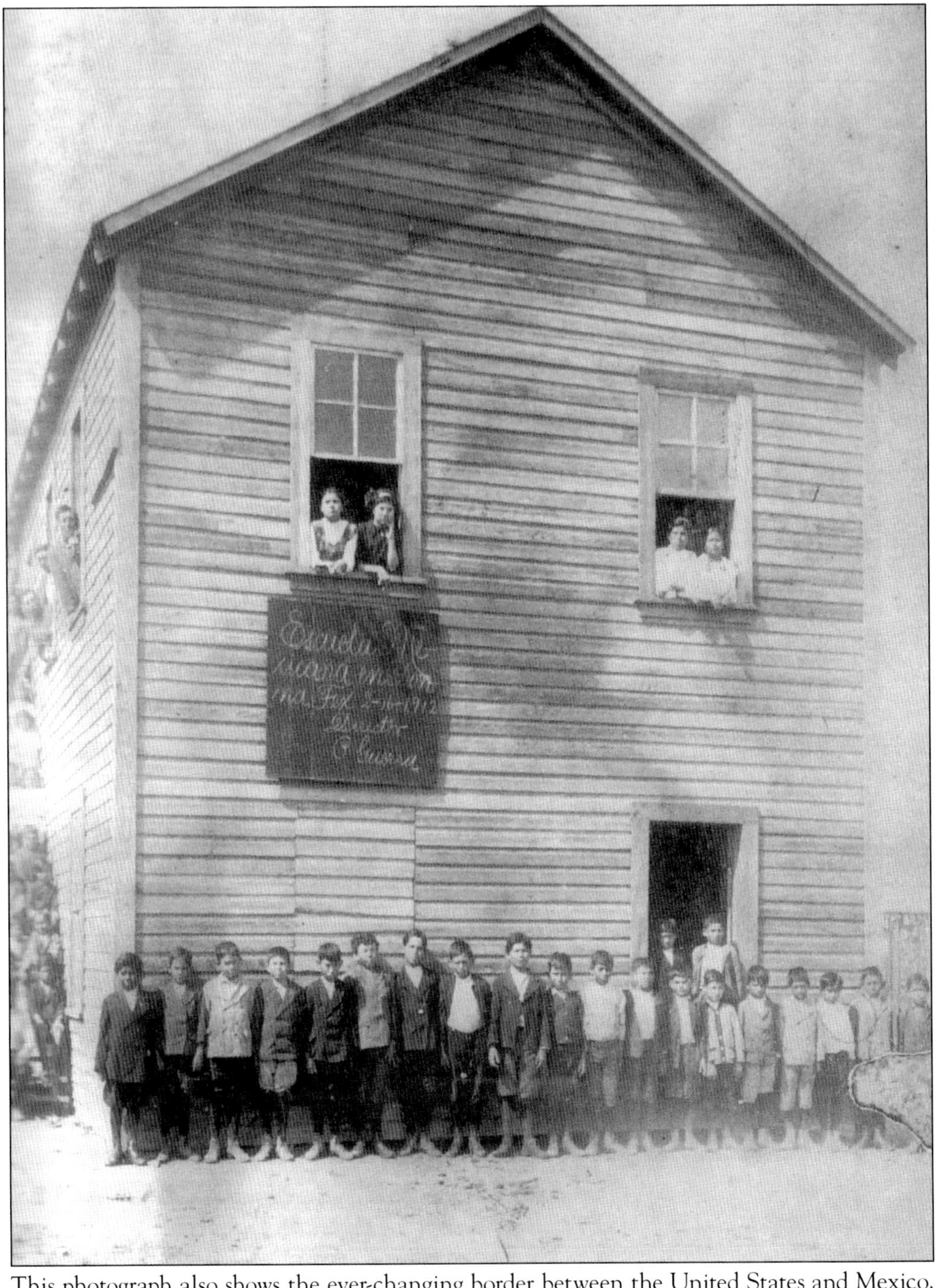

This photograph also shows the ever-changing border between the United States and Mexico. This school, known as Escuela Mexicana in Donna, Texas, was established in 1912. The director of the school was P. Guerra. Donna is northwest of modern-day Progreso. (Courtesy Weslaco Museum.)

# *Three*

# INDUSTRY BOOM

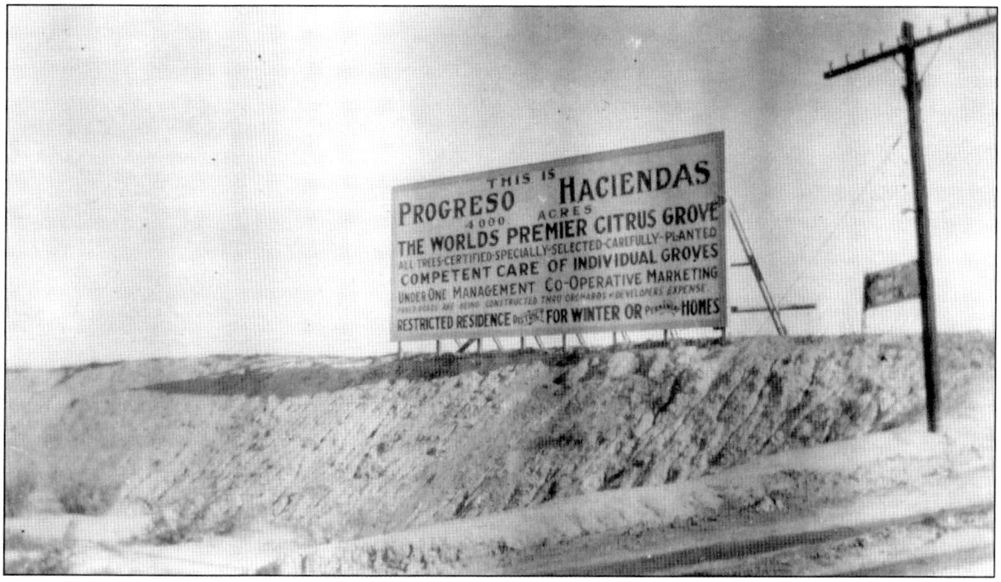


This sign proclaims "Progreso Haciendas . . . the World's Premier Citrus Grove" and perhaps explains the vision investors had for Progreso. Jack Holcomb managed the Progreso Haciendas Company in 1948, after he bought the company from his father, Blaine. But the Progreso Citrus boom was short-lived as two disastrous freezes—one in 1949 and another in 1951—literally killed the industry in Progreso. After that point, people farmed cotton and vegetables. (Courtesy Buddy and Gretchen Hovda.)

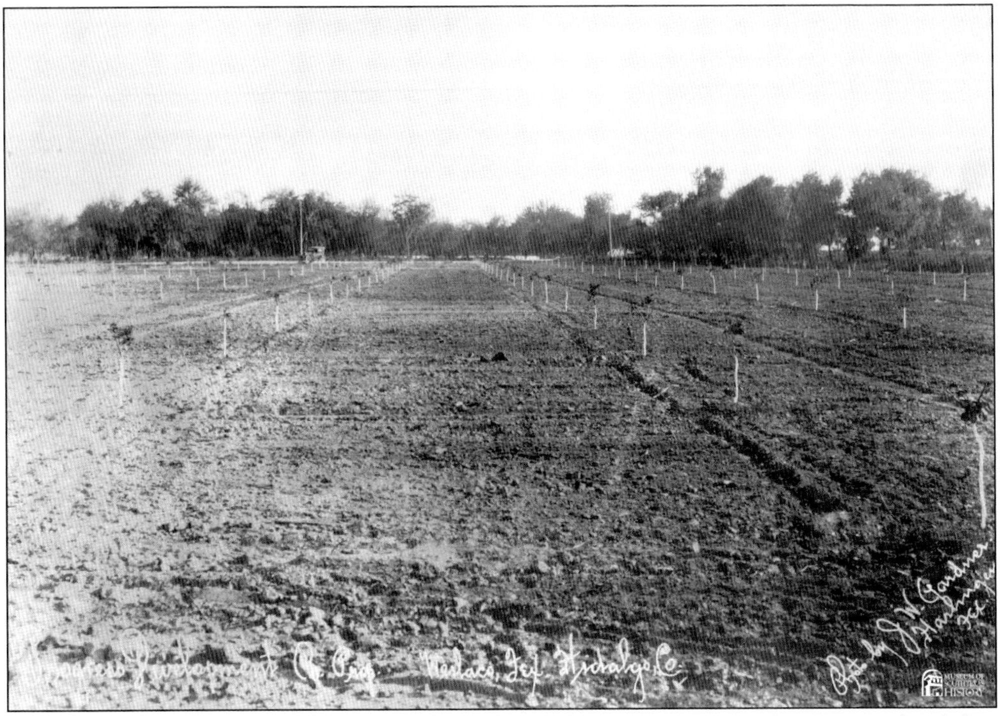

The Progreso Development Company planted these new citrus groves in the 1920s on land that is just north of the Rio Grande. Local farmers had high hopes for the citrus industry, but Mother Nature would later destroy the citrus industry in Progreso. Records indicate that the trees here are grapefruit. (Both, courtesy Museum of South Texas History.)

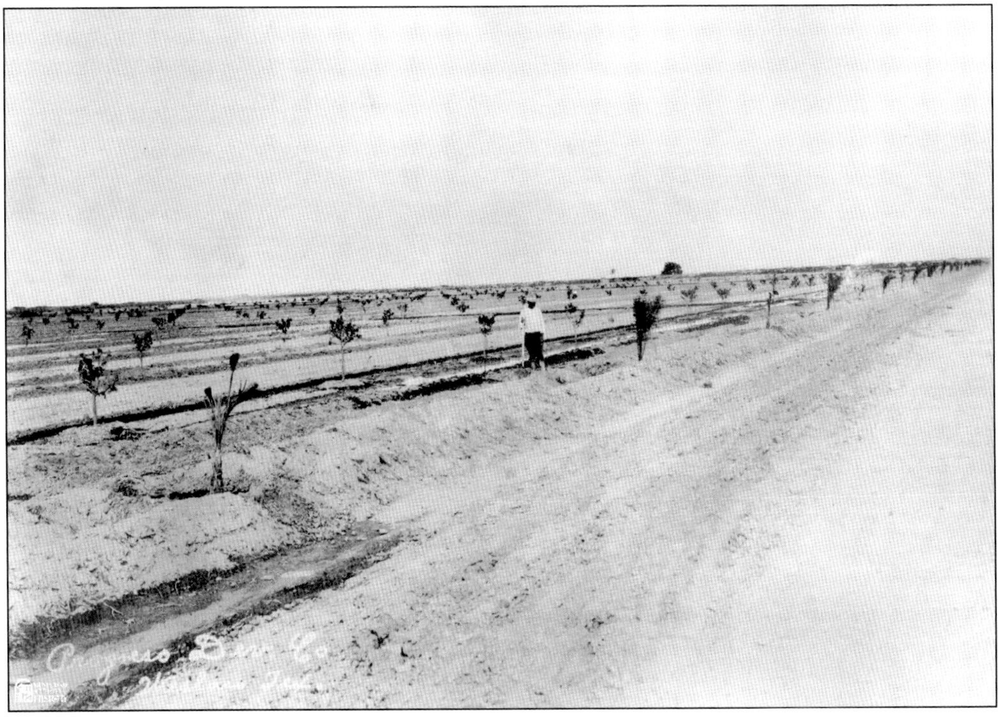

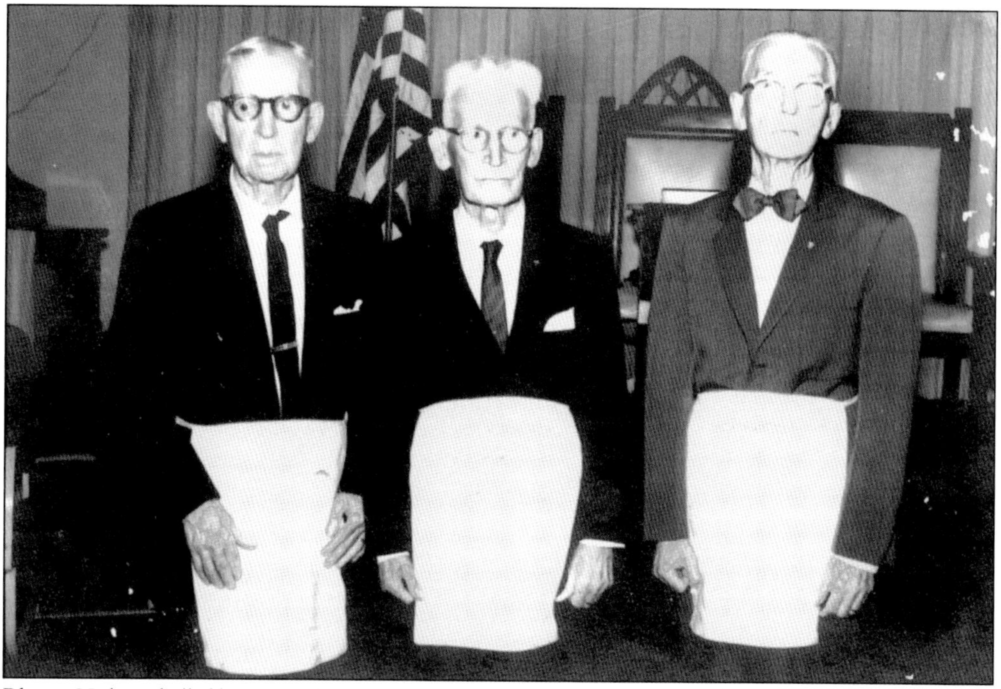

Blaine Holcomb (left) invested in Progreso in the early 1930s. He and his brothers Earl Holcomb (center) and C. H. Holcomb (right) were honored for 170 years of collective Masonic service. This photograph was taken in 1965 at the Weslaco Masonic Lodge. (Courtesy Jack Holcomb.)

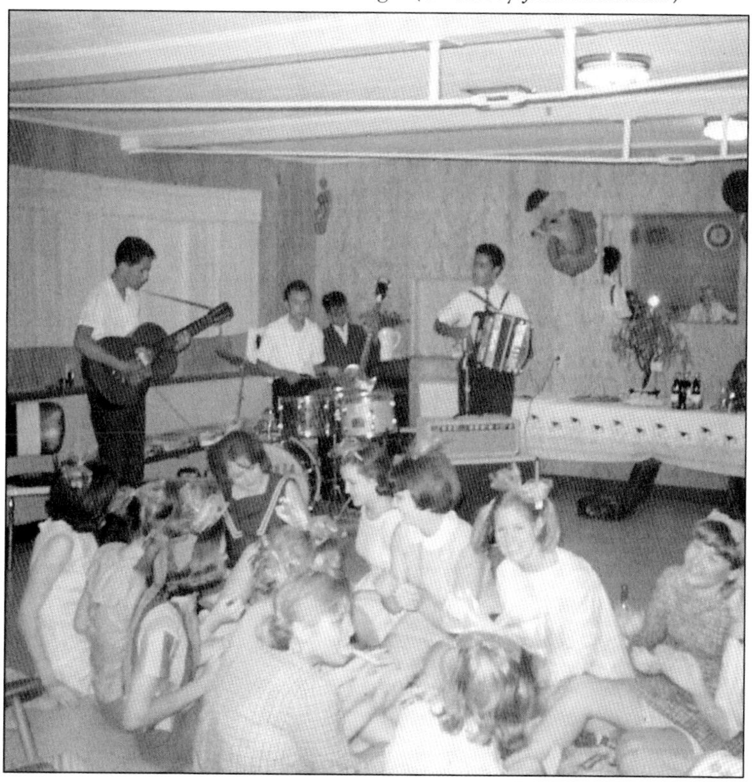

Jack and Ann Holcomb lived on the corner of Baker Street and FM 1015 in Progreso. This image shows one of the many parties the Holcombs hosted for the young people of Progreso. The couple realized that entertainment in town was limited, so they hired bands like Jose Garza y su Conjunto. (Courtesy Jack Holcomb.)

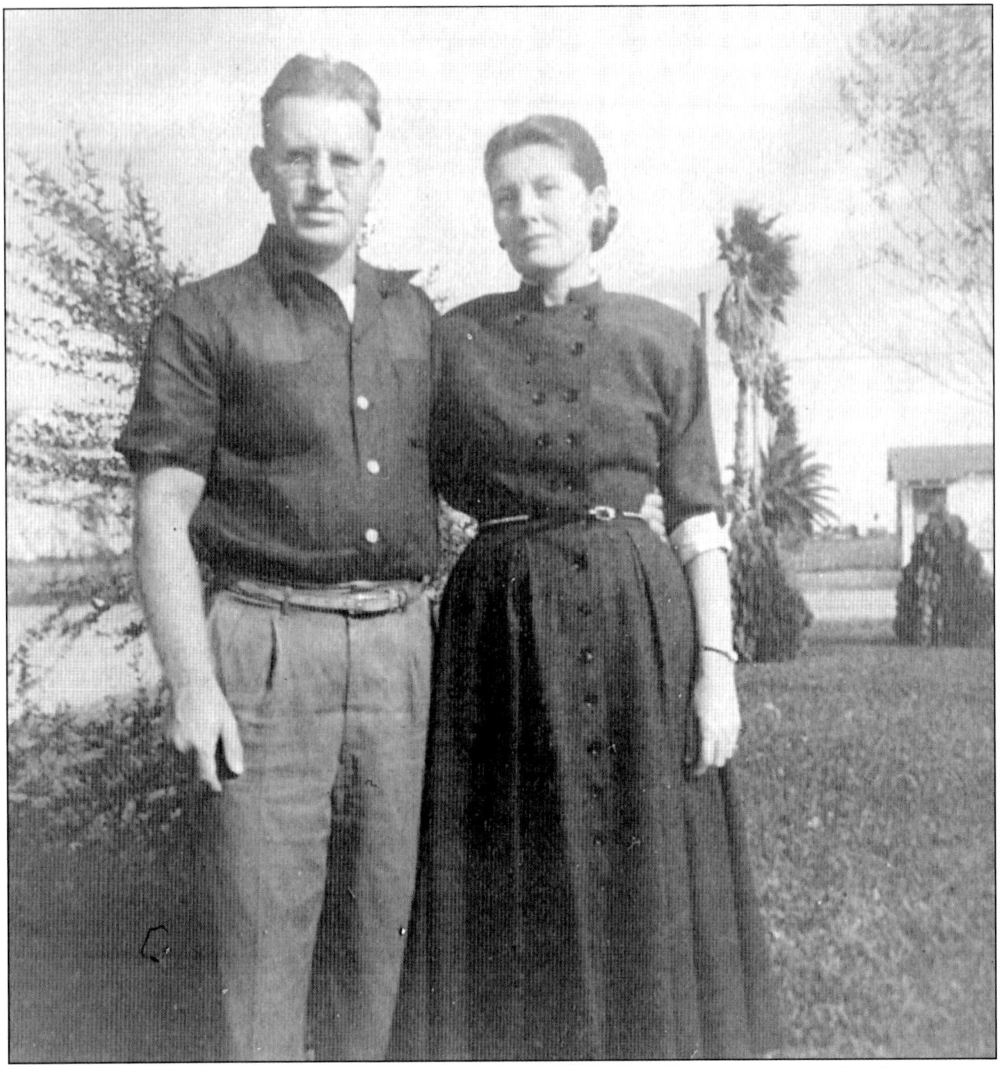

Jack and Ann Holcomb purchased 20 acres of land, for $20 an acre, and moved to Progreso in 1937. Jack took over the Progreso Haciendas Company in 1948 and later purchased another 700 acres of farmland to grow citrus, vegetables, and sugarcane. This photograph was taken in 1953. (Courtesy Jack Holcomb.)

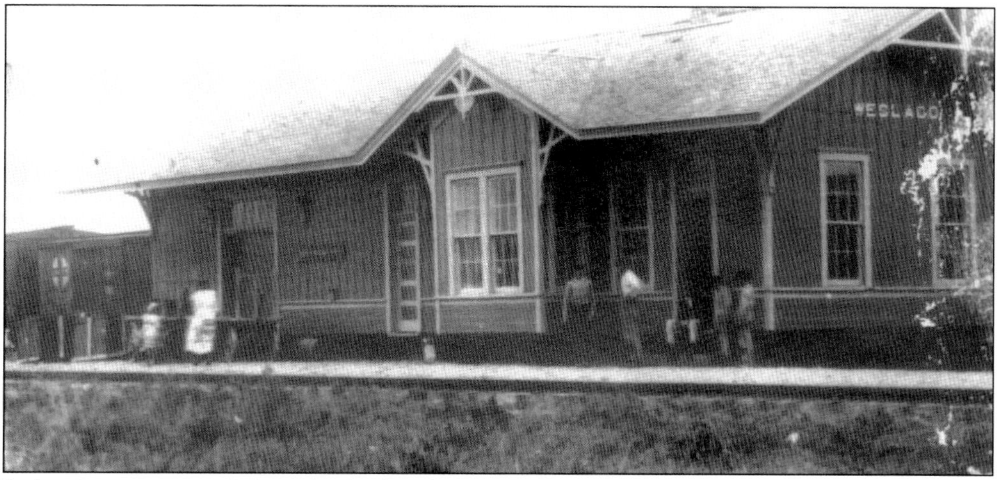


Before Progreso joined the web of railroad tracks that went up and down the Rio Grande Valley, business owners used trucks to transport cotton and citrus produced in the area to the Weslaco depot. This 1920 photograph shows the Weslaco railroad station, where farmers took their crops to market. (Courtesy Weslaco Museum.)

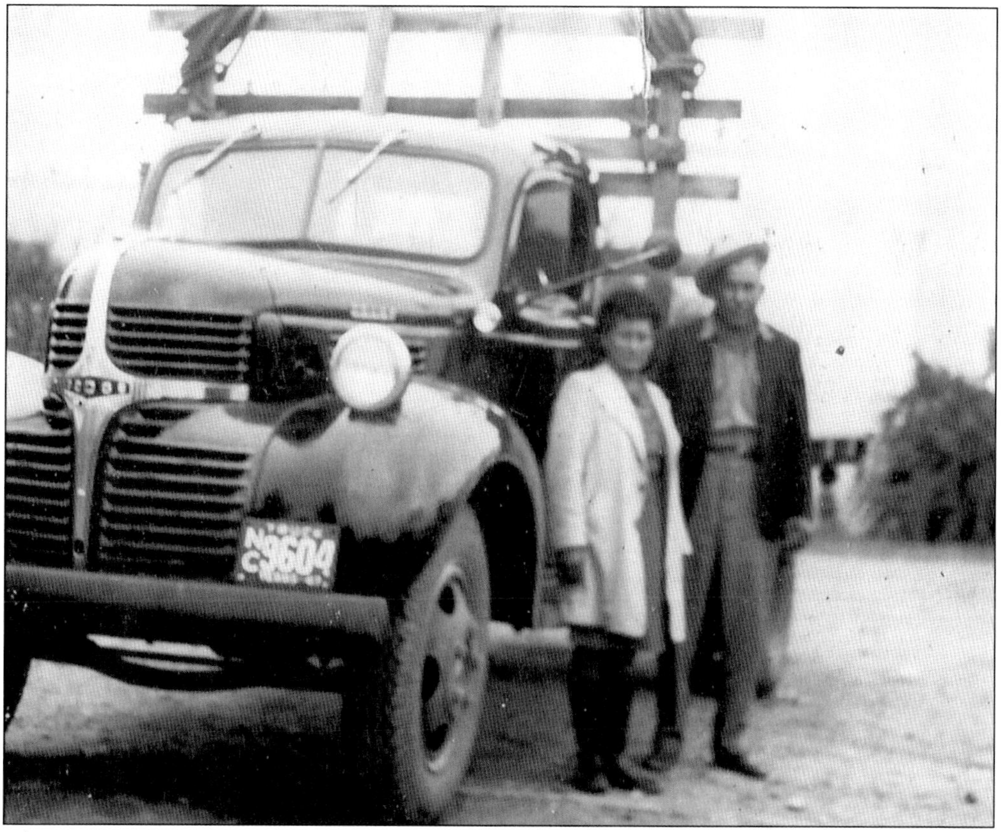

This 1943 or 1944 photograph shows Pedro and Lorenza Garza by their cotton truck, used to transport cotton from Progreso to Weslaco. At that time, cotton was the cash crop, but getting the product to market involved driving the bales of cotton to the Weslaco depot. Dozens of people like the Garzas made a living by transporting cotton. (Courtesy Soledad G. Rodriguez.)

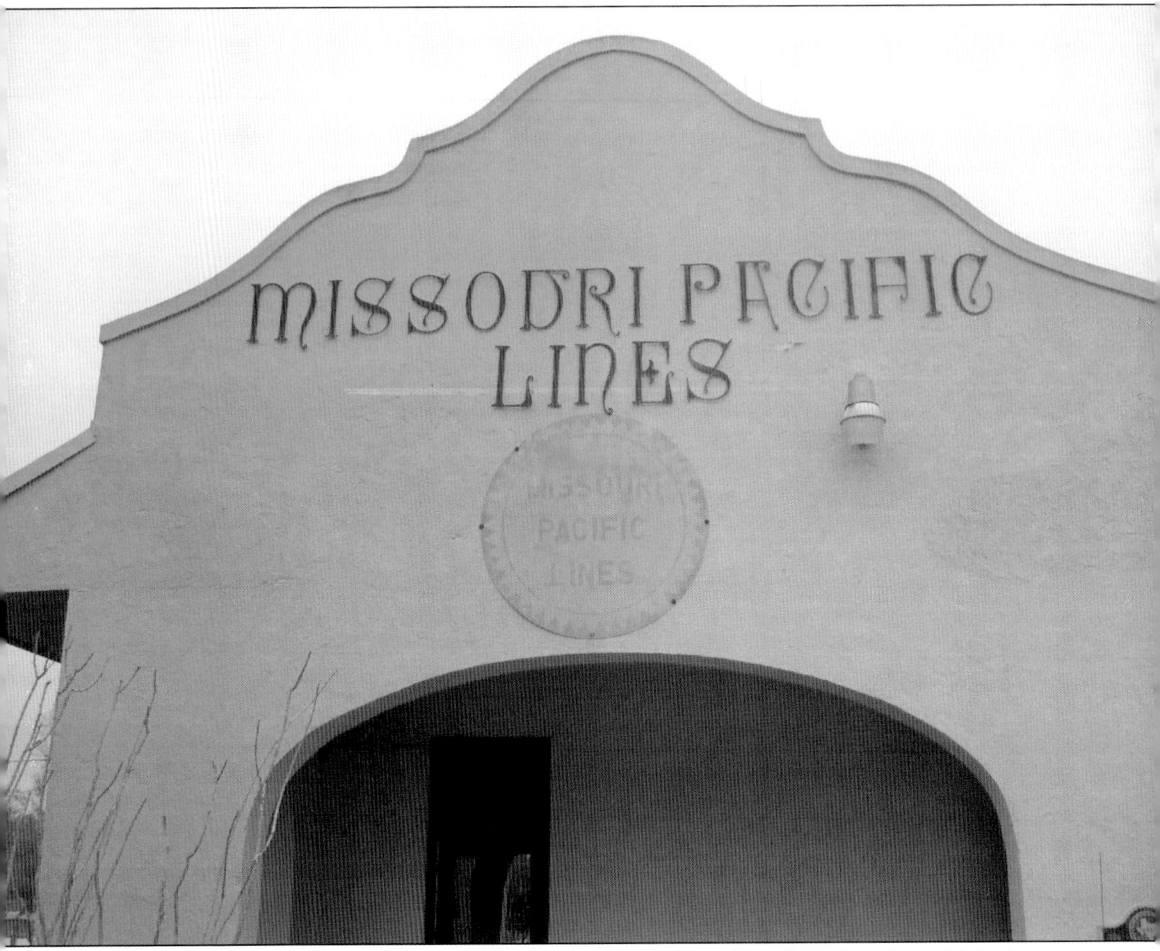


When Progreso was added to the route of the so-called Spiderweb Railroad in 1926, the town experienced a commercial boom. The Progreso Missouri Pacific Depot was recently restored by the Beckwith family, its present owners. The doorknobs are original and are inscribed with the name Missouri Pacific. (Courtesy author's collection.)

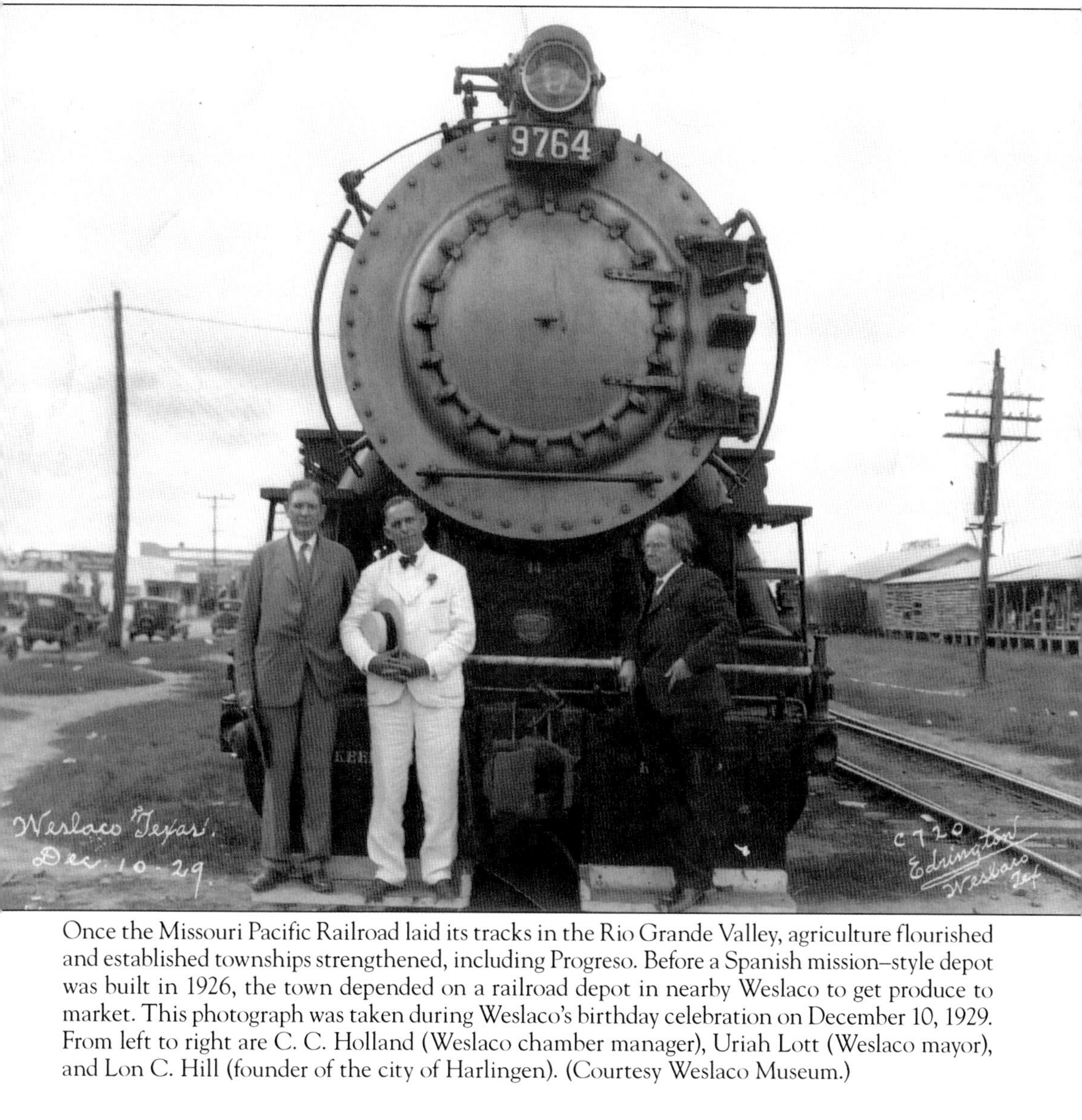


Once the Missouri Pacific Railroad laid its tracks in the Rio Grande Valley, agriculture flourished and established townships strengthened, including Progreso. Before a Spanish mission–style depot was built in 1926, the town depended on a railroad depot in nearby Weslaco to get produce to market. This photograph was taken during Weslaco's birthday celebration on December 10, 1929. From left to right are C. C. Holland (Weslaco chamber manager), Uriah Lott (Weslaco mayor), and Lon C. Hill (founder of the city of Harlingen). (Courtesy Weslaco Museum.)

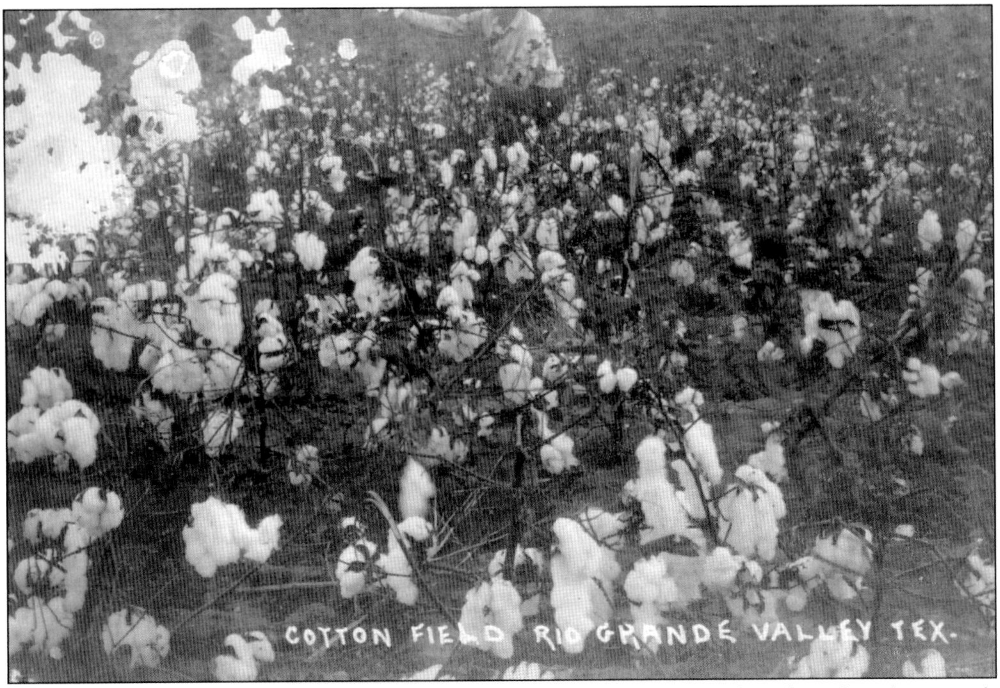


The cotton business has been part of Progreso's agricultural history for decades. This photograph was taken in an undisclosed field in the Rio Grande Valley. Progreso made news headlines after the first U.S. bale of cotton in 1984 was produced by Progreso resident Balde Gonzalez. (Courtesy Weslaco Museum.)

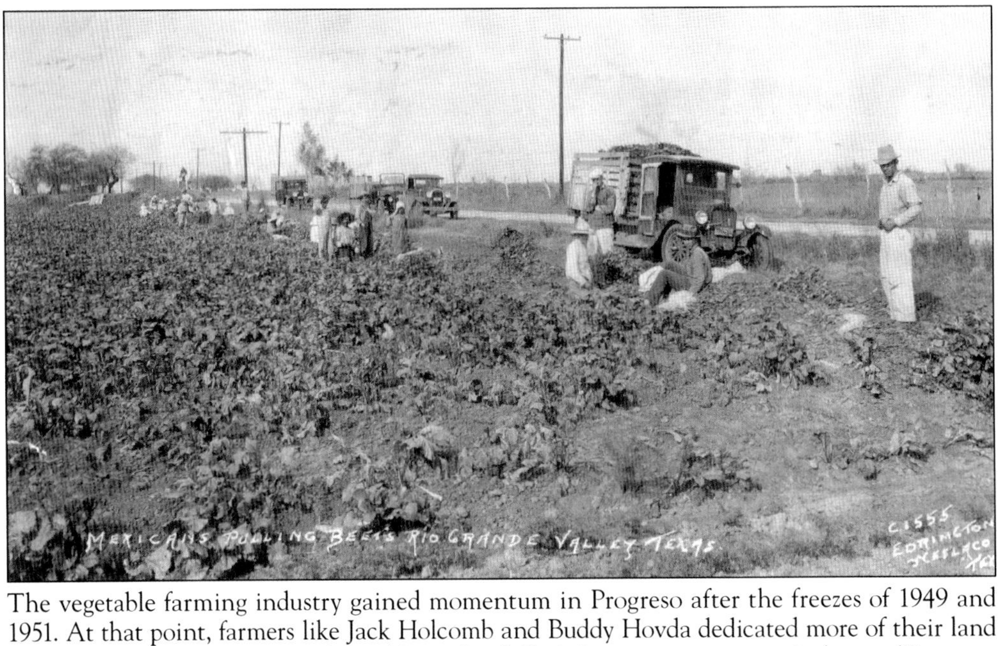


The vegetable farming industry gained momentum in Progreso after the freezes of 1949 and 1951. At that point, farmers like Jack Holcomb and Buddy Hovda dedicated more of their land to vegetable farming because the cold weather killed the promising citrus industry. (Courtesy Weslaco Museum.)

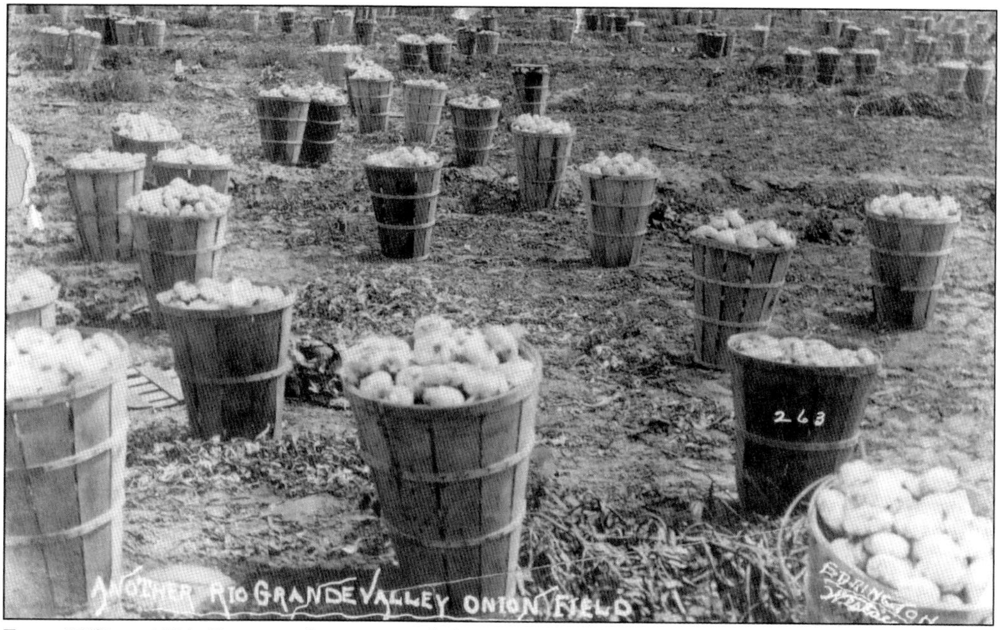


From 1952 to 1971, Progreso farmers used the majority of their land for vegetable farming. Jack Holcomb employed between 1,500 and 1,800 people to work the fields at the height of the season. (Courtesy Weslaco Museum.)

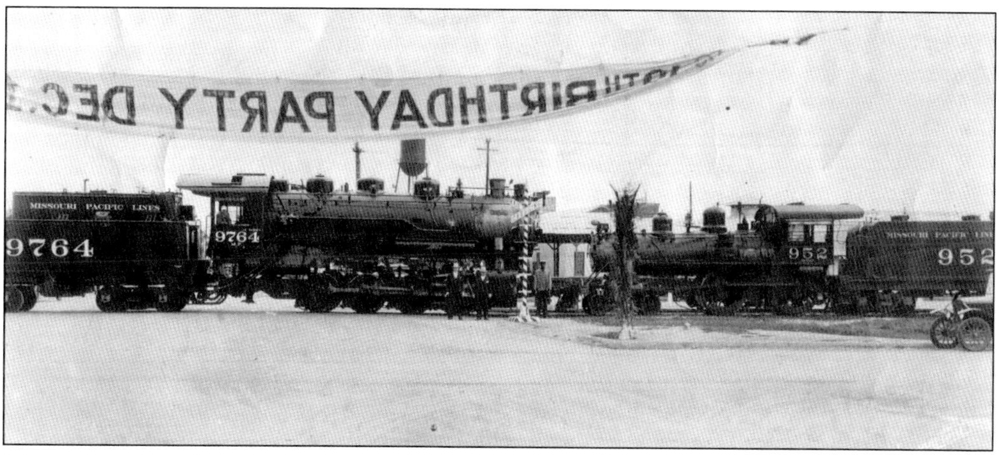


The locomotives shown here carried the cotton and produce grown in Progreso to markets in Houston, Dallas, and San Antonio. The Spiderweb Railroad, later absorbed by the Missouri Pacific Railroad, maintained a stop in Progreso from 1926 to 1931. During those years, the Progreso agricultural industry boomed. Farmers say the line made it easy for growers to sell their goods in major markets. (Courtesy Weslaco Museum.)

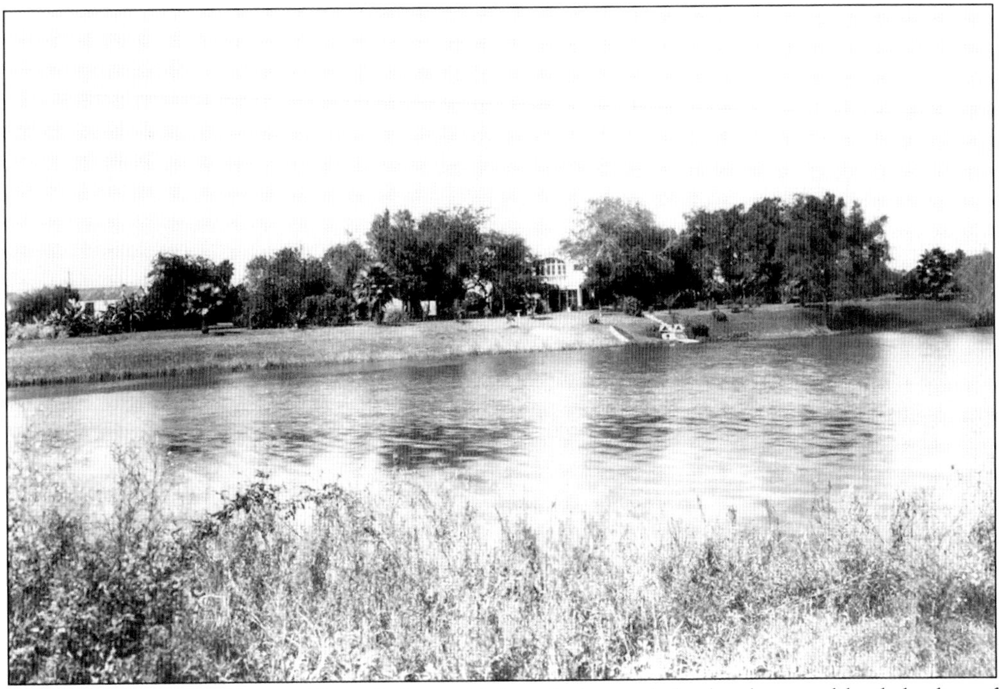

Progreso Lakes is made up of Lion Lake and Moon Lake, and the land around both bodies of water is prime real estate. These two photographs show views of Lion Lake (above) and of Dr. Larry M. Dubuisson's home (below). The Mediterranean architecture shows the type of homes built by the investors of the Progreso Development Company. Progreso Lakes was established as a city in 1979; before then, Progreso and Progreso Lakes shared a common history. (Both, courtesy Weslaco Museum.)

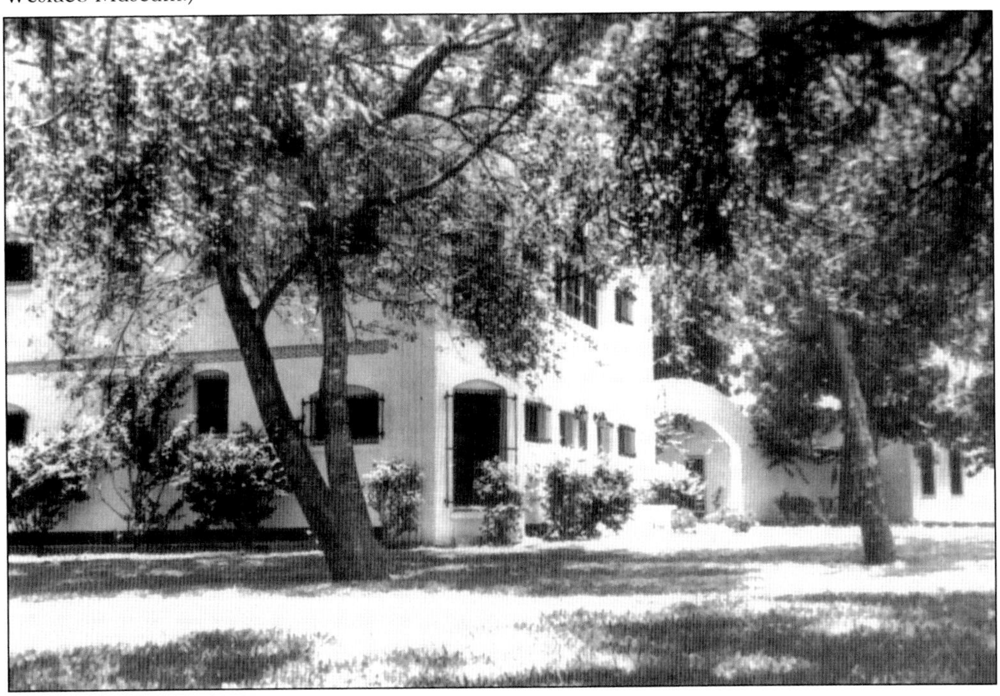

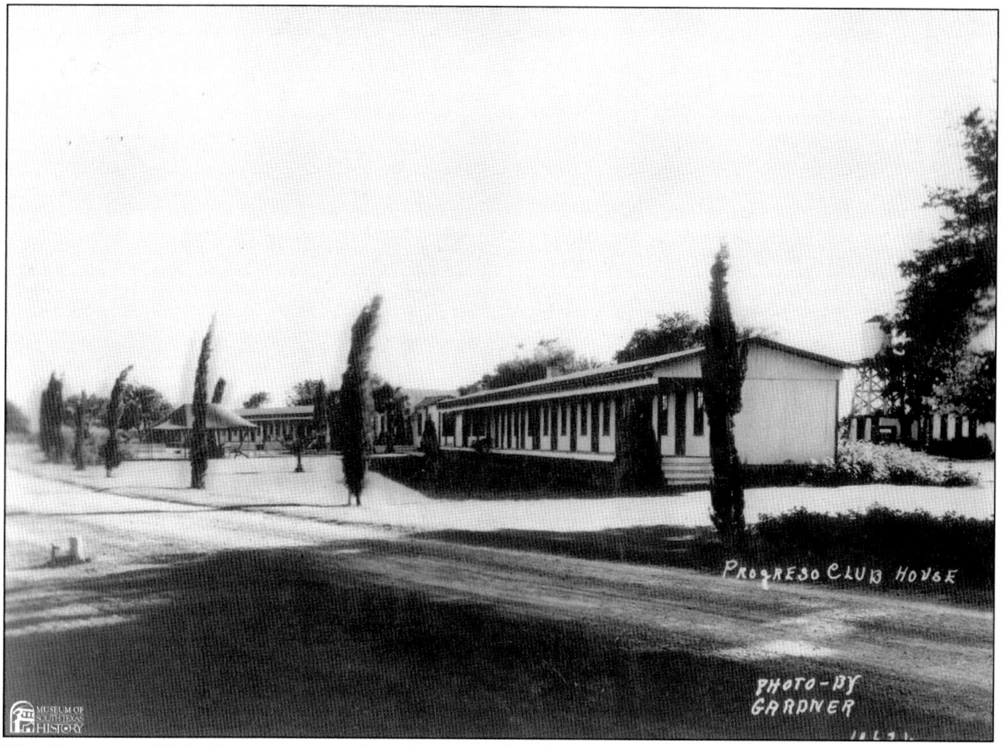


The Progreso Club House was used in the 1930s by the Progreso Development Company and its investors. The company recruited investors from as far north as Chicago. Locals say the investors wined and dined in nearby Rio Rico, Mexico. This photograph was taken by Gardner in 1930. (Courtesy Museum of South Texas History.)

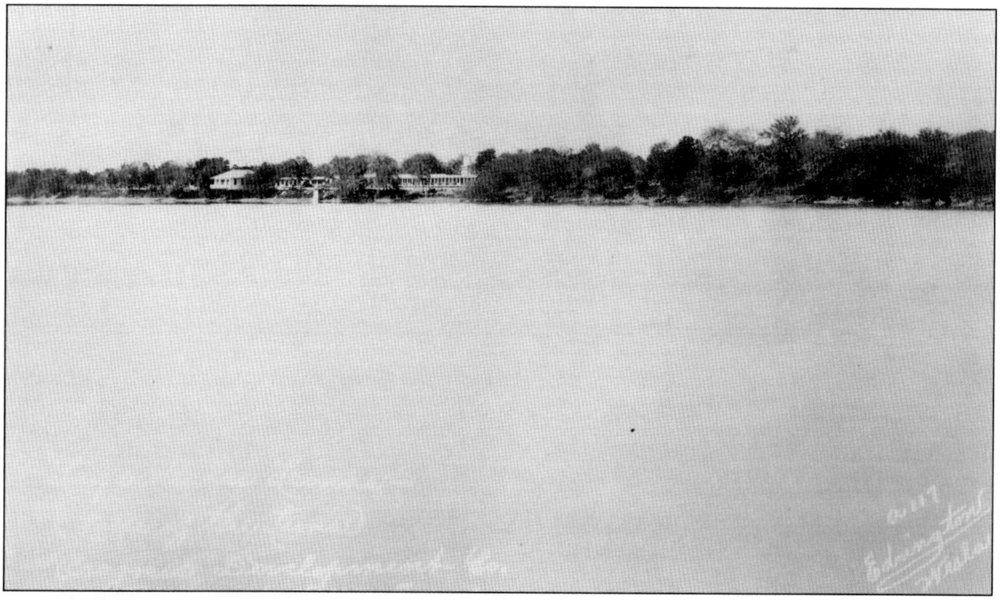

Lago de los Leones is another Progreso Development Company project in the Rio Grande Valley. This photograph was taken at Progreso Lakes in 1927. (Courtesy Museum of South Texas History.)

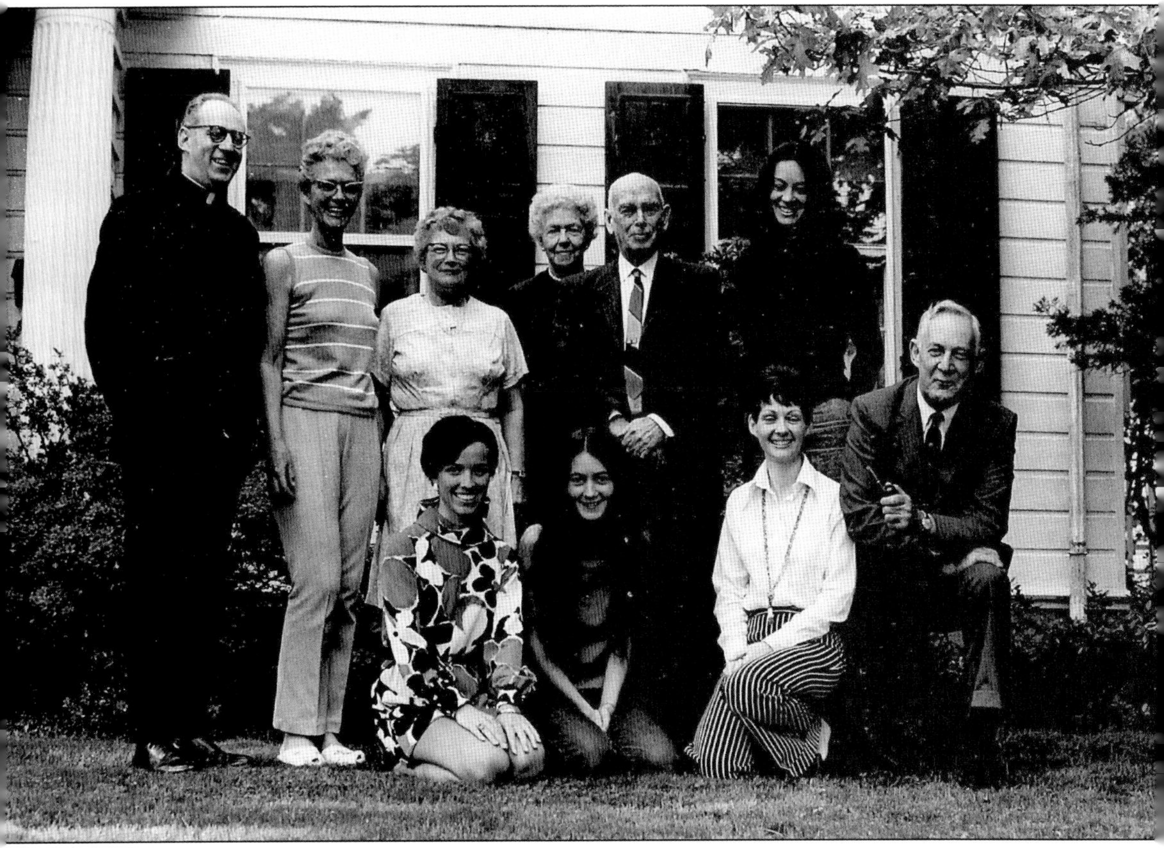

The Progreso Development Company invested a lot of time and money in Progreso. Bill Fitzgerald worked for the Progreso Development Company and lived just east of FM 1015 and north of Baker Street in Progreso. This family photograph was taken in 1958 or 1959. (Courtesy Jack Holcomb.)

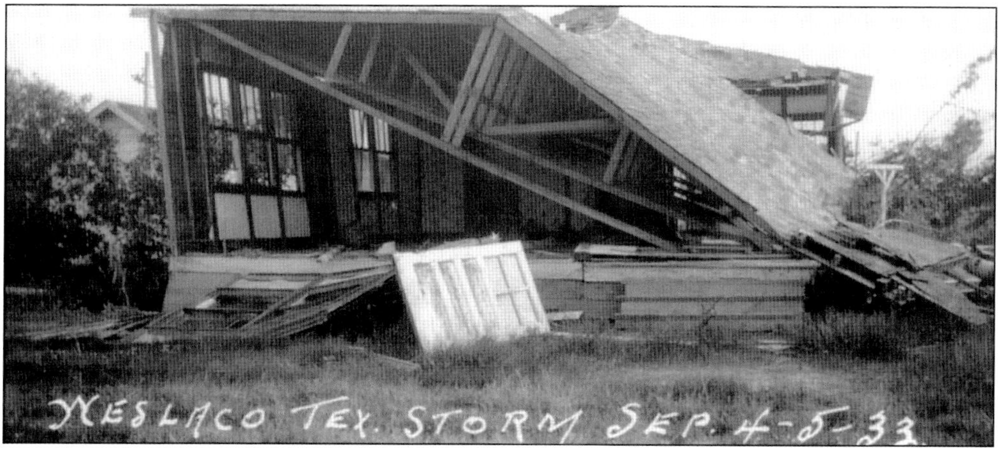


These two photographs show the damage to homes and property caused by the 1933 hurricane. Combined with the market crash of 1929, this major hurricane destroyed the Progreso Development Company, which eventually declared bankruptcy. (Both, courtesy Weslaco Museum.)

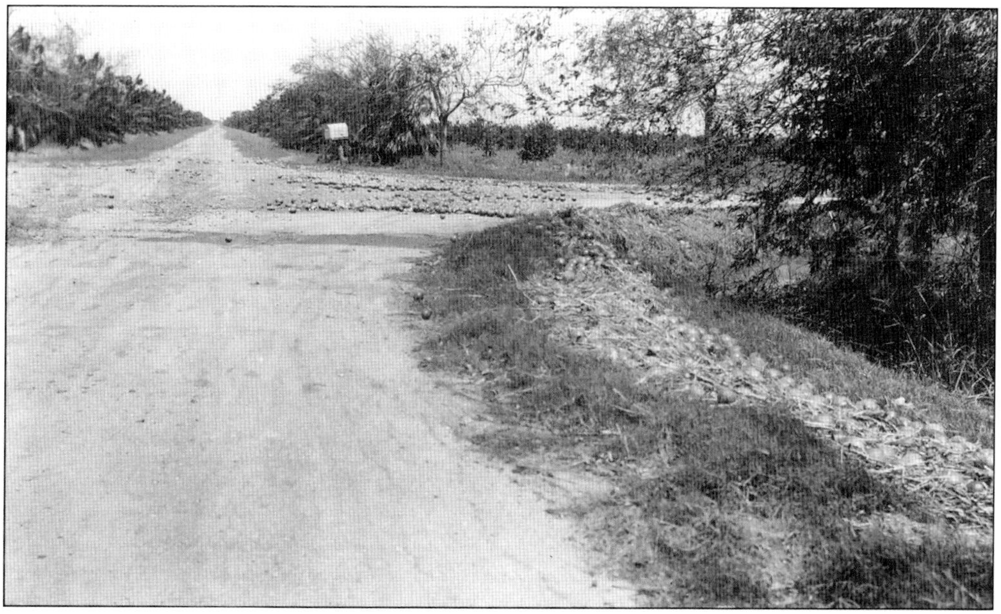

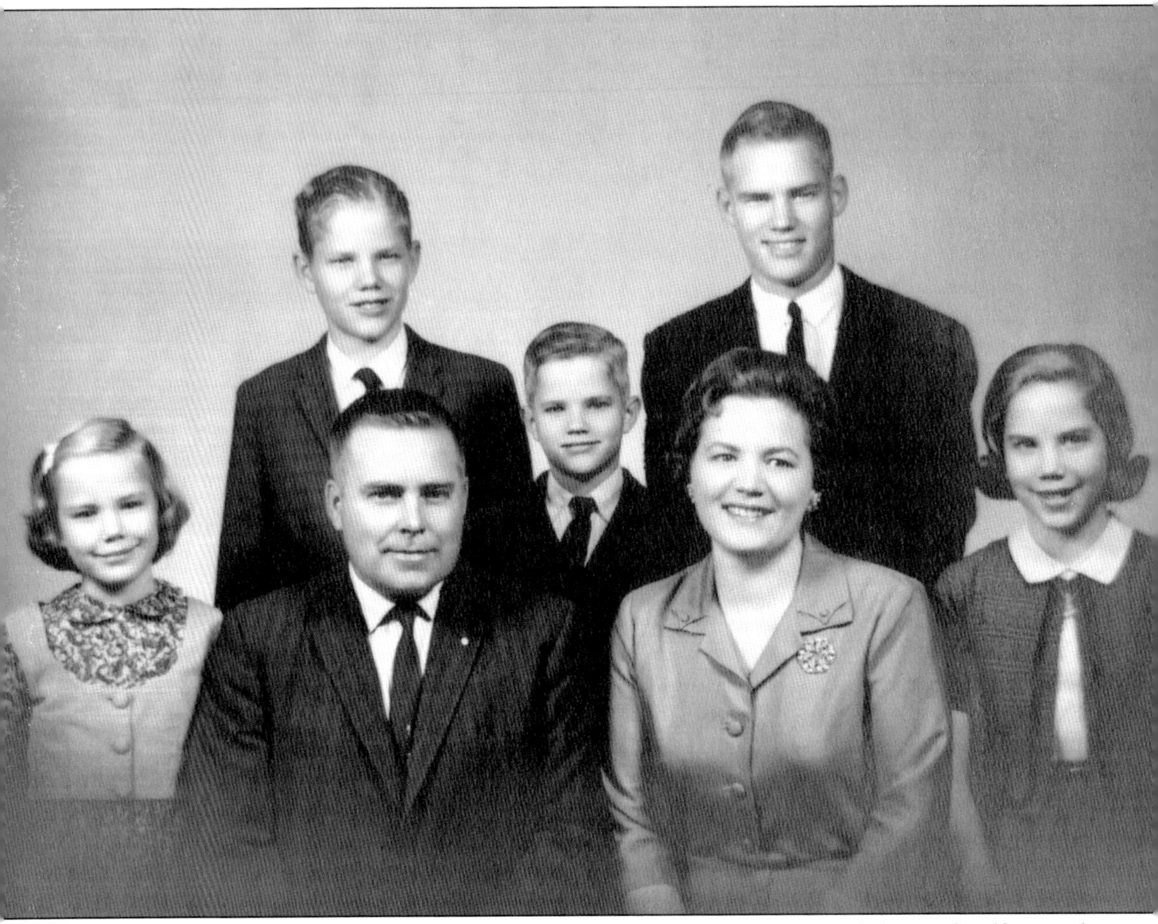

The Hovda family moved to Progreso in 1952. Family members are, from left to right, (first row) Hanna, Buddy, Gretchen, and daughter Gretchen; (second row) David, Hans, and Allen. The Hovdas have farmed in Progreso for about half a century. They are members of the Progreso Co-op and its group of local farmers. (Courtesy Buddy and Gretchen Hovda.)

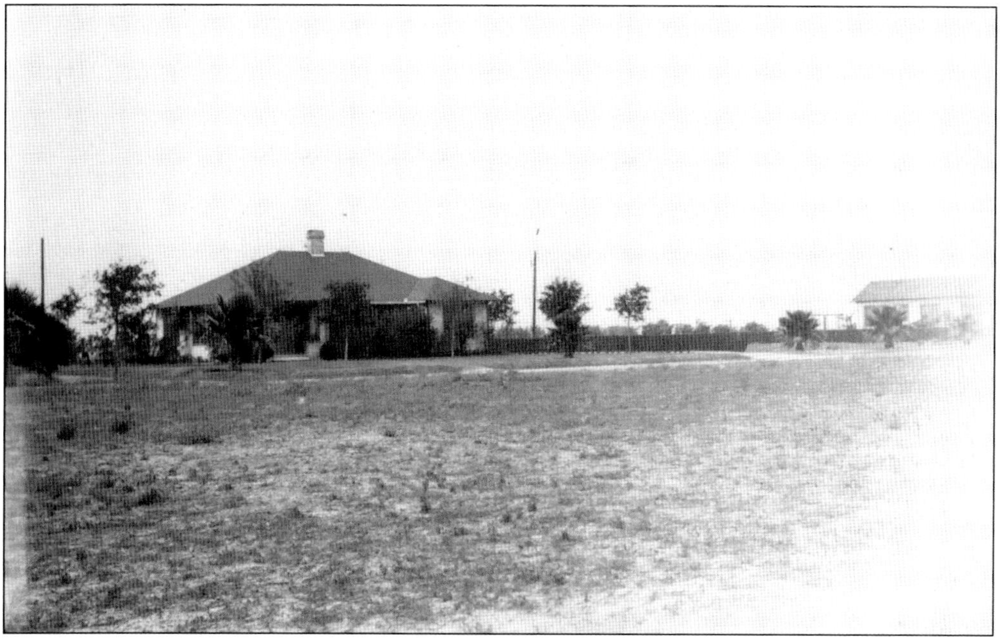

Originally built for a Progreso Development Company investor in 1926, the ranch house in this photograph became the Progreso home of the Buddy Hovda family. The family lived in the home from 1952 to 1989. This photograph was taken in 1933. (Courtesy Buddy and Gretchen Hovda.)

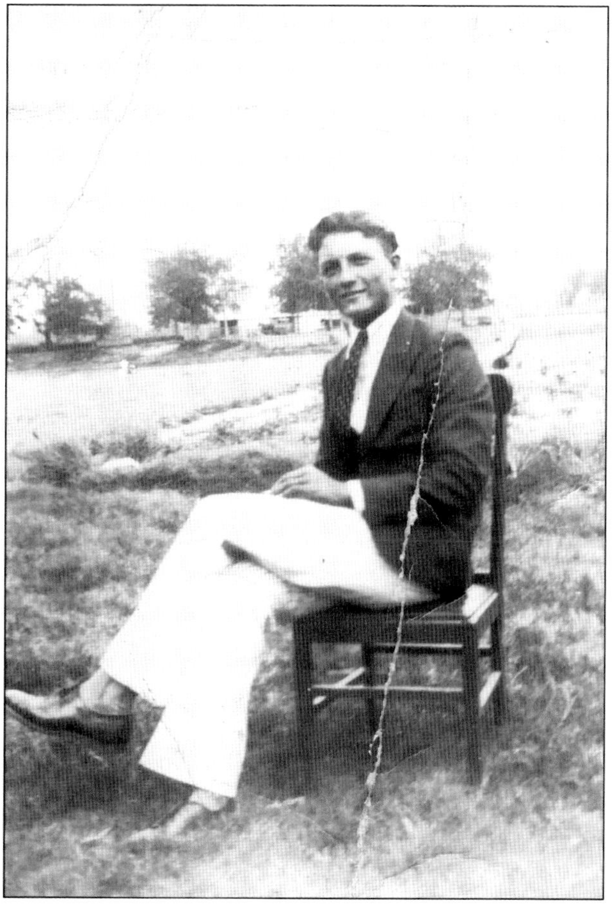

Roberto Champion is from the historic Italian Campeoni family who settled in Point Isabel in the mid-1800s. This photograph was taken along the Rio Grande on his 17th birthday. Roberto eventually became the first part-time deputy sheriff in Hidalgo County. For many years, he enforced law and order north of the Rio Grande, including in Progreso. (Courtesy Gloria C. Garcia.)

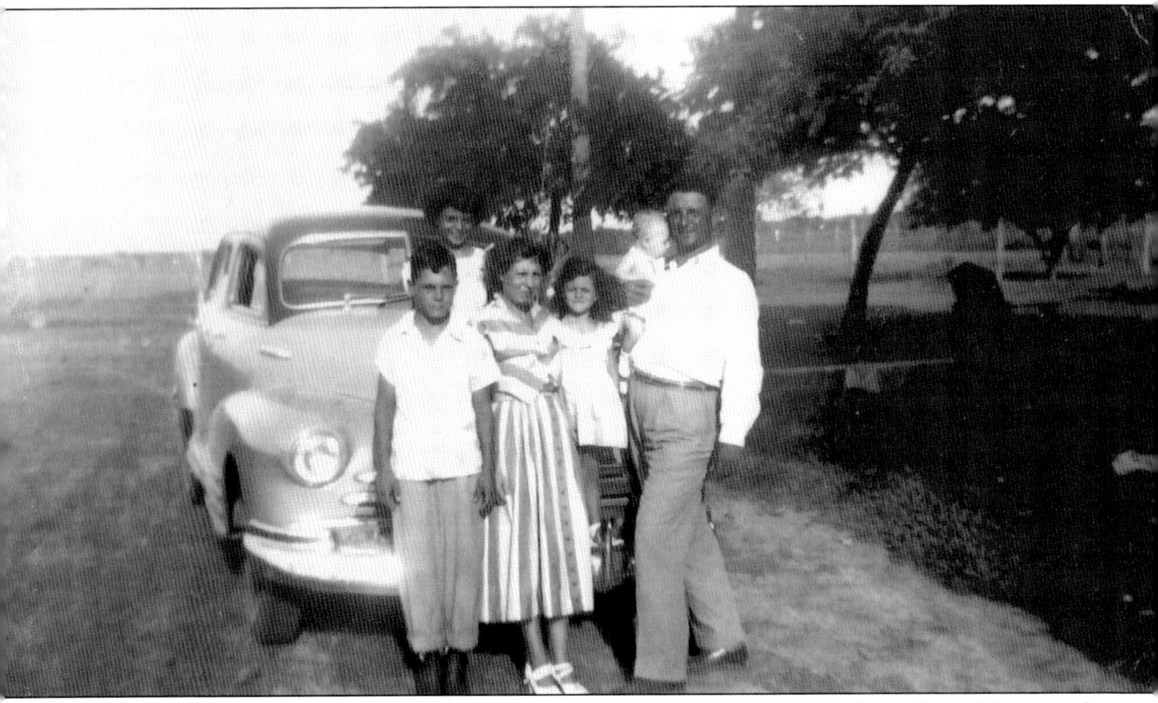

Roberto and Santitos Champion and their children—from left to right, Robert, Dora, Gloria, and Ernesto—are in front of their Progreso home on R. C. Champion Road. The street dead ends at a plot of pasture land; the Champion family still owns that property today. This photograph was taken in 1949. (Courtesy Gloria C. Garcia.)

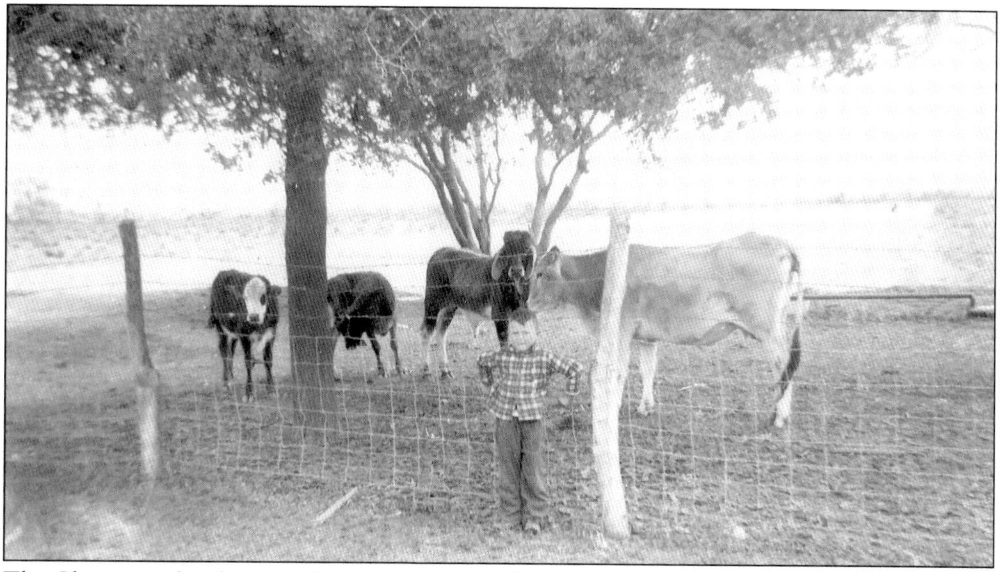

The Champion family not only owned a pool hall, a store, and a string of apartments, but they also owned a farm in Progreso. This image shows Ernesto Champion standing in front of the Champion pastureland located on the east side of the Champion home on R. C. Champion Road. This photograph was taken in 1953. (Courtesy Gloria C. Garcia.)

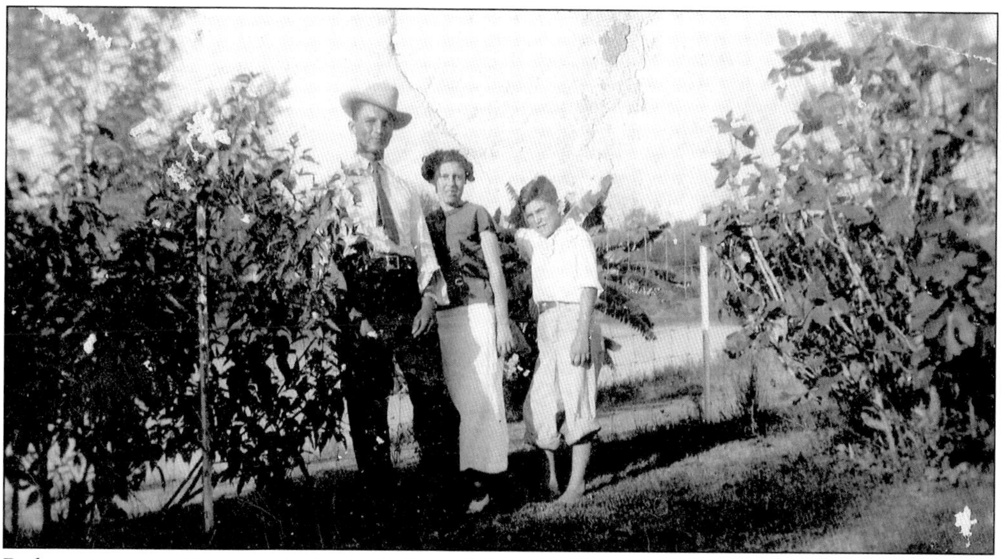

Before moving to Progreso, Roberto (left) and Santitos Champion (center) lived along Lion Lake in what is now Progreso Lakes. In this 1936 or 1937 photograph, the Champions and Arturo "Buddy" Treviño, Santitos's brother, are standing by fig trees on the banks of the lake. (Courtesy Gloria C. Garcia.)

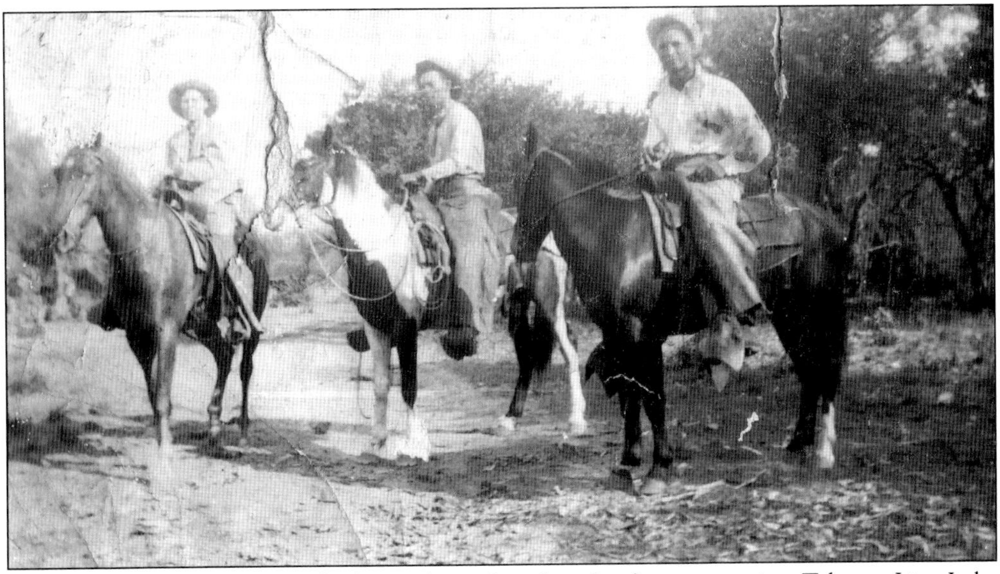

For many years, riding on horseback was the preferred mode of transportation. Taken at Lion Lake in 1936 or 1937, this photograph shows, from left to right, Santitos Treviño Champion, Pedro Champion, and Roberto Champion. (Courtesy Gloria C. Garcia.)

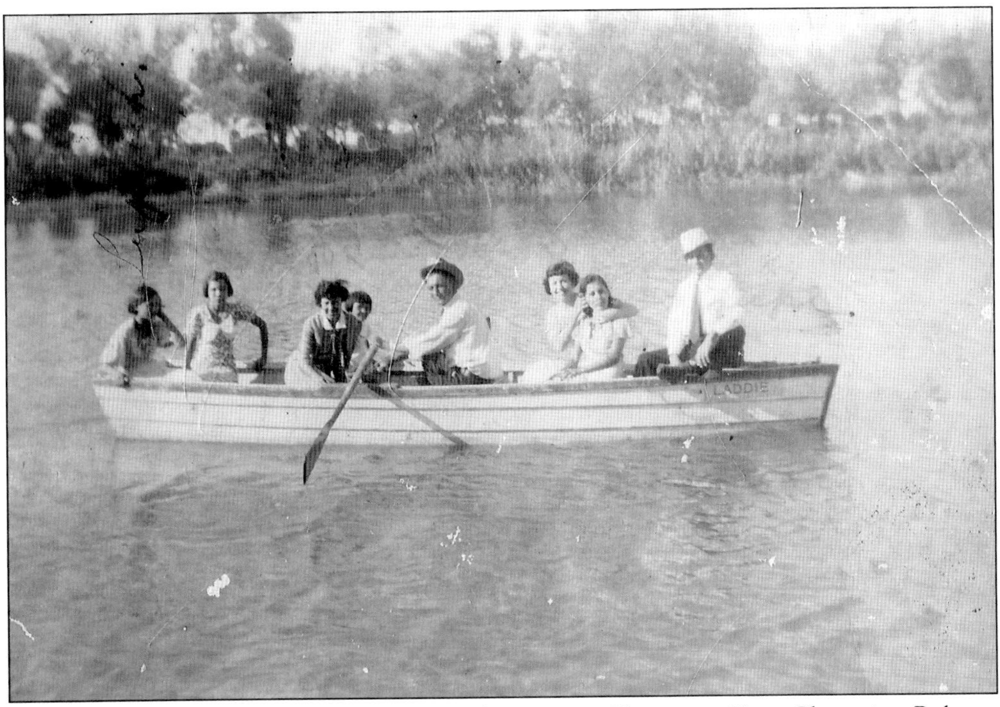


From left to right are Lupe Champion, Julia Solis, Santitos Champion, Nena Champion, Roberto Champion, Emma Treviño, Alicia Solis, and Lupe Hinojosa. Santitos Champion used this boat, the *Laddie*, to deliver fresh lunch and breakfast to Roberto Champion daily. On weekends and when people visited the Champion family, *Laddie* was used for entertainment. This photograph was taken in 1936 or 1937. (Courtesy Gloria C. Garcia.)

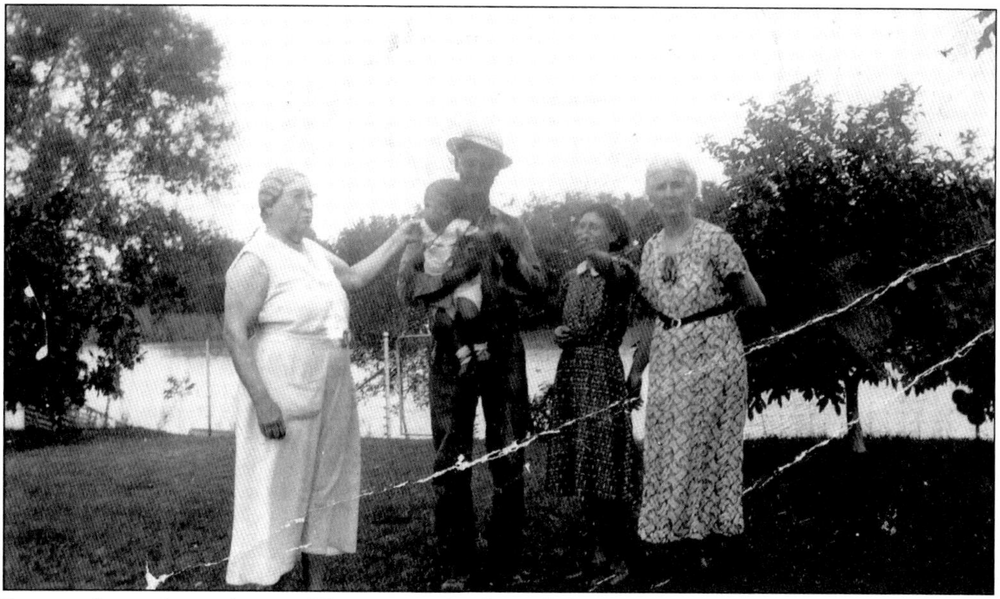

Progreso has welcomed winter Texans, people who call the Rio Grande Valley home for the winter, for decades. From left to right are a Mrs. B'gole, Roberto Champion holding Bobby Champion, Santitos Champion, and an unidentified person from Missouri. This 1938 photograph shows a glimpse of Progreso's southern hospitality. Just visible at left is the family boat, *Laddie*. The Champions used the craft to entertain guests. (Courtesy Gloria C. Garcia.)

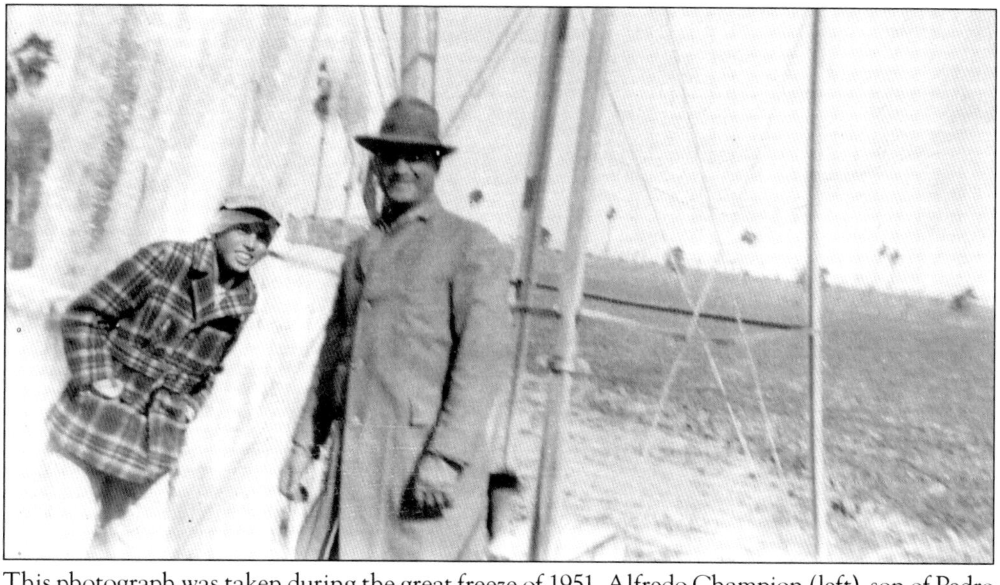

This photograph was taken during the great freeze of 1951. Alfredo Champion (left), son of Pedro B. Champion and Petra Adame Champion, and Roberto Champion (right) are standing next to the Champion family *papalote*, colloquial Spanish for "windmill." This photograph was taken just north of the Champion house located at the center of the Progreso township. (Courtesy Gloria C. Garcia.)

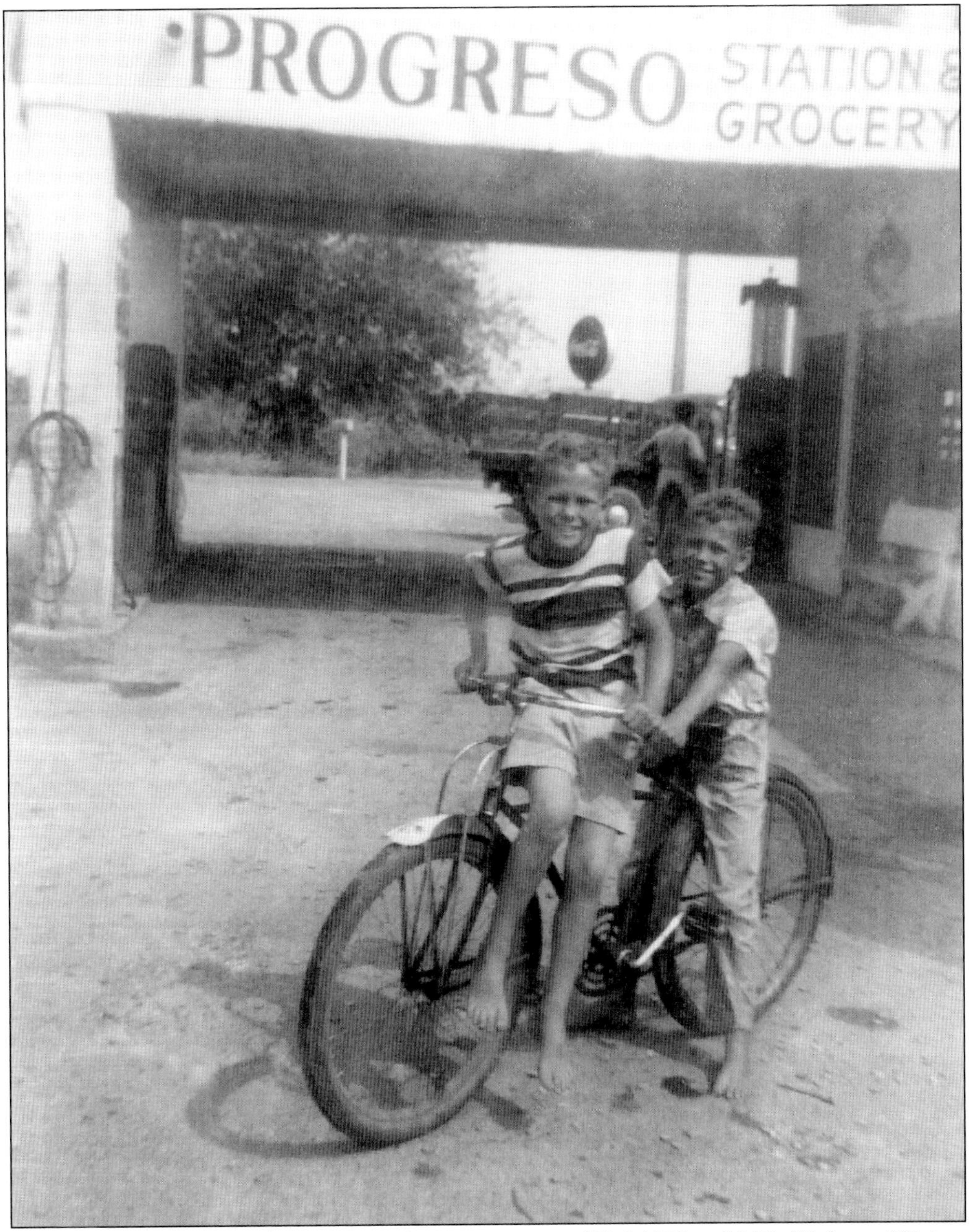


The Progreso Station and Grocery at the intersection of FM 1015 and U.S. Highway 281 is a community landmark. The business has switched hands over the years, but a store still stands in that particular location today. In this photograph Michael "Mike" Madden (left) and Gerald B. "Jerry" Madden (right) are riding a bicycle. (Courtesy Jay Madden.)

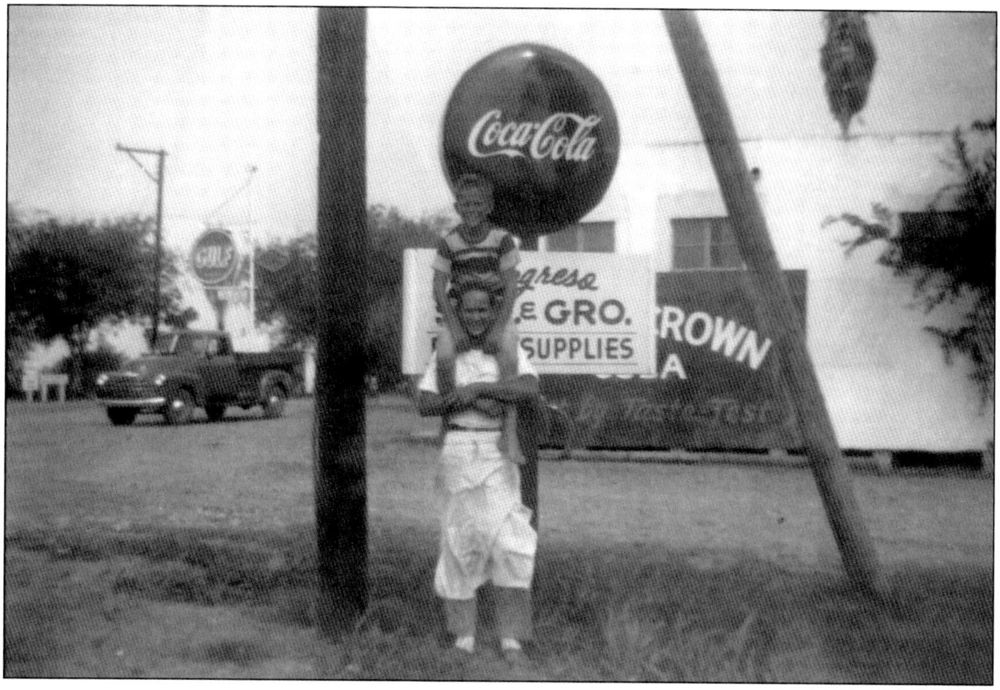


George "Bubba" Madden and Mike Madden (on shoulders) worked with their father, Gerald W. Madden, at the Progreso Station and Grocery. The grocery store sold everything from fishing supplies to Mexican *pan dulce* (sweet bread). These two photographs were taken in 1951. (Both, courtesy Jay Madden.)

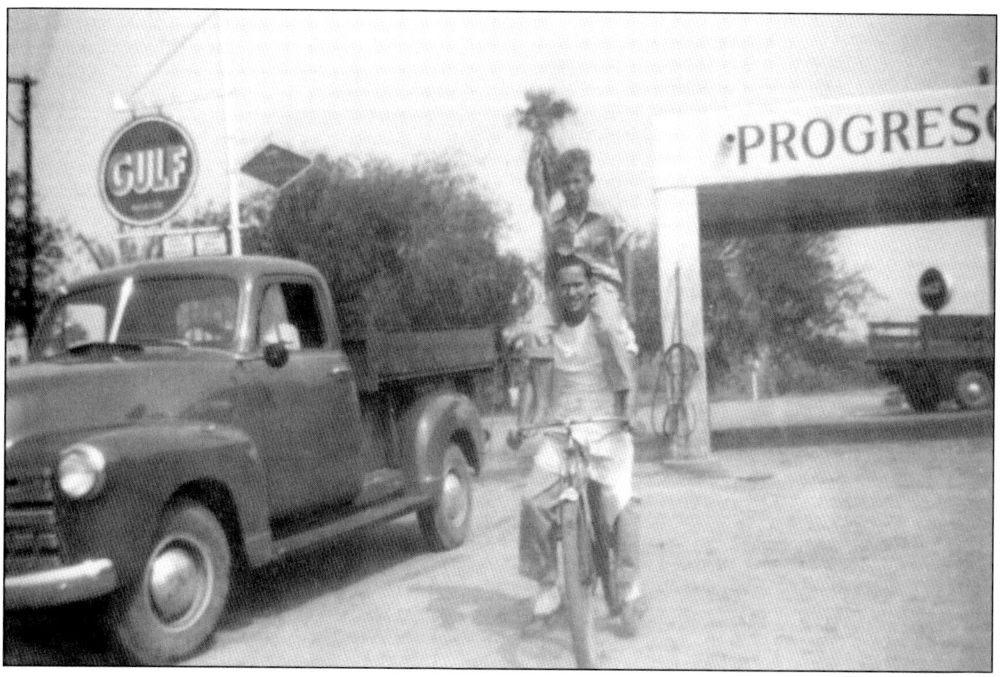

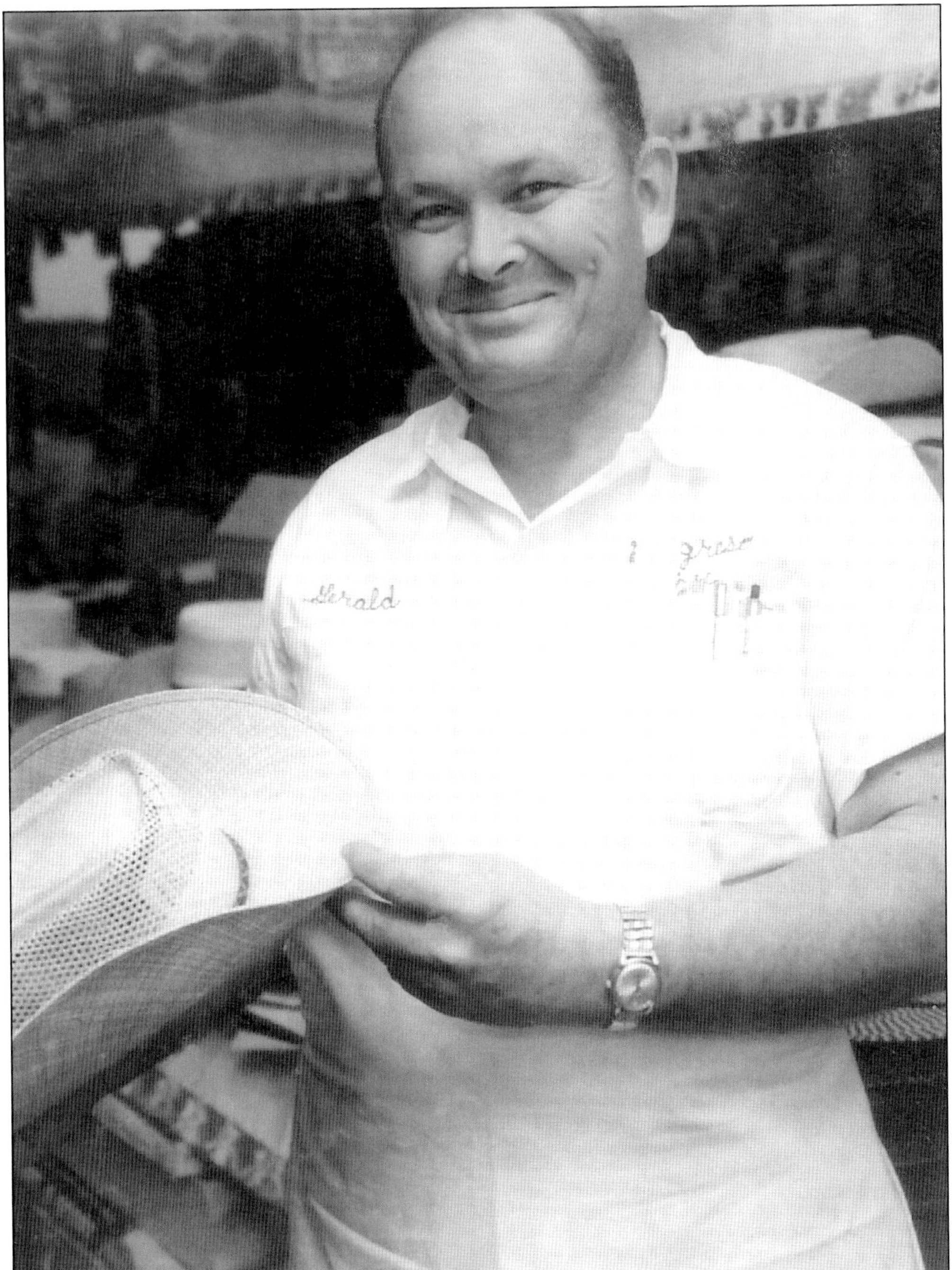

Gerald W. Madden is shown inside the Progreso Station and Grocery. The Maddens sold everything from baked goods to clothing on credit, and they were known for forgiving people's debts during the holidays. During the Bracero Program (an agreement between the United States and Mexico that allowed Mexican workers to take agricultural jobs in America), the store delivered food to Mexicans working in the fields of Progreso. This photograph was taken in the early 1950s. (Courtesy Jay Madden.)

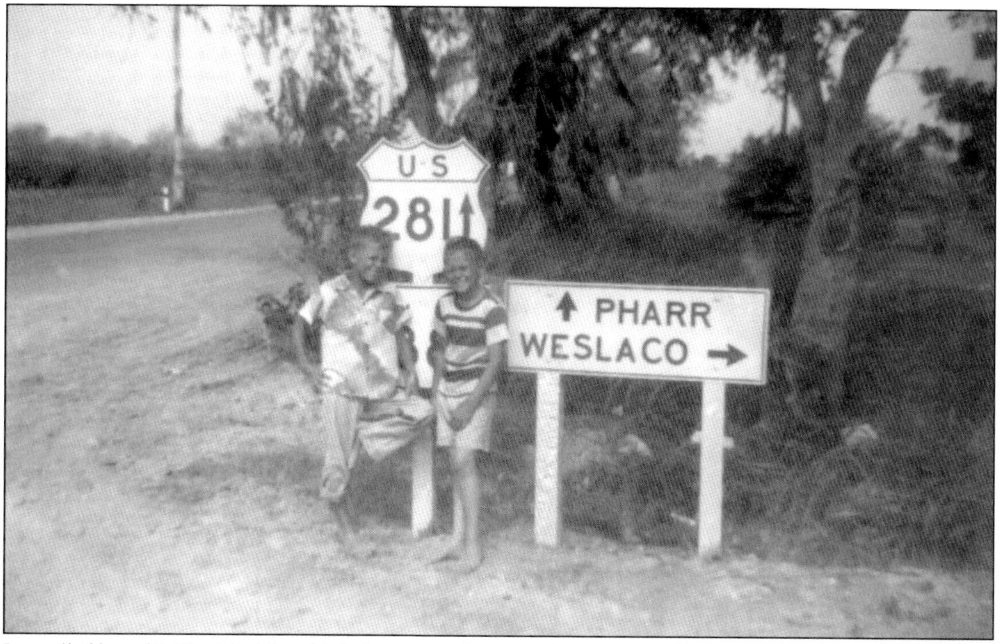


Jerry (left) and Mike Madden (right) are standing on the corner of FM 1015 and Military Highway 281. This 1951 photograph shows the location of the Progreso Station and Grocery and the directions to two nearby towns. Weslaco is about 5 miles north of Progreso, and Pharr is about 22 miles to the west. (Courtesy Jay Madden.)

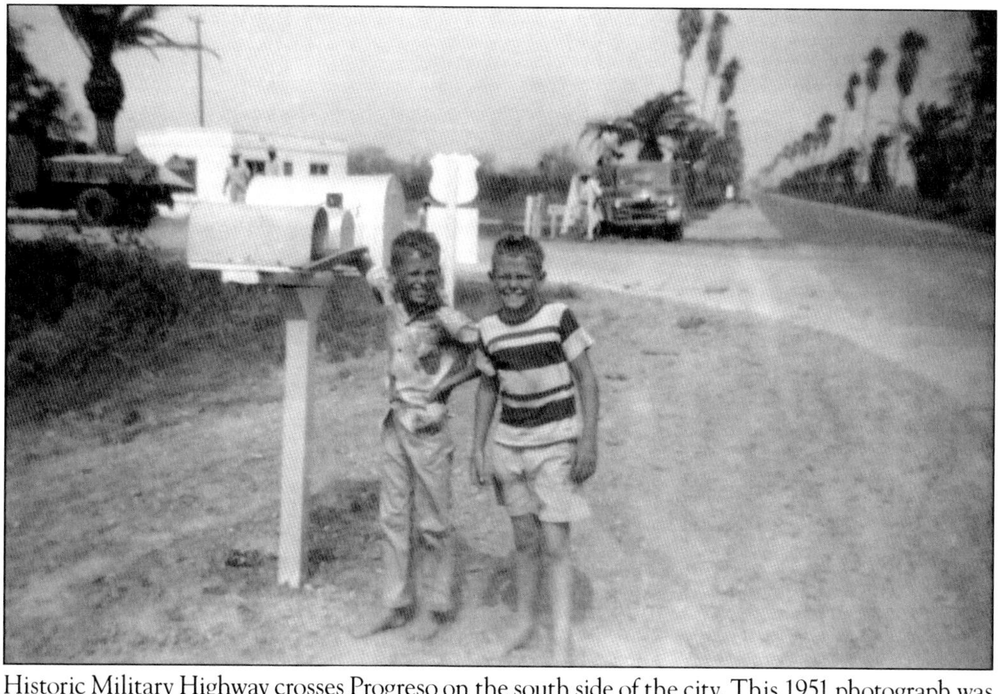

Historic Military Highway crosses Progreso on the south side of the city. This 1951 photograph was taken across the street from the Progreso Station and Grocery and shows Jerry and Mike Madden standing by a mailbox. A corner café can be seen at rear left, as well as a few farm workers and trucks of the time. (Courtesy Jay Madden.)

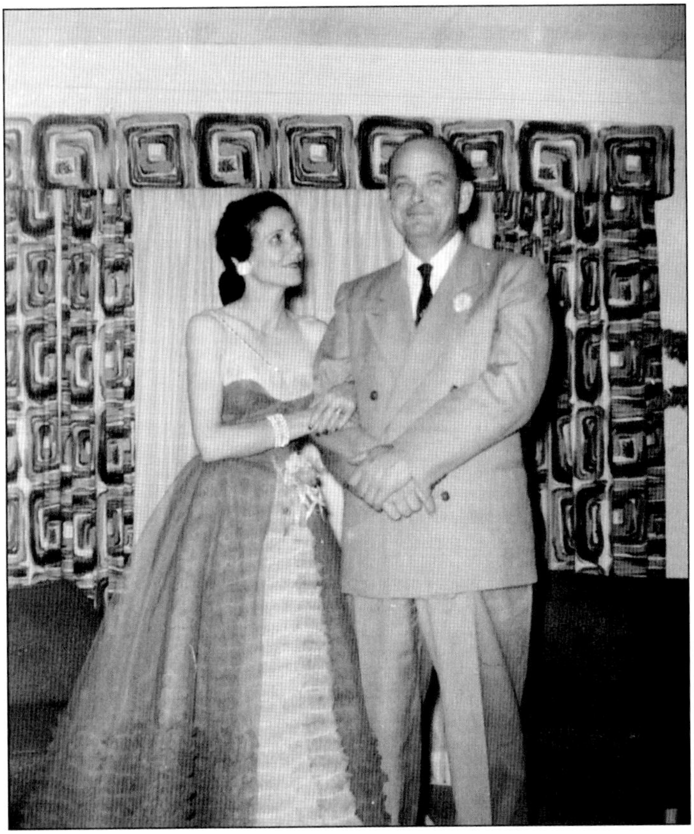

Gerald W. Madden and Roberta Madden owned the Progreso Station and Grocery from the late 1940s to the late 1960s. This photograph of the Maddens was taken in 1955. Locals say the couple was loved by Progreso residents. (Courtesy Jay Madden.)

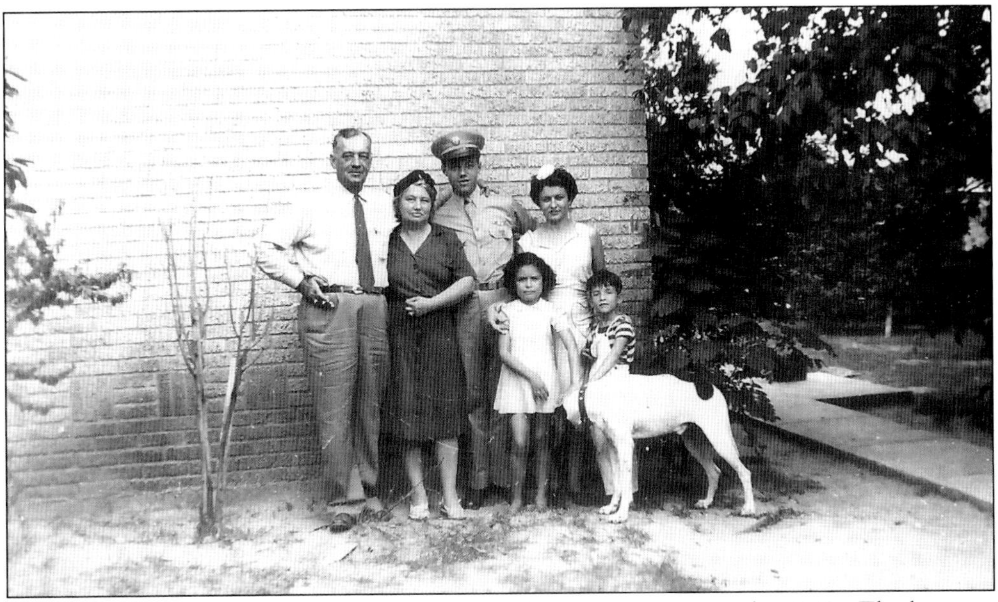

Al Cain owned about 80 percent of the B and P Bridge Company in the 1940s. The business eventually erected the Progreso International Bridge in 1953. This 1945 photograph shows the Cain family home in Progreso. From left to right are Al Cain, Christine Chadick Cain, William C. Cain, Margarita ?, and Margarita's children, Sylvia and Leo. (Courtesy William C. Cain family.)

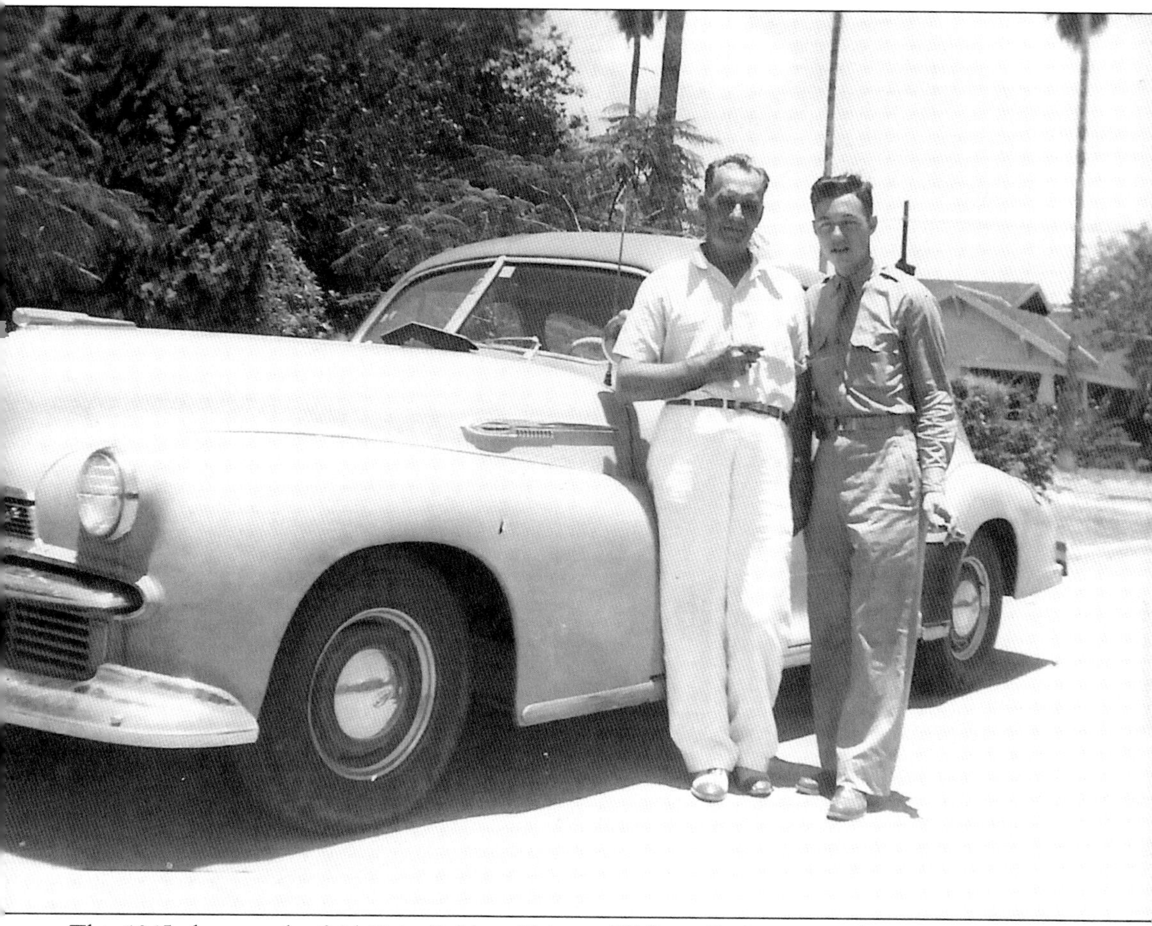

This 1945 photograph of Al Cain (left) and his son William C. Cain was taken in Mercedes. It captured two generations of Progreso businessmen, whose vision of the Progreso International Bridge joined Mexico and the United States and perhaps changed the course of Progreso's history. (Courtesy William C. Cain family.)

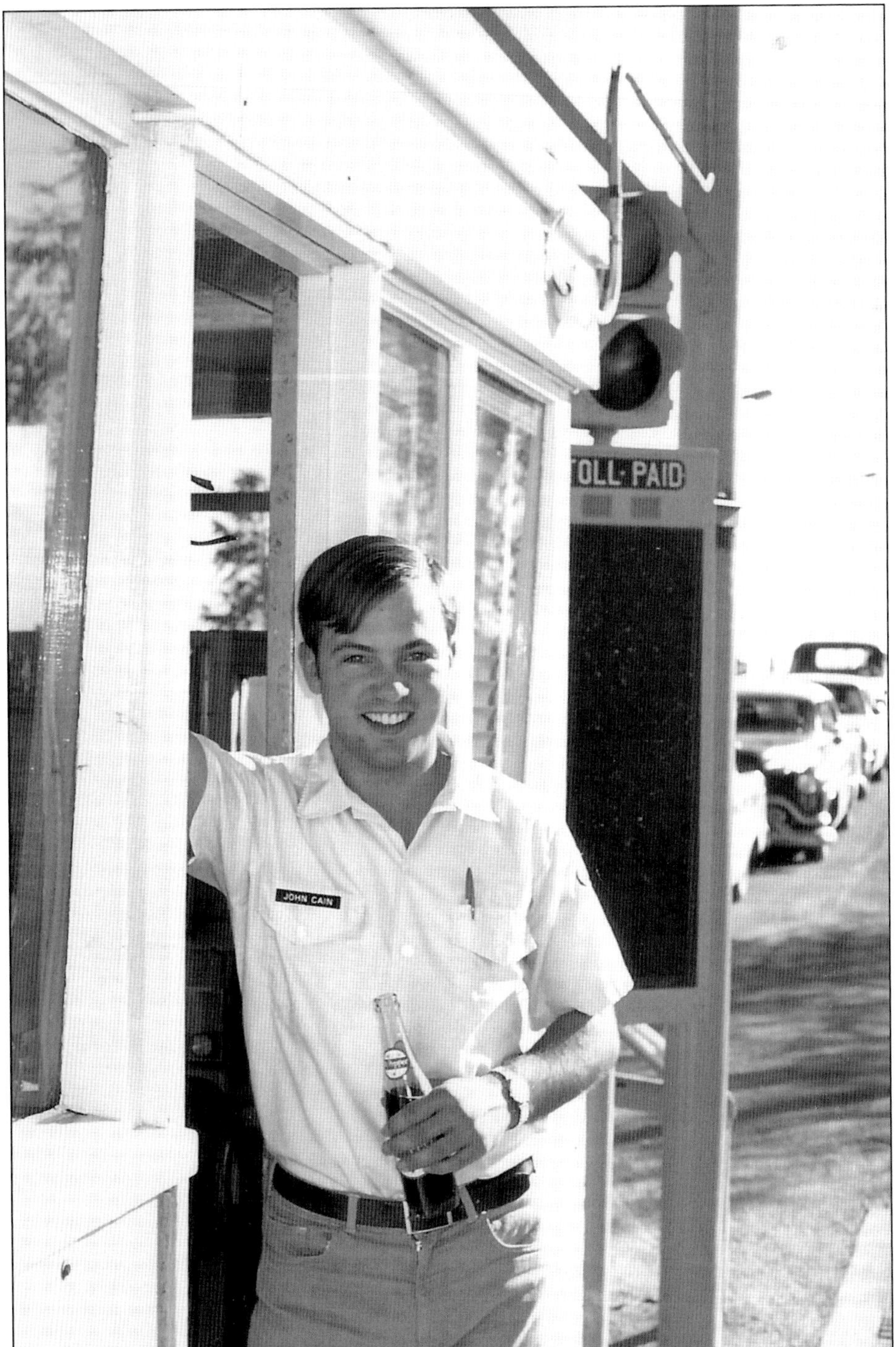


John Cain, son of William C. Cain, continued his family's legacy when he worked at the Progreso International Bridge during college summer breaks. This photograph was taken in 1972 while John Cain attended the University of Texas at Austin. It shows the Progreso International Bridge tollbooth and cars waiting to drive into Mexico. (Courtesy William C. Cain family.)

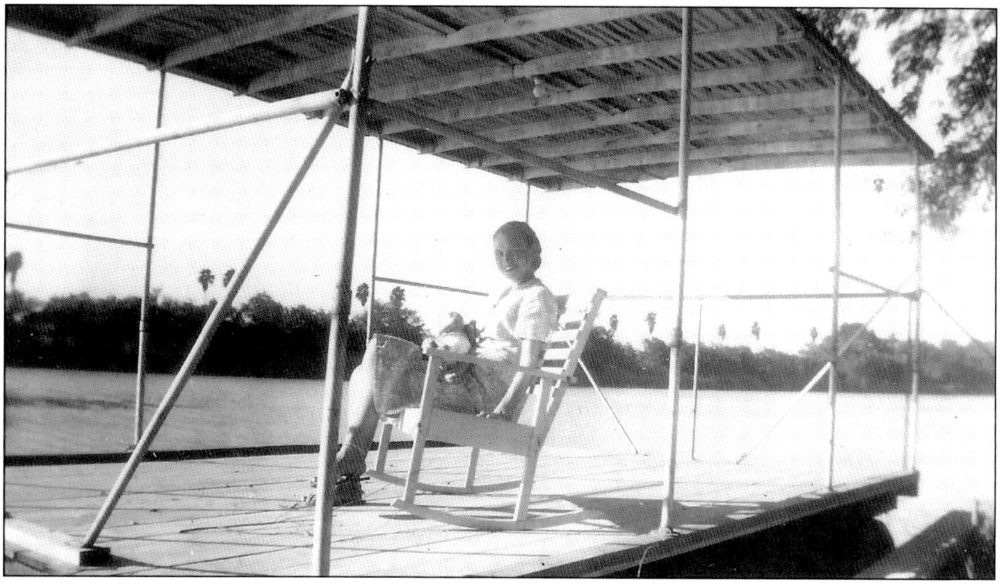

The Cain family made tremendous contributions to the growth and development of Progreso. The family lived on Moon Lake for many years. In this 1948 photograph, Kathryn Cain is shown soaking up the sun on the family pontoon boat on Moon Lake, holding her six-week-old daughter Frances. Al Cain put several pontoon boats into circulation at the Rio Rico crossing after the devastating flood of 1941 washed away the Rio Rico Bridge. When the boats were taken out of circulation, Al Cain gave the boat shown in this photograph to the family of William C. Cain. (Courtesy William C. Cain family.)

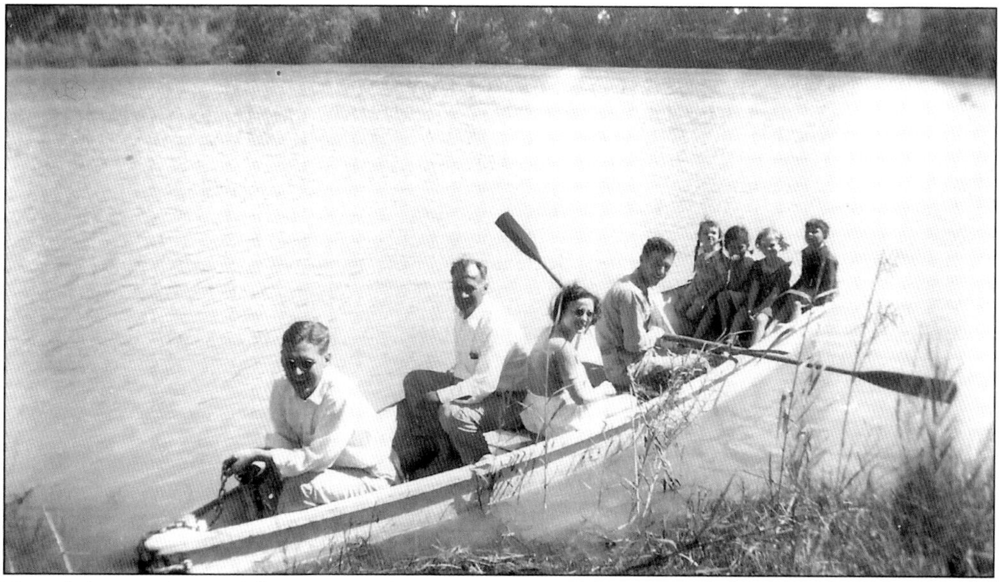

From left to right are Allen Cain, Al Cain, Kathleen Cain, unidentified, Diana Cain, Pammy Cain, and other unidentified children. This photograph shows the Cain family on their lakefront property on Moon Lake, named for its crescent shape. This lake sits next to Lion Lake, named after a passerby found a dead mountain lion on the property. (Courtesy William C. Cain family.)

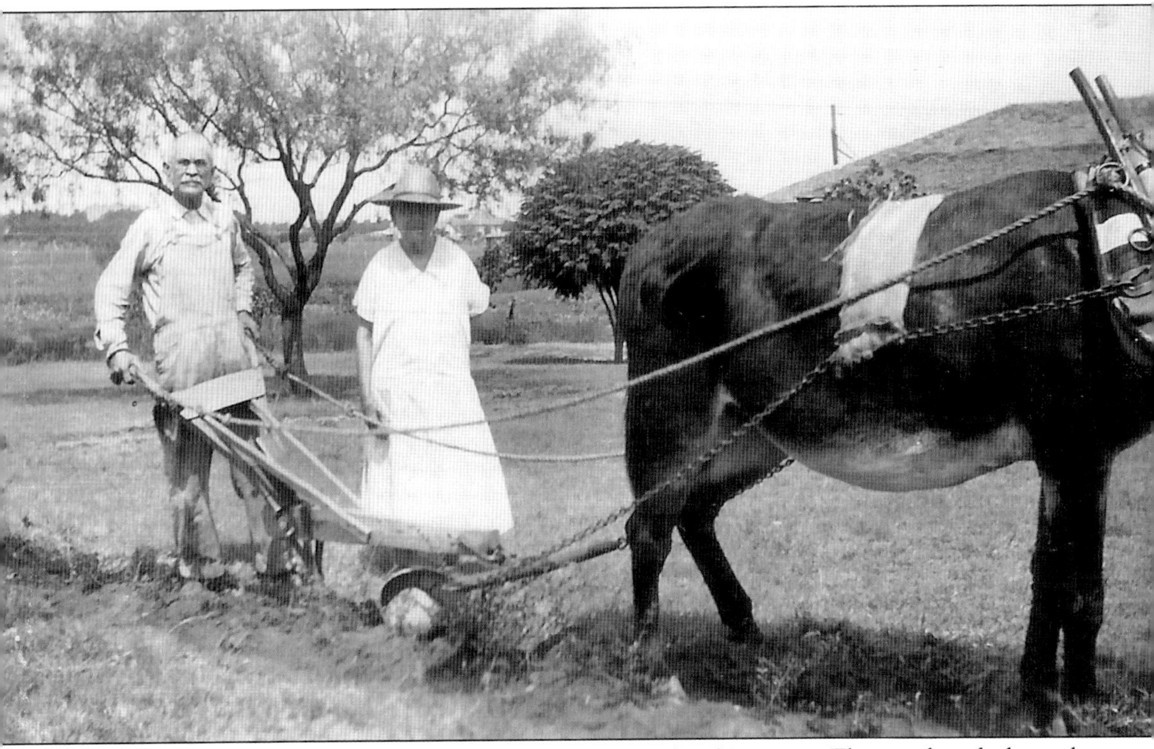

This photograph is testament to the hardworking people of Progreso. This unidentified couple is shown plowing a field with a donkey. The mesquite tree behind them is native to the Progreso area. (Courtesy William C. Cain family.)

These mailboxes were donated to the Progreso Co-op Gin, Inc. The origin of the boxes is debatable, but locals believe they were used in one of the original Progreso post offices. The first Progreso post office was requested in 1896 for Toluca Ranch, but the Post Office Department named the town Progreso. (Courtesy Progreso Co-op Gin, Inc.)

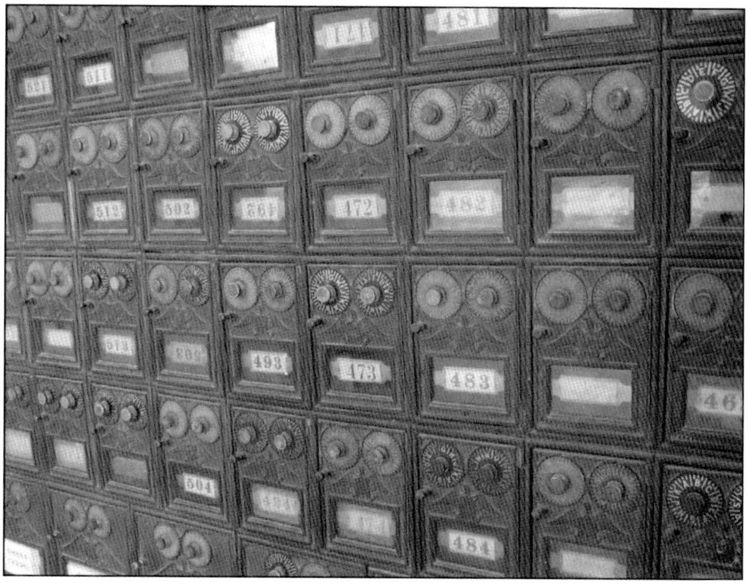

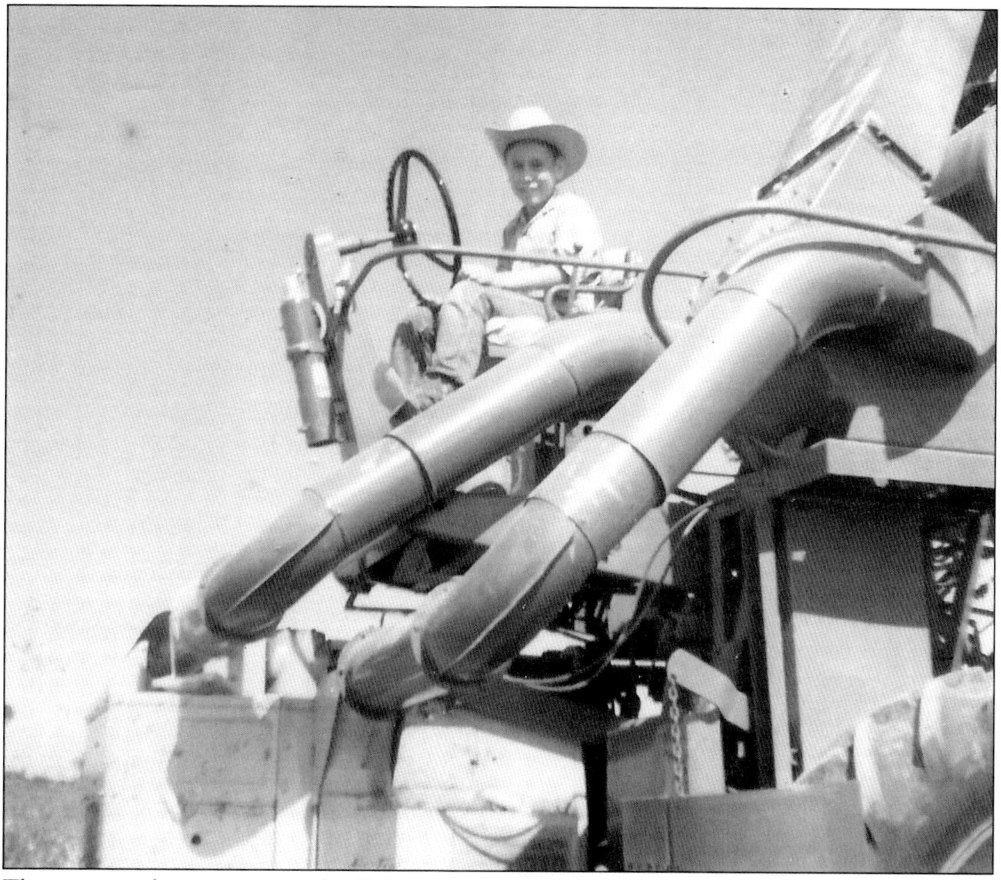

The cotton industry was critical to Progreso's growth and development, especially after the freezes of 1949 and 1951 killed citrus groves in the area. This 1950s photograph shows Gilberto Rodriguez working a cotton picking machine of the time. (Courtesy Soledad G. Rodriguez.)

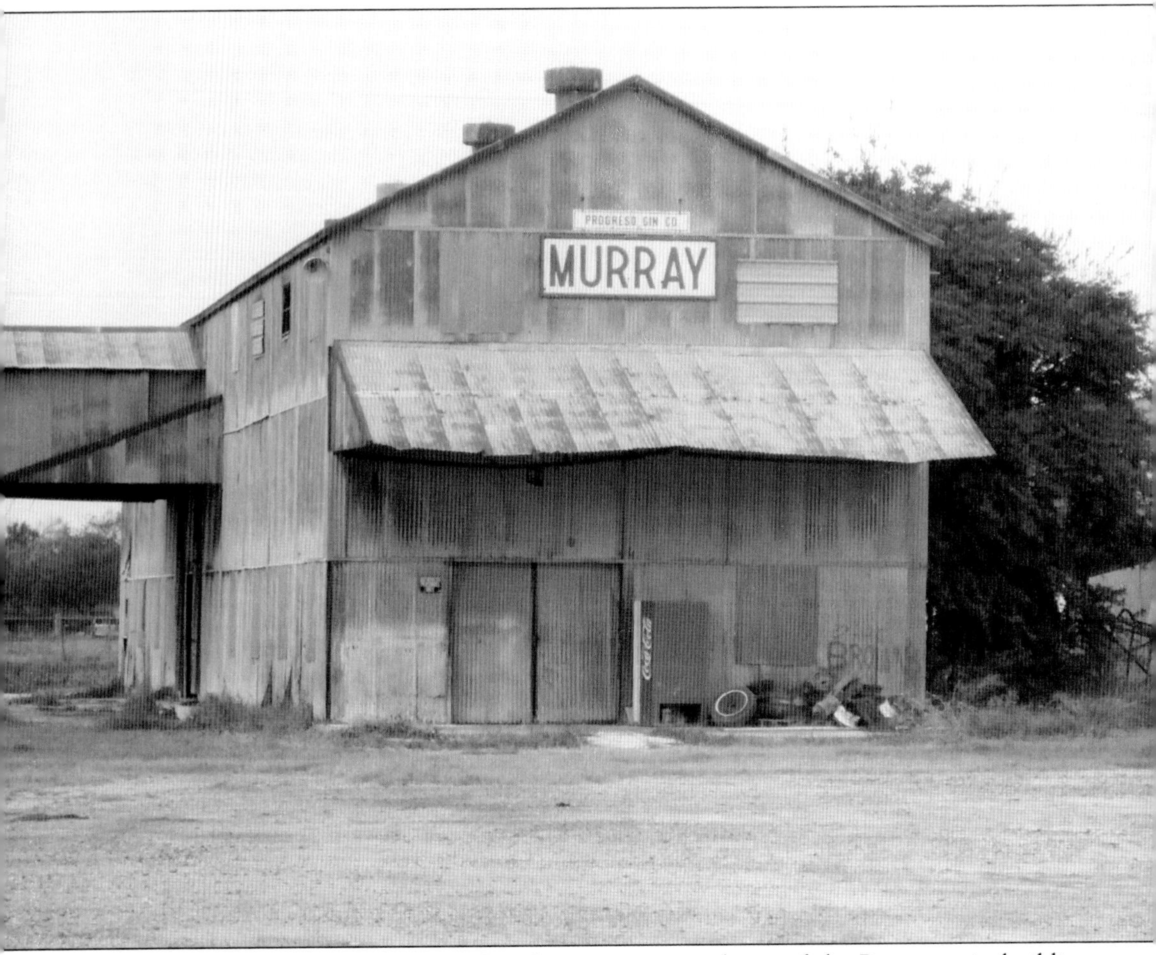


The offices of the Progreso Co-op Gin, Inc., are just southeast of the Progreso gin building depicted here. A group of farmers formed the co-op in the late 1960s, and to this day the sons of many of the original members still get together to share ideas and drink coffee. (Courtesy Progreso Co-op Gin, Inc.)

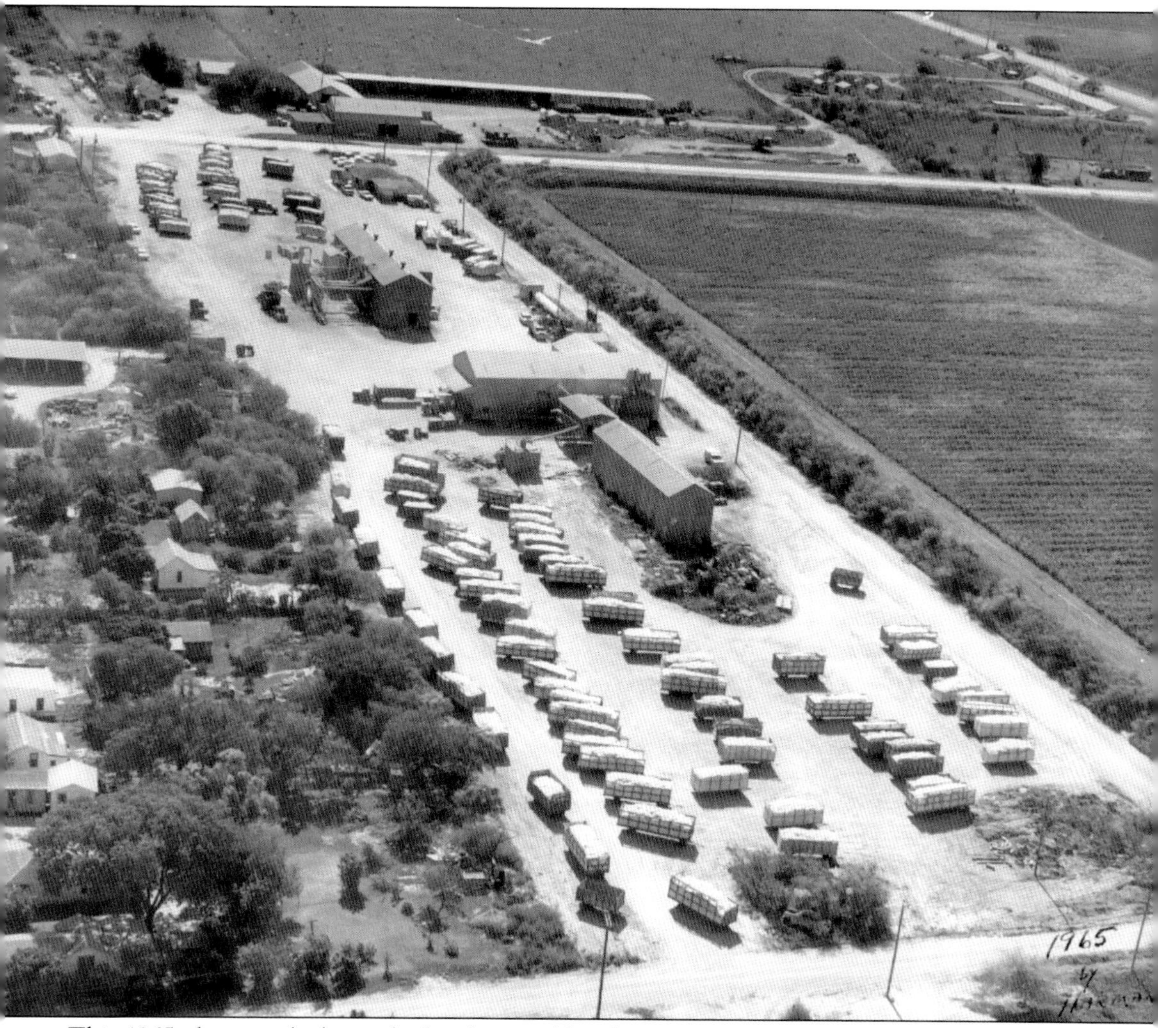

This 1965 photograph shows the hustling and bustling Progreso Cotton Gin. Cotton was big business in Progreso in the 1960s, and the Progreso Cotton Gin was at the center of it all. Later farmers also diversified their agricultural investments to include sugarcane, vegetables, corn, and grain. (Courtesy Progreso Co-op Gin, Inc.)

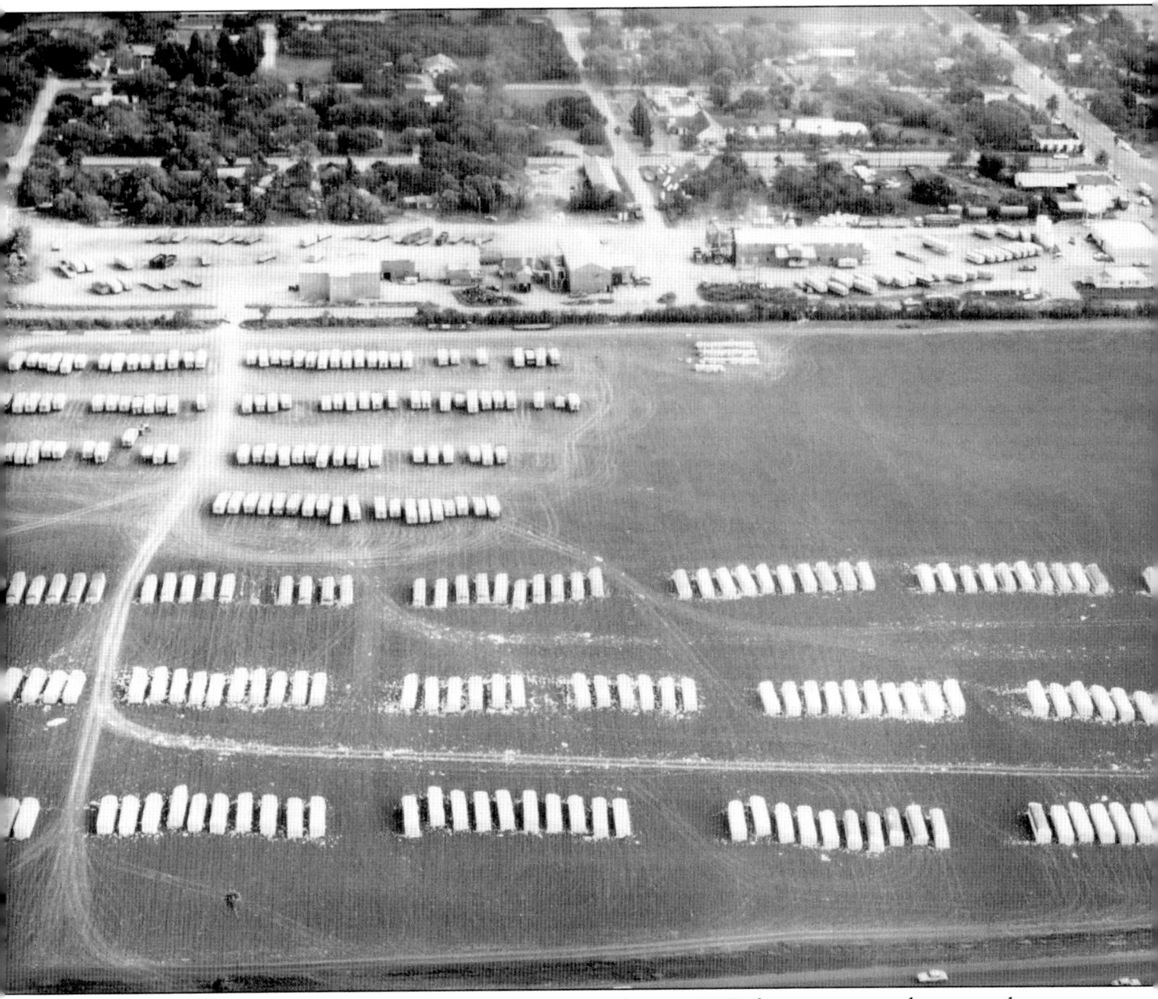

Cotton was such an important crop in Progreso that in 1952 farmers erected a second cotton gin to meet demand. This photograph shows the two gin buildings, dozens of bales of cotton, and the Progreso township. About 28 farmers formed the Progreso Co-op Gin, Inc., in 1968. The gin buildings are no longer in business, but the co-op still exists. (Courtesy Progreso Co-op Gin, Inc.)

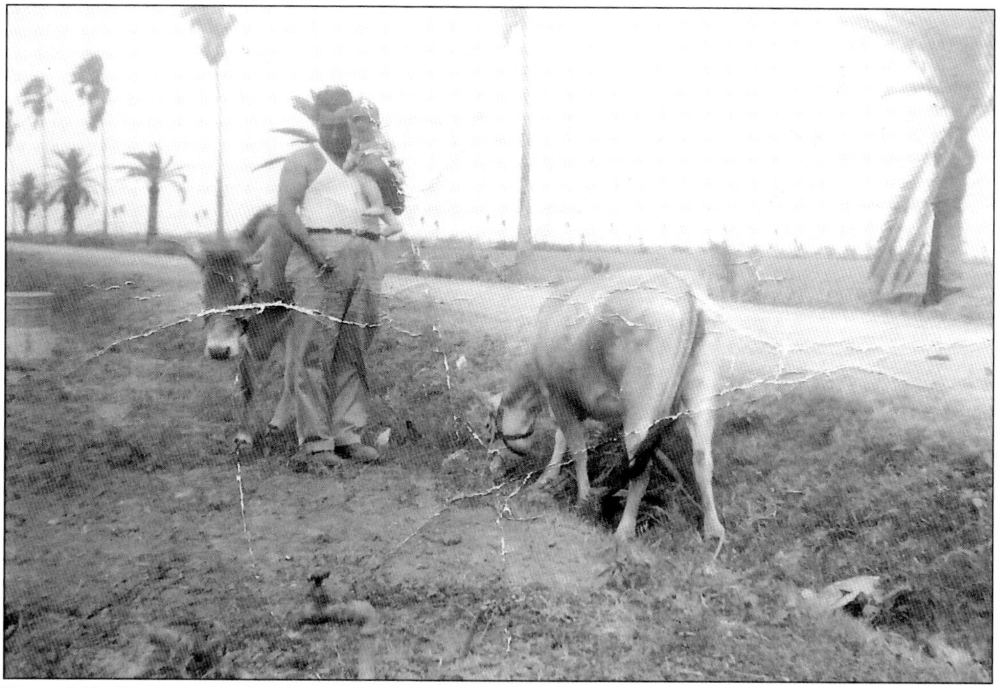

Ysmael Rodriguez was the foremen of the George Harren Ranch in Progreso. This photograph was taken in 1952. Some families in the area raised cattle to supplement their income. (Courtesy Soledad G. Rodriguez.)

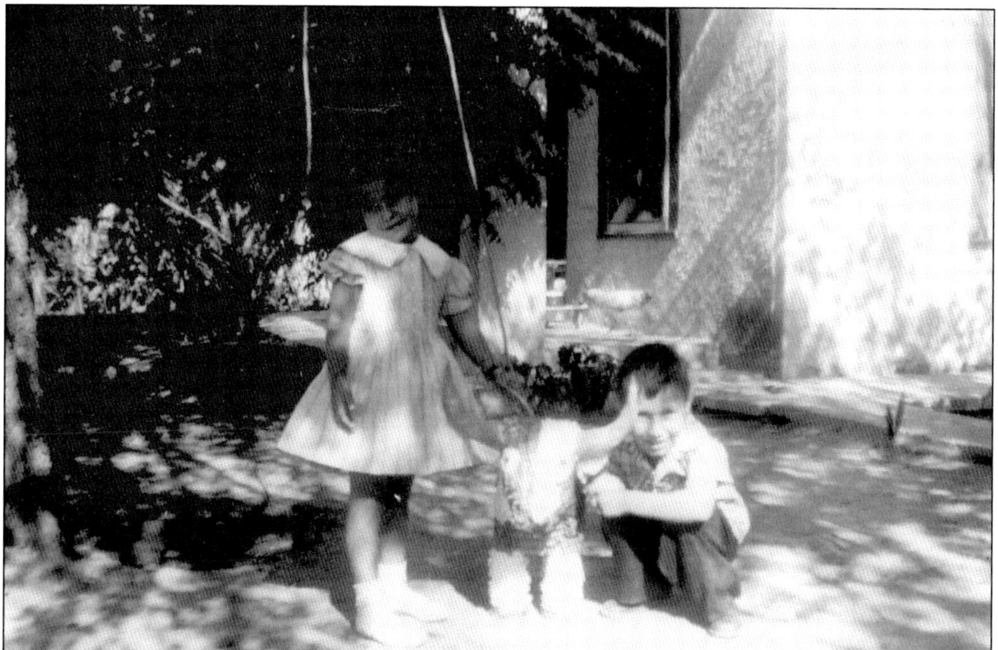

This August 1957 photograph of Magdalena and Gilberto Rodriguez was taken near Holy Spirit Church. The piñata shows the Mexican influence in the everyday lives of Progreso residents. (Courtesy Soledad G. Rodriguez.)

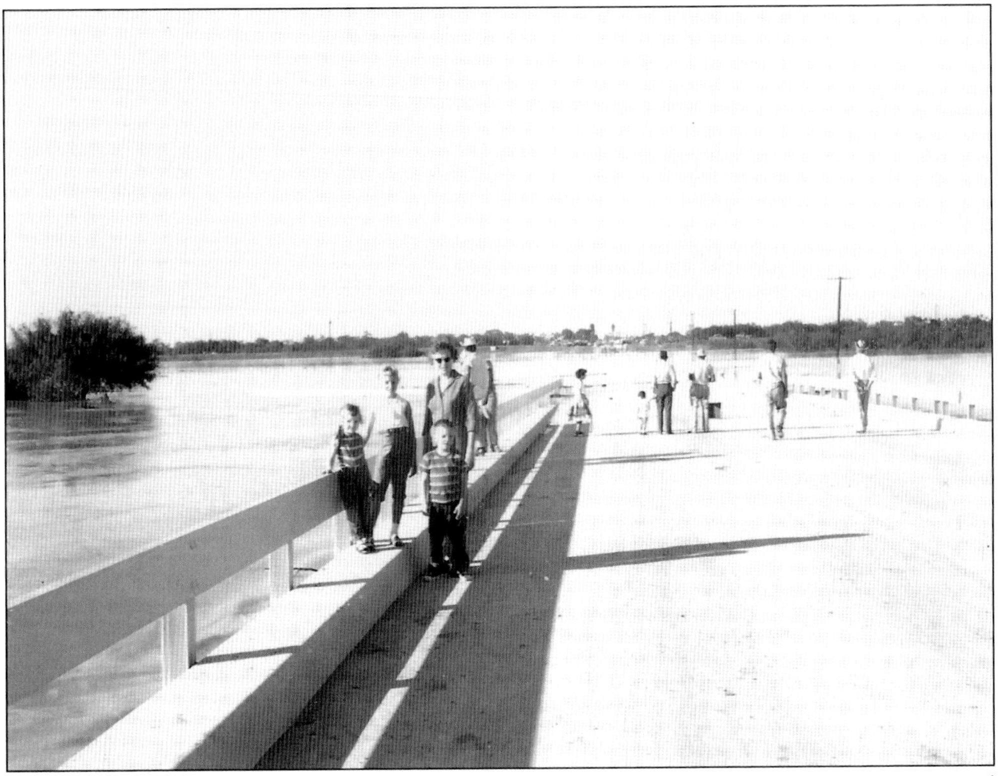

Hurricane Carla hit Progreso as a Category 4 storm in 1961. The waters rose, and the rivers and canals spilled over their banks. These photographs show families surveying the damage (above), while others evacuate the flooded area by boat (below). (Both, courtesy William C. Cain family.)

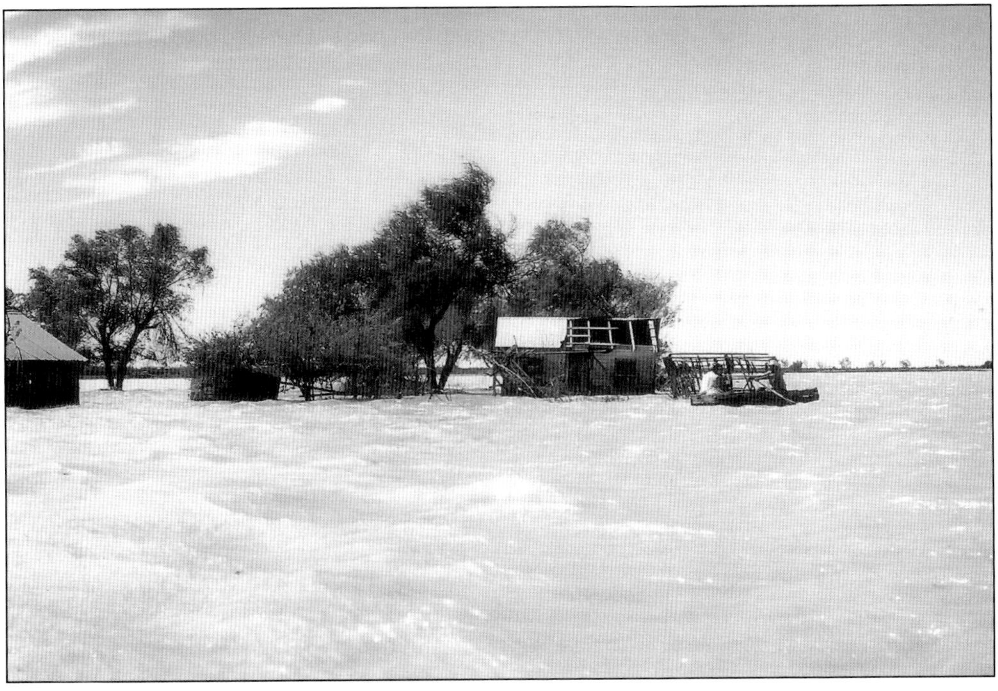

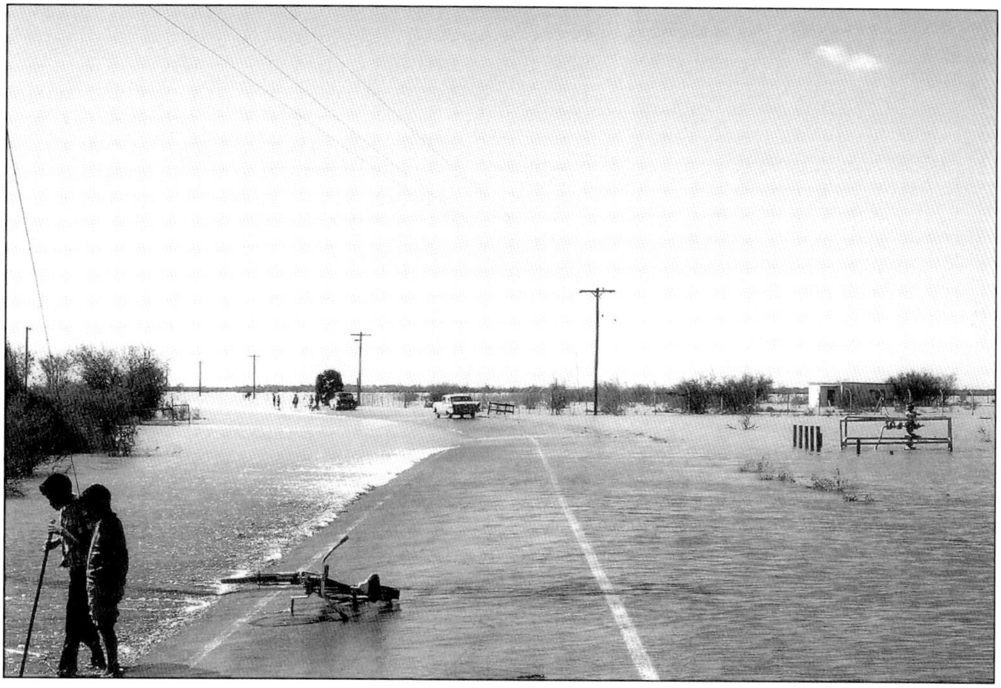

Calculating the destruction left behind by Hurricane Carla was difficult. The storm hit Progreso in 1961 and caused the Rio Grande to overflow its banks. The water rose to such a degree that main streets were impassable by car. (Both, courtesy William C. Cain family.)

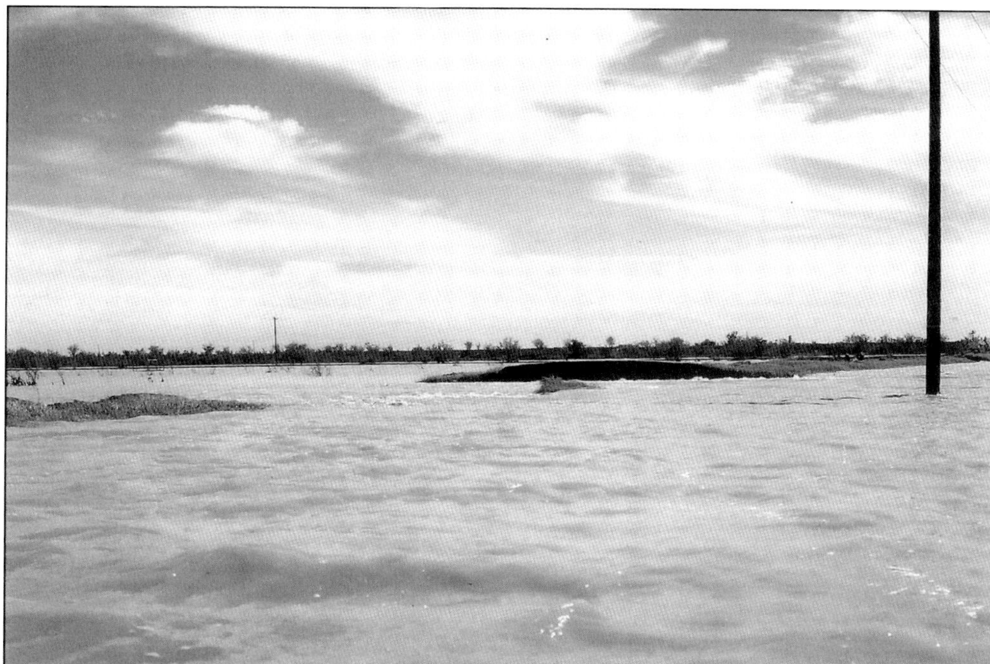

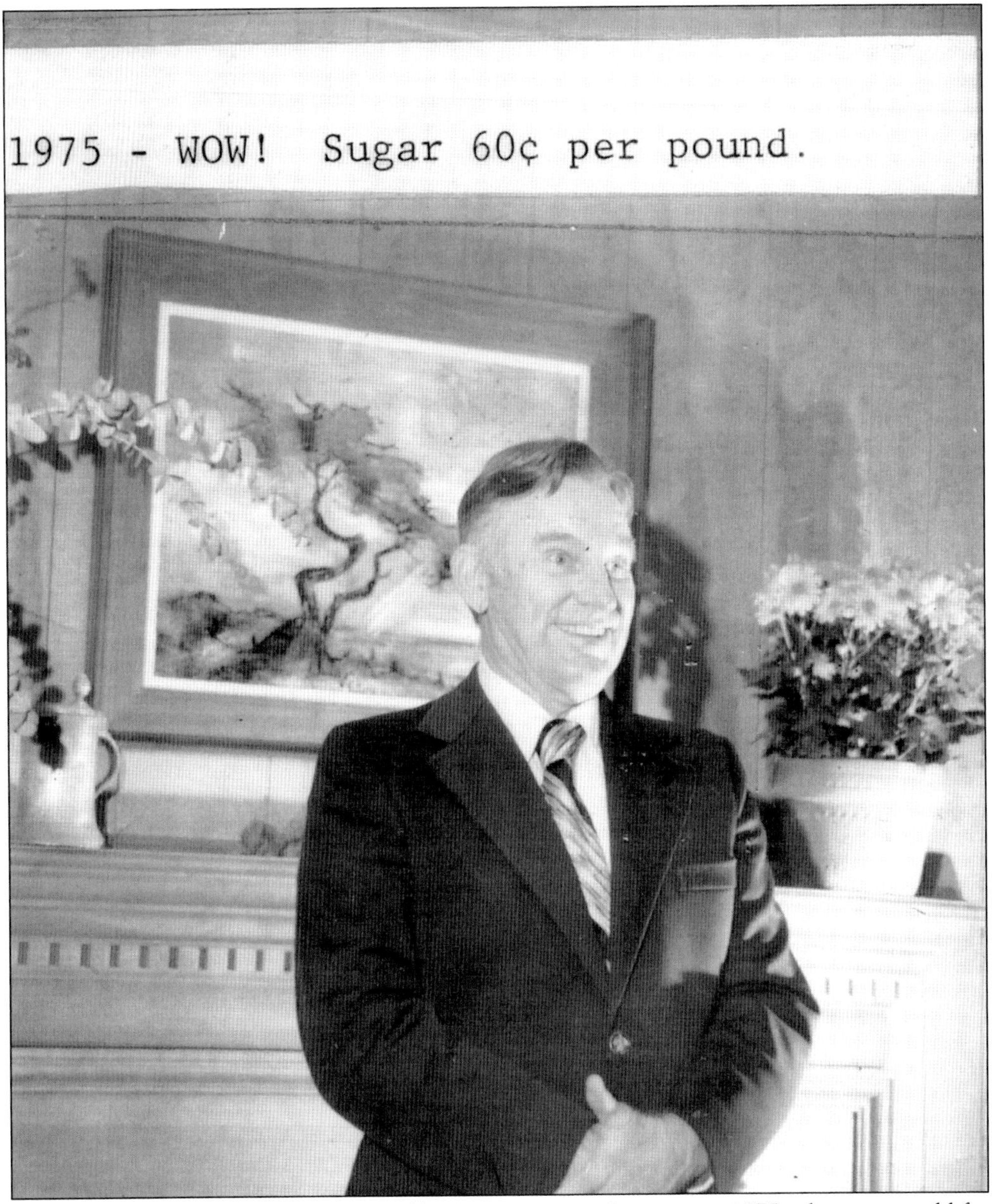


Jack Holcomb celebrated the success of his Progreso sugar business in 1975, when sugar sold for 60¢ a pound. Holcomb has produced thousands of pounds of sugar over the years. In 1976, he was appointed director of the Federal Reserve Bank of Dallas for a three-year term. (Courtesy Jack Holcomb.)

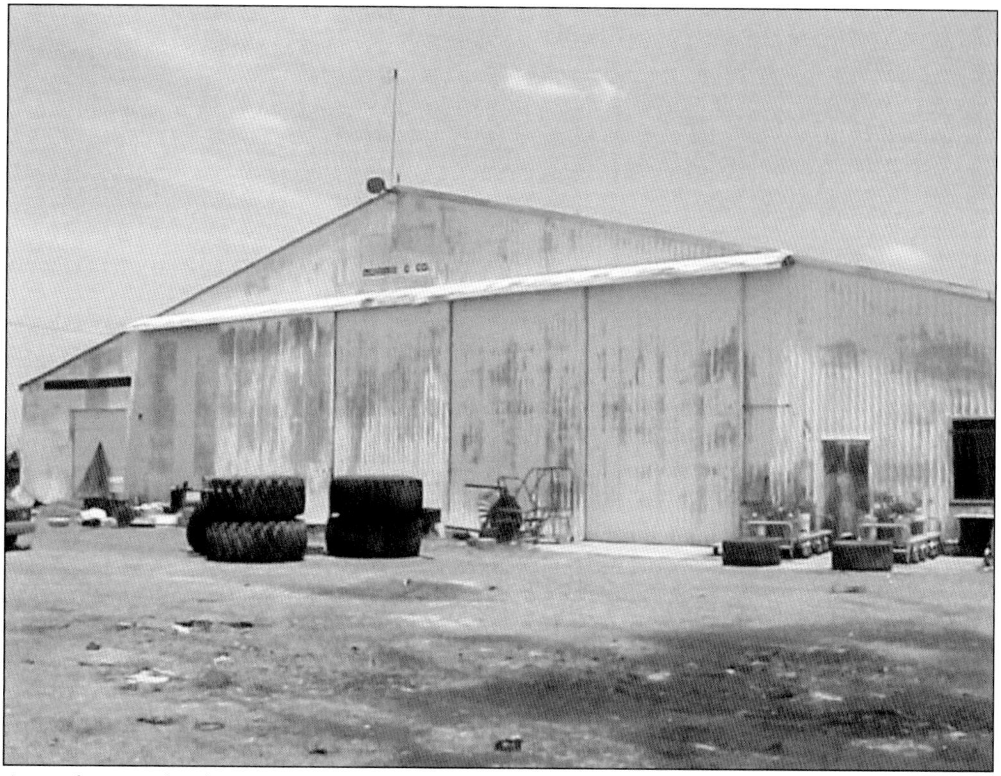

Aircraft, even fuselages of military planes like the ones depicted below, can be found on the grounds of the former Progreso Airport. The facility has been closed for years, but the owner of the property, Dale Roberts, says the airport manufactured speed modifications and auxiliary tip tanks for Beechcraft planes. (Both, courtesy Dale Roberts.)

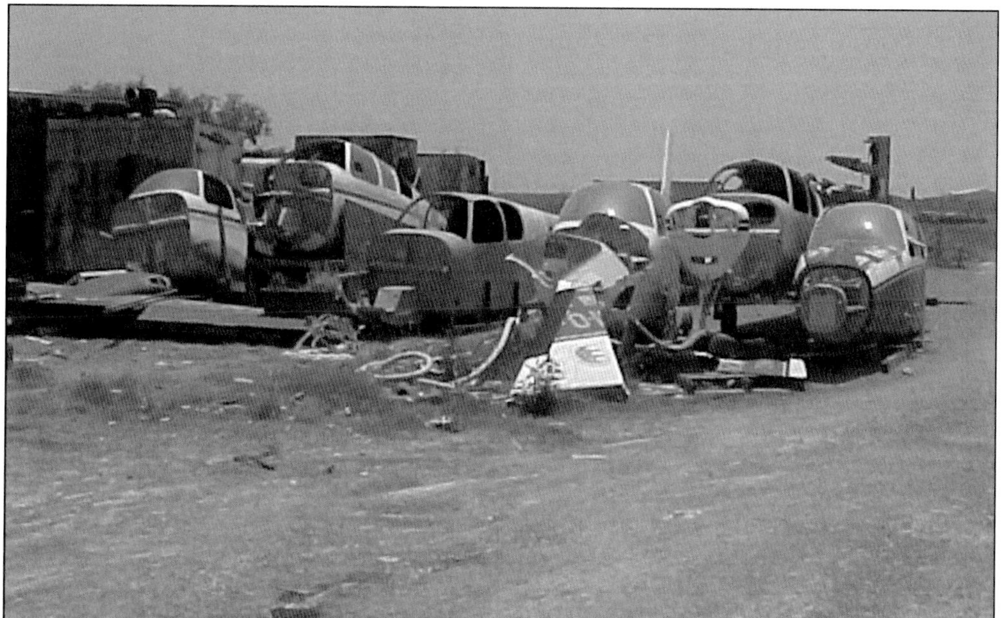

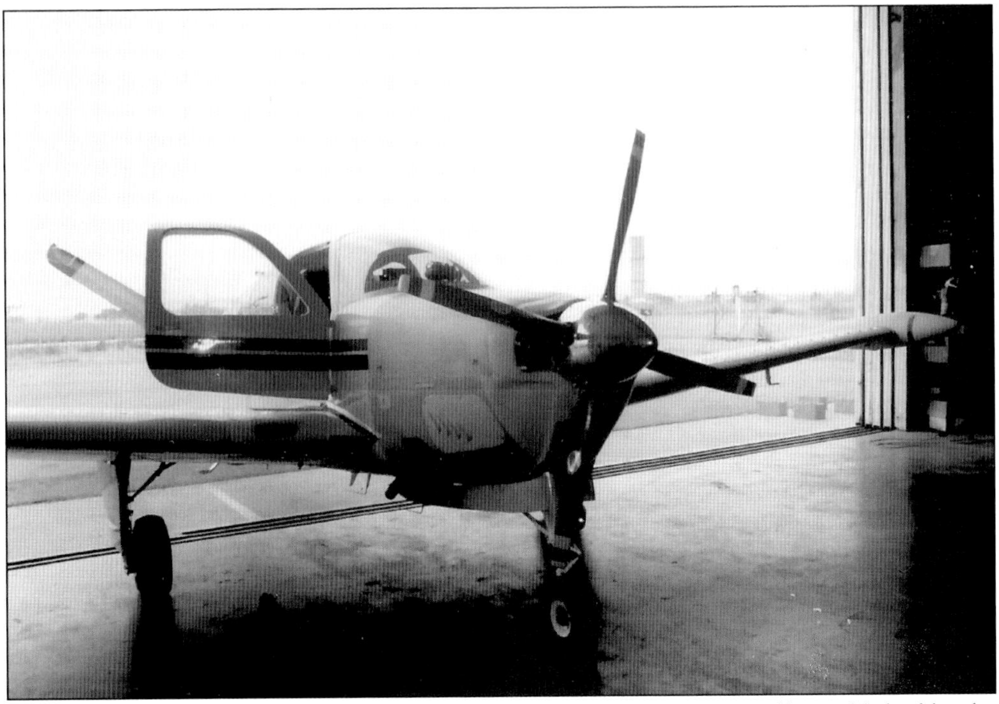

According to the Roberts's family records, the Progreso Airport was initially established by the U.S. military. It was later turned over to the U.S. Border Patrol and then sold to John Roberts and Allen Peterson. Roberts bought out Peterson and manufactured speed modifications and auxiliary tip tanks for Beechcraft aircraft. The airport hanger in this photograph is no longer used for business, but the building and the landing strip are still intact. (Both, courtesy Dale Roberts.)

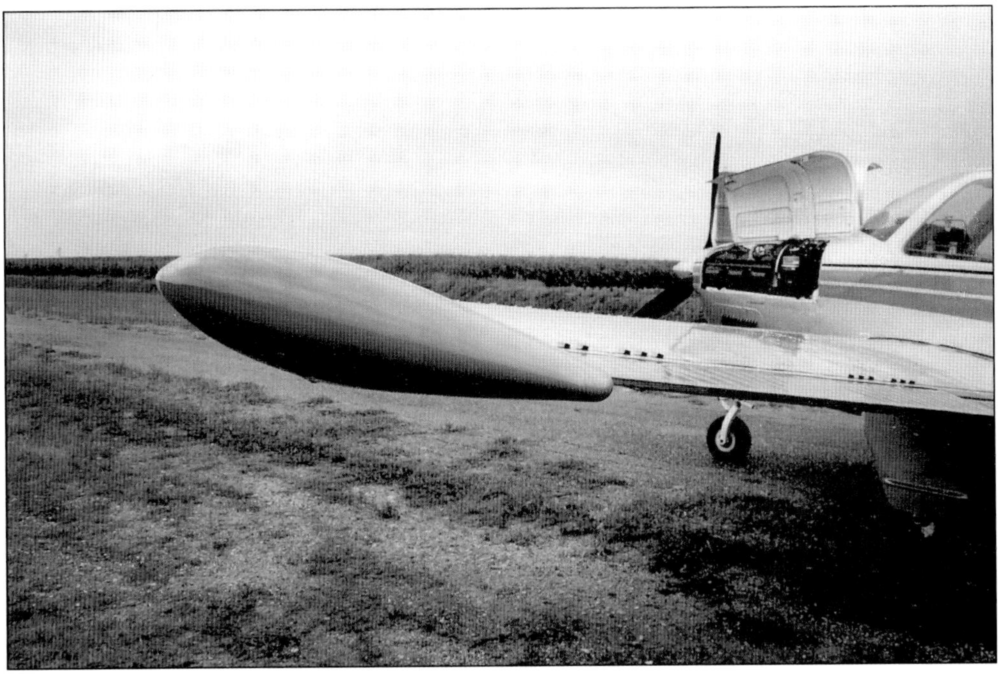

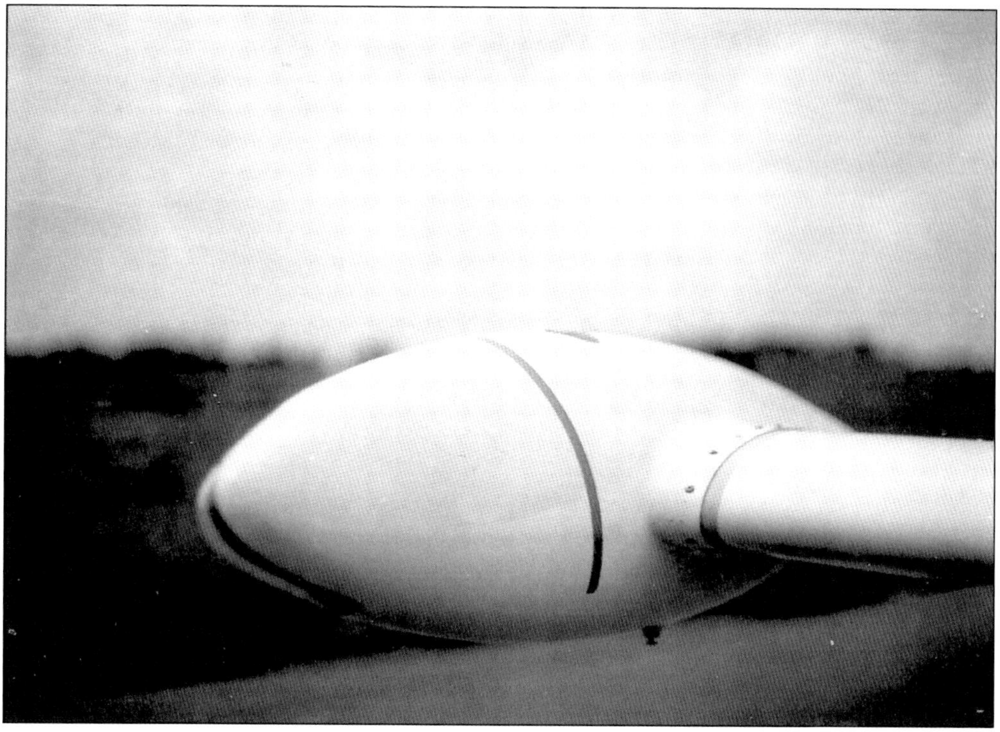

Precise and aerodynamic, the parts shown in these photographs were manufactured for Beechcraft airplanes at the Progreso Airport. The company made light single-engine aircraft for business jets and military aircraft. The tip tanks shown in these photographs are examples of the work developed at the Progreso Airport. (Both, courtesy Dale Roberts.)

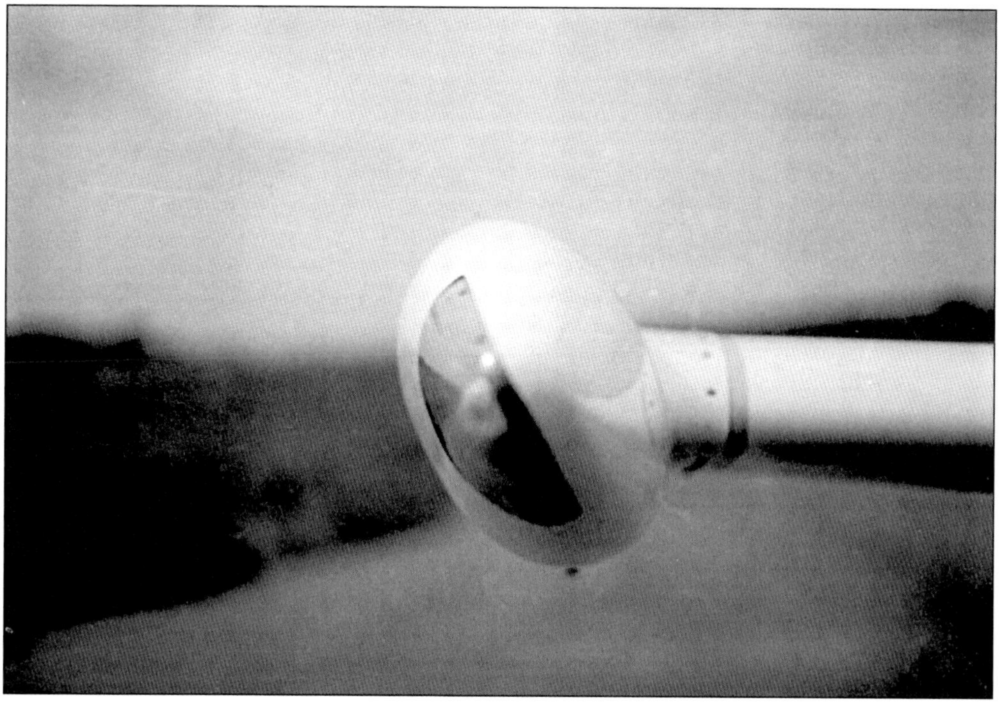

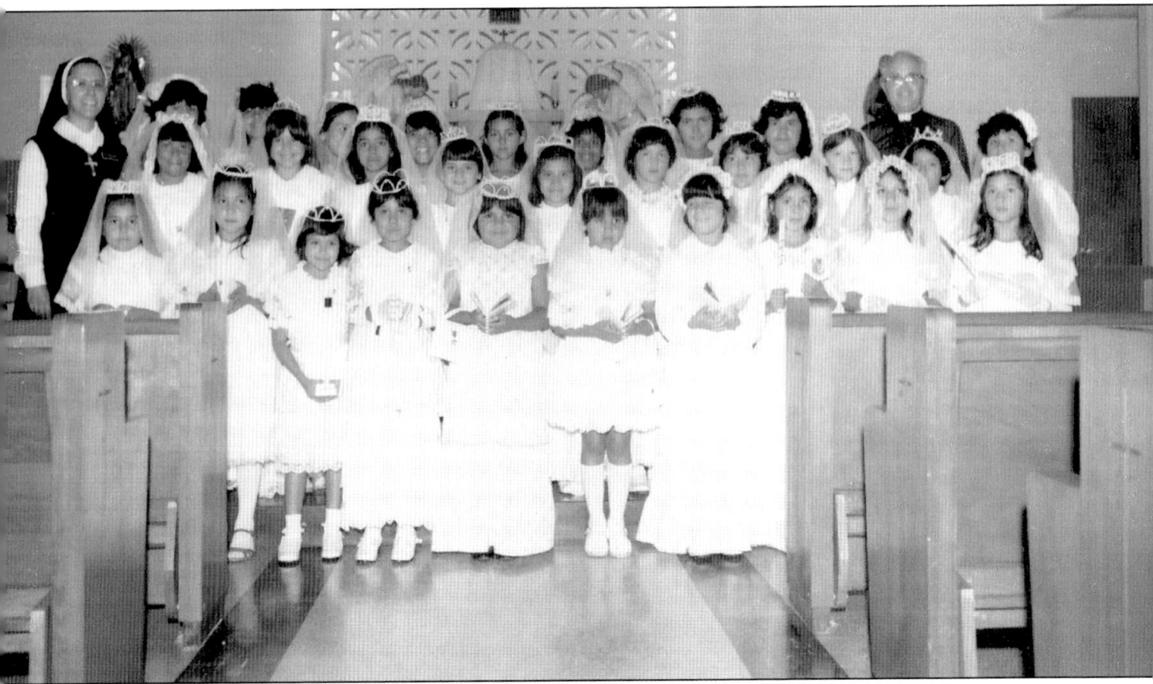

These girls received the Catholic sacrament of communion at Holy Spirit Church on November 26, 1978. On the far right side of the group is Fr. Francis Schoutteten. He was the first priest permanently assigned to Progreso. Before Schoutteten, oblate fathers, known as "saddlebag priests," traveled throughout the Rio Grande conducting masses and performing sacraments. (Courtesy Holy Spirit Church.)

Holy Spirit Church was dedicated on May 25, 1969, but the first mass was held under a tent in 1957. Before then, Progreso Catholics attended mass in Weslaco and Mercedes. In 1962, church service was held inside E. D'Hemecourt's Roof Tile Building Store. The D'Hemecourts later donated land for the construction of Holy Spirit Church. (Courtesy Holy Spirit Church.)

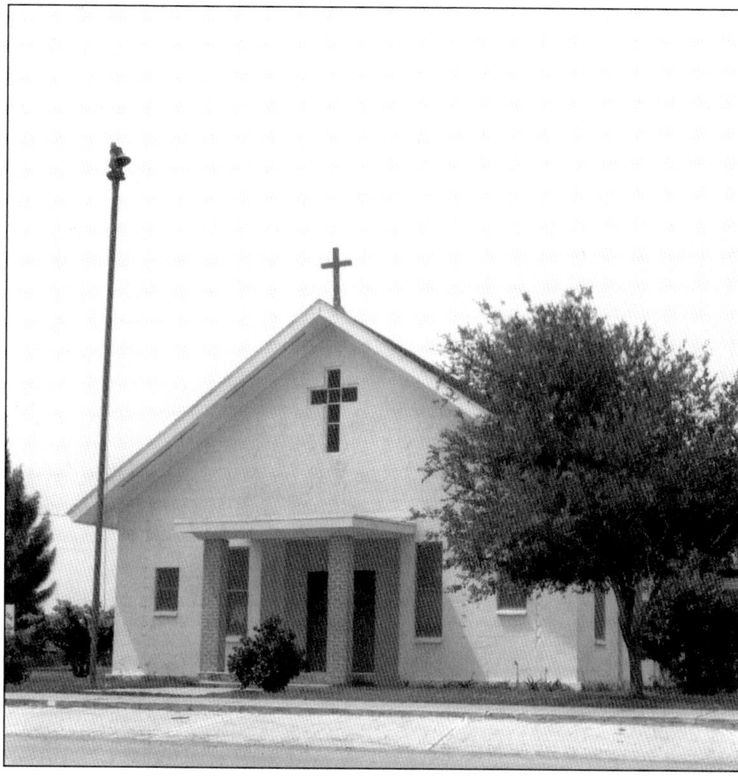

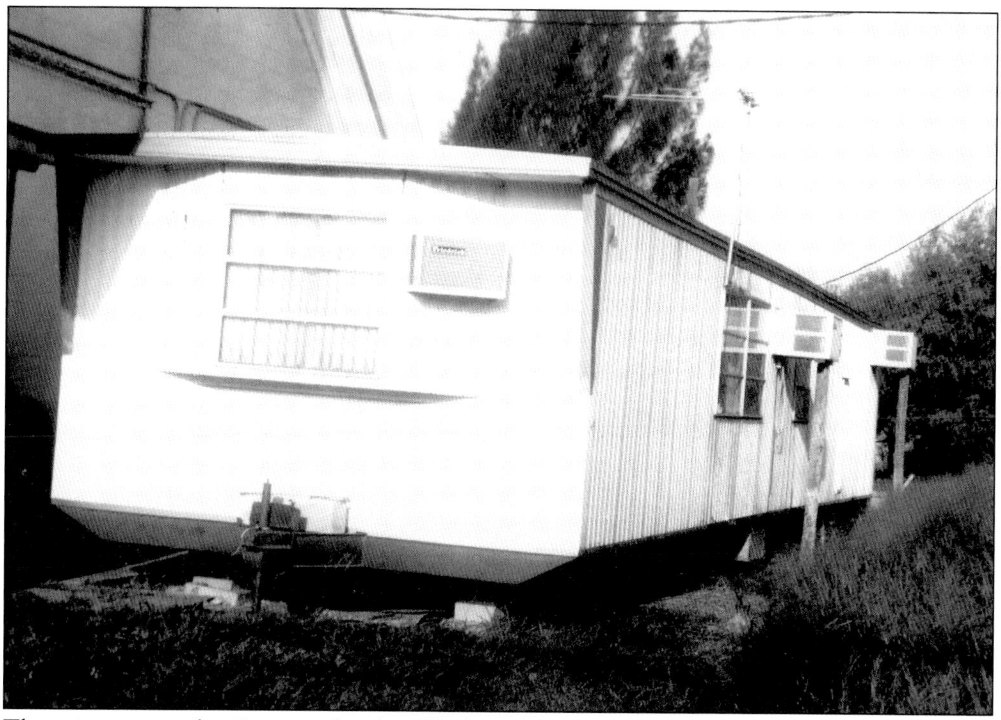

The priest assigned to Progreso lived in Weslaco until the mobile home in this photograph was purchased. The church paid about $6,100 for the residence. (Courtesy Holy Spirit Church.)

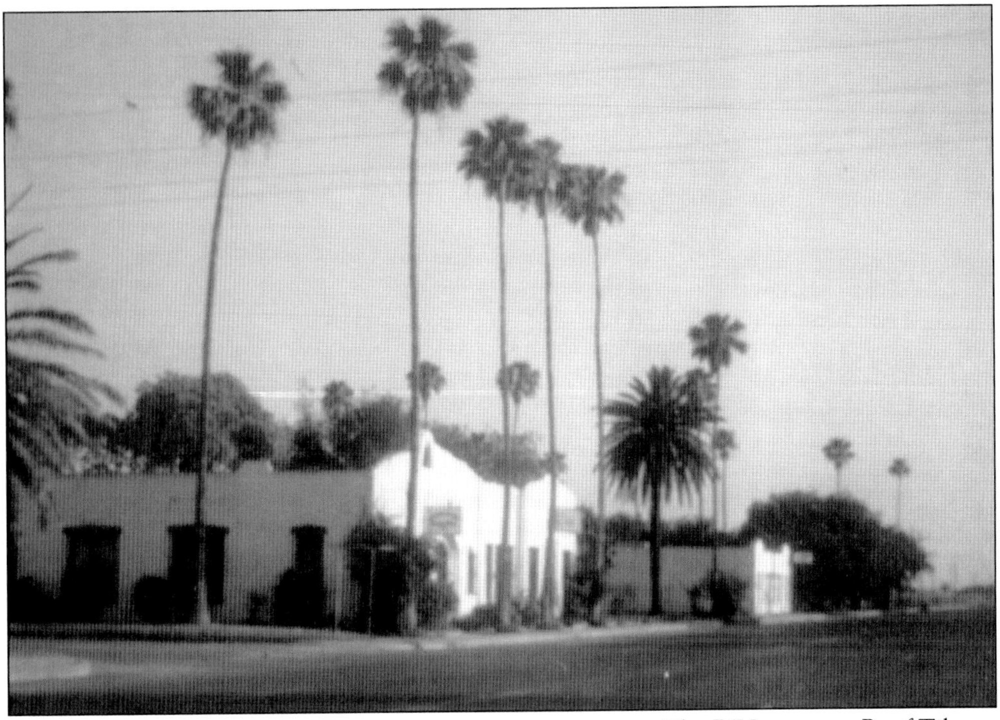

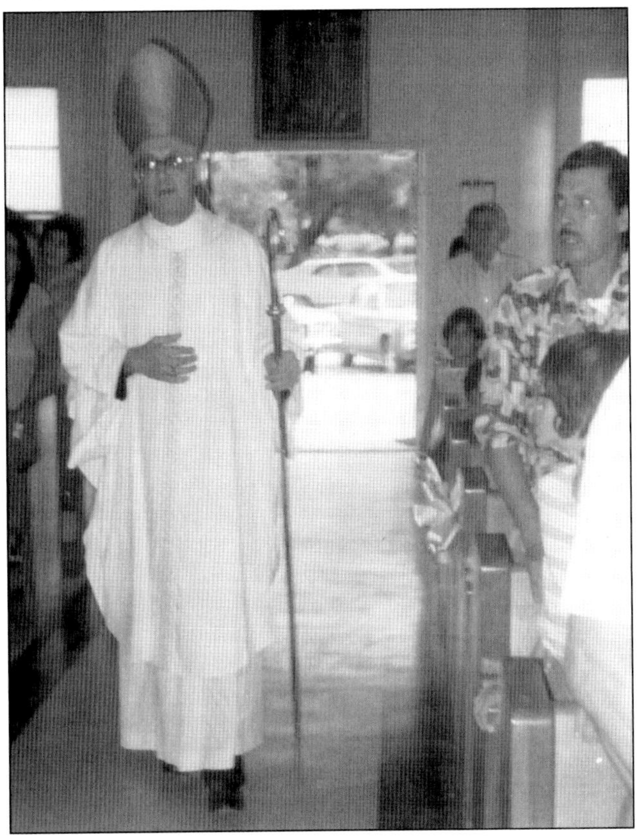

The D'Hemecourt Roof Tile Building Store was used as a temporary Catholic church in the early 1960s, until Holy Spirit Church was erected in 1969. (Courtesy Holy Spirit Church.)

On October 21, 1977, Bishop John J. Fitzpatrick of the Diocese of Brownsville celebrated a special sacrament for the sick at Holy Spirit Church in Progreso. (Courtesy Holy Spirit Church.)

# *Four*

# Progreso International Bridge

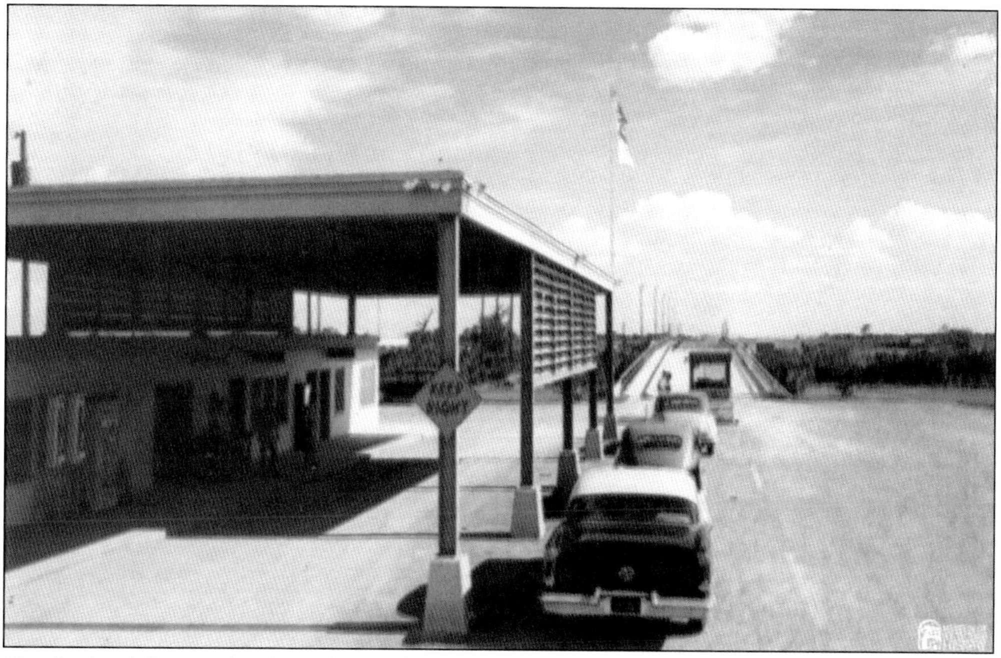


Hundreds of thousands of people use the Progreso International Bridge to cross over to Mexico by car and by foot every year. The bridge is a favorite crossing for winter Texans, tourists from cold northern states who enjoy the mild South Texas winters in the Rio Grande Valley. This 1950s photograph of the Progreso International Bridge shows U.S. Customs on the left and the tollbooth to the far right. In the 1980s, the bridge was expanded to make room for more customs activity. The land the bridge sits on was leased from the owners of Toluca Ranch for 99 years. (Courtesy Museum of South Texas History.)

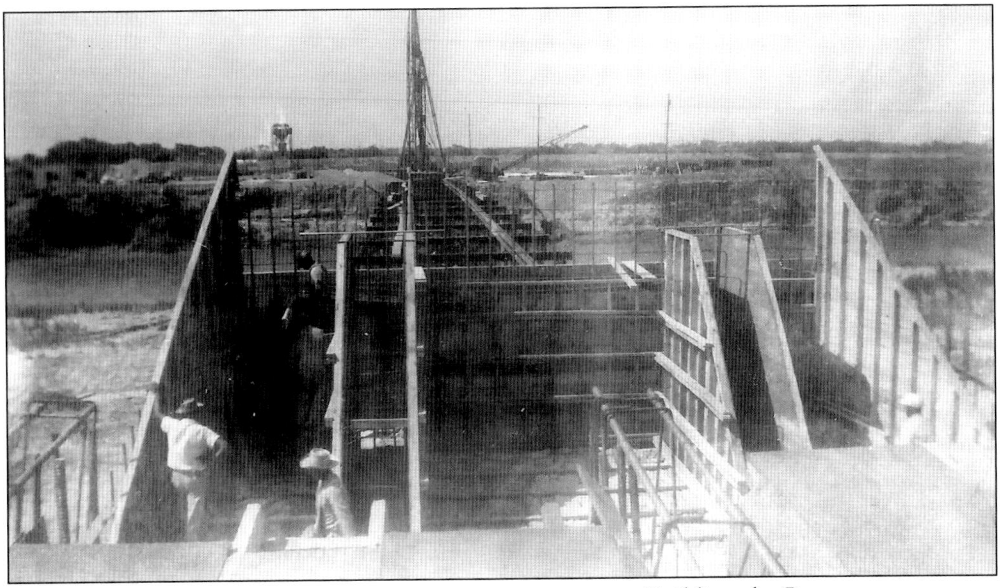

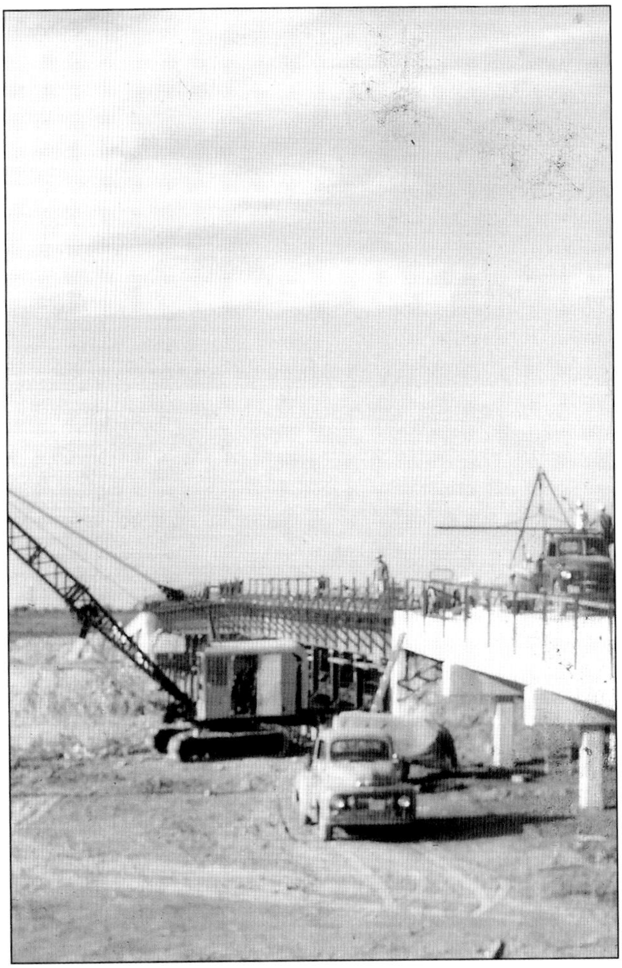

Building the Progreso International Bridge required more than just solid materials—it required vision. William C. Cain and the rest of the B and P Bridge Company convinced Weslaco citizens to invest their money in a bridge that went nowhere. It was said to go nowhere because there was nothing on the Mexican side of the border but an open field. (Courtesy William C. Cain family.)

This photograph shows the machinery used to construct the Progreso International Bridge. At a cost of about $300,000, the bridge was built 980 feet long and 25 feet wide. (Courtesy William C. Cain family.)

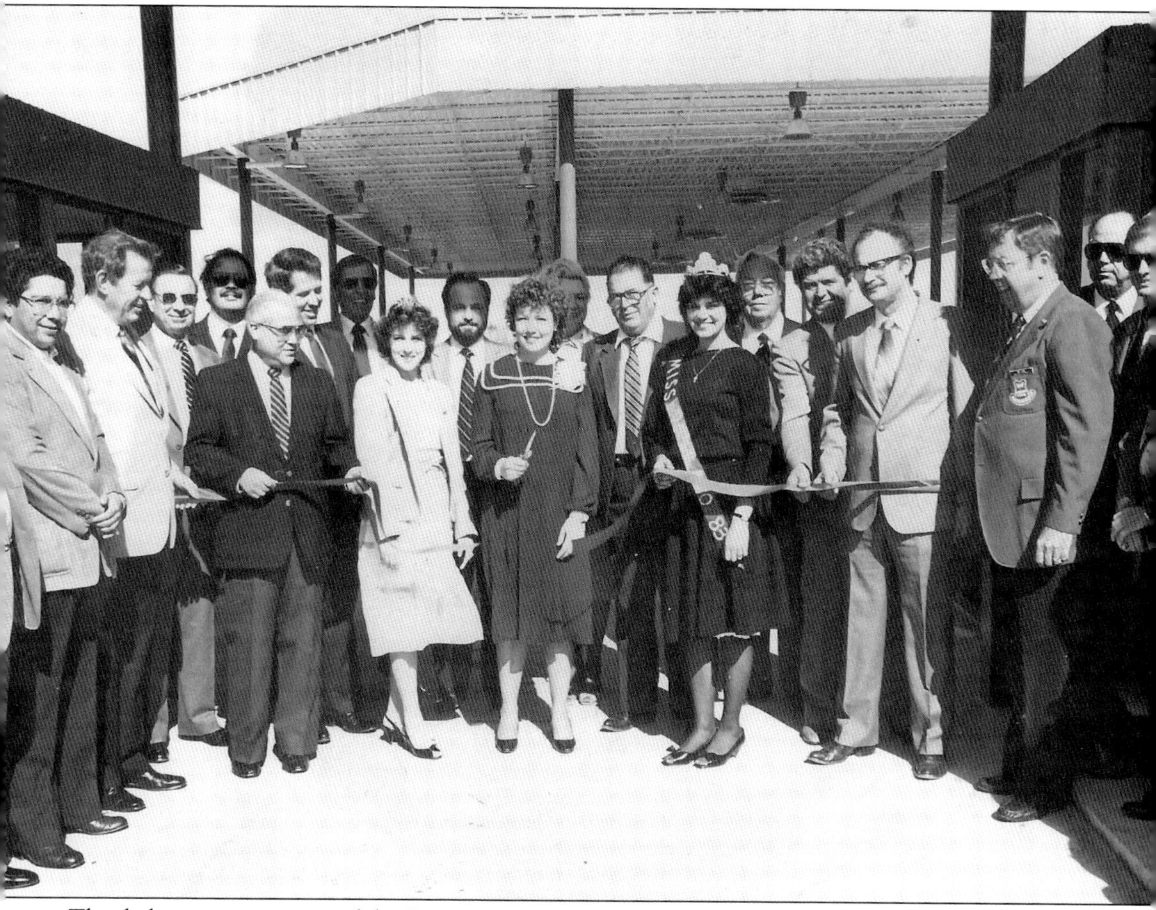

The dedication ceremony of the Progreso International Bridge was big news on both sides of the border. The bridge was built in 1953, after the Rio Rico suspension bridge collapsed during the great flood of 1941. In this photograph are, in no particular order, former U.S. Rep. Kika De La Garza, Mary Angela Cain, William C. Cain, Johnny Jones, Shelly Collier, Jay Jones, and John Cain. (Courtesy William C. Cain family.)

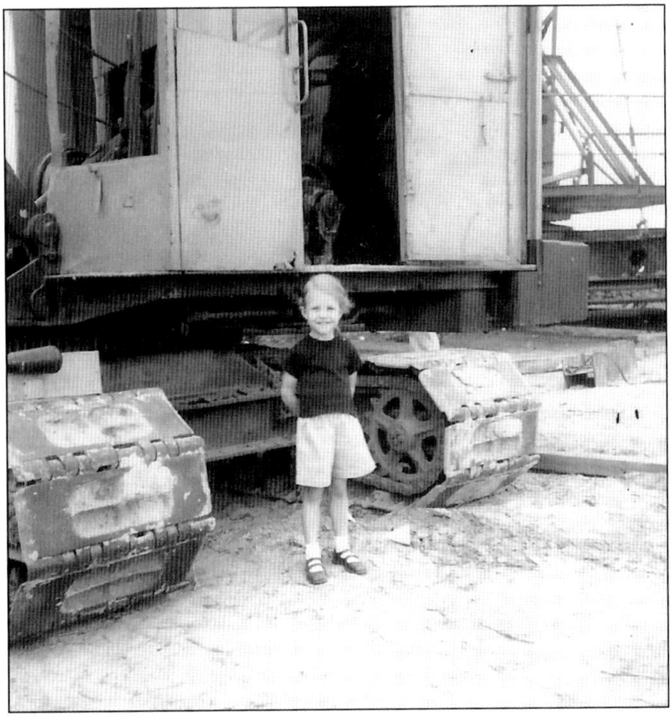

Members of the Cain family grew up surrounded by the events of the Progreso and Rio Rico Bridges. This 1952 photograph shows four-year-old Frances Cain in front of the machinery used to build the bridge. (Courtesy William C. Cain family.)

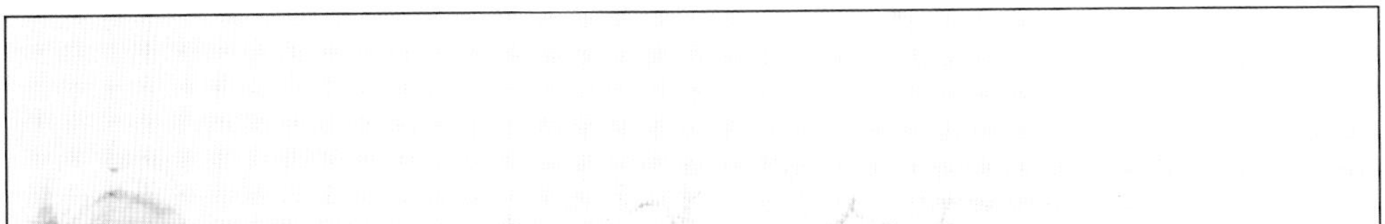

This photograph of the dedication ceremony of a road that connected Nuevo Progreso to Rio Bravo, Mexico, captured the anxiety of a crowd awaiting perhaps the most celebrated guest, former Mexican president Gustavo Díaz Ordaz Bolaños. From left to right are Kathryn Cain, John Cain, Frances Cain, Mary Angela Cain, Odilia Marroquin, and several unidentified people. (Courtesy William C. Cain family.)

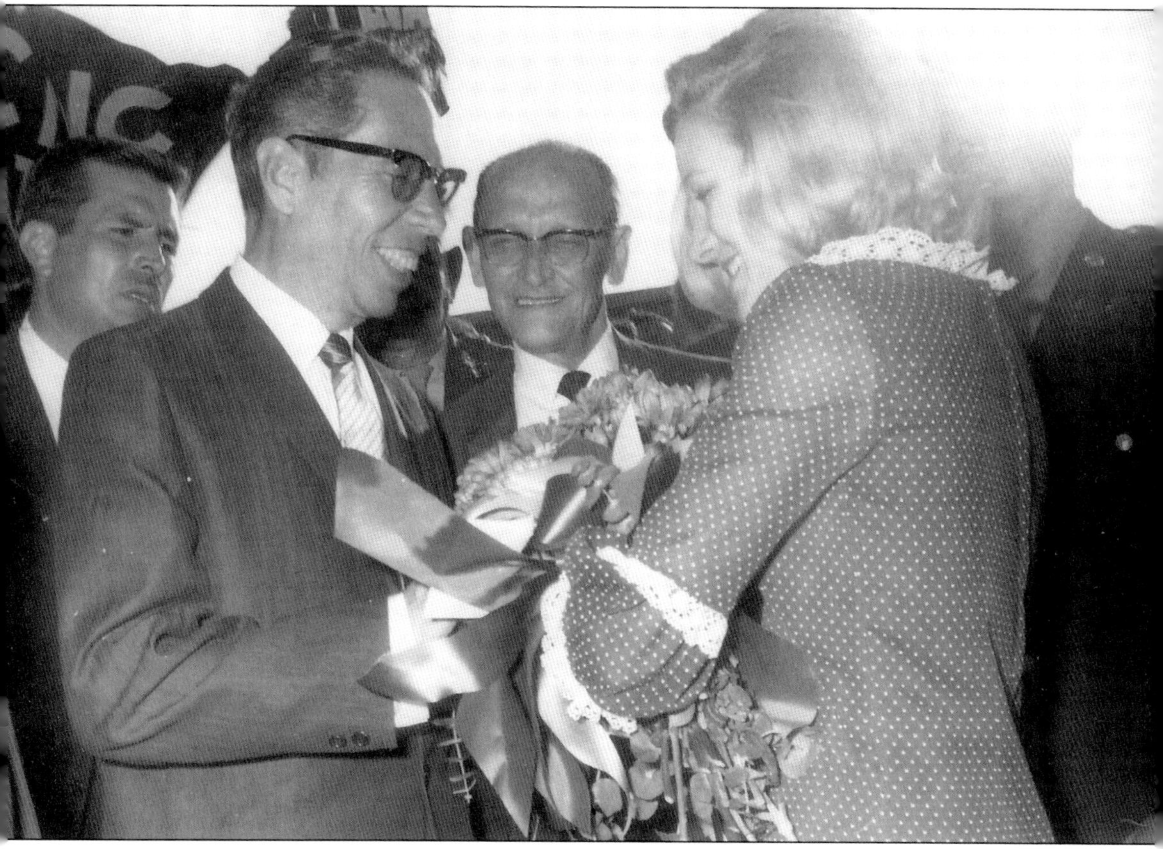

Frances Cain is shown here with former Mexican president Gustavo Díaz Ordaz Bolaños during the dedication of a new road connecting Rio Bravo to Nuevo Progreso, Mexico. The Cain family gave former president Díaz Ordaz Bolaños a big welcome and presented him with flowers. Díaz Ordaz Bolaños served as Mexico's president from 1964 to 1970. (Courtesy William C. Cain family.)

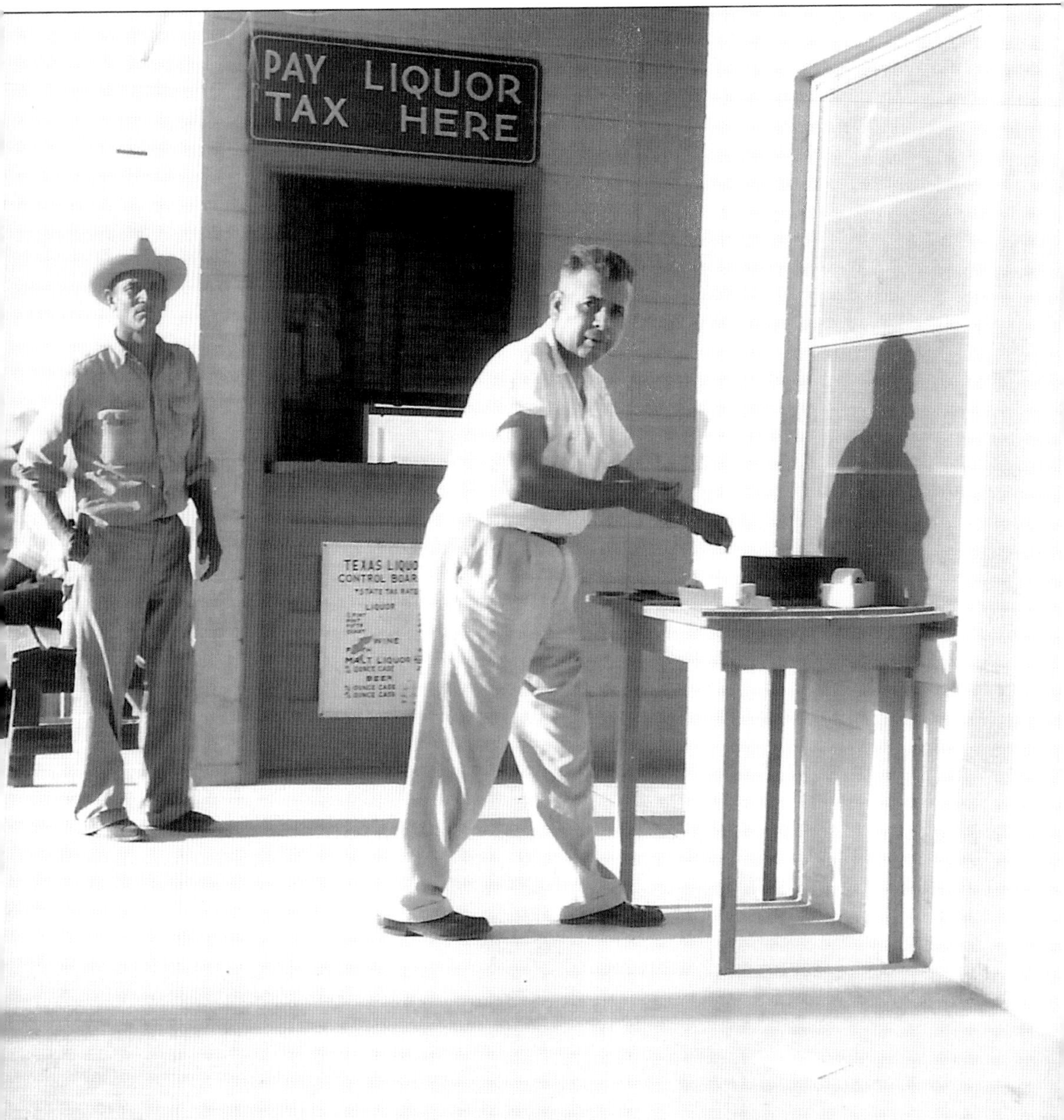


Silverio Hinojosa is shown in an area of the Progreso International Bridge that thousands of people can identify with, those who travel to Mexico to buy alcohol and liquor. People who buy alcohol in Mexico visit a liquor tax booth, like the one shown in this photograph, on their way back to the United States and pay taxes. (Courtesy William C. Cain family.)

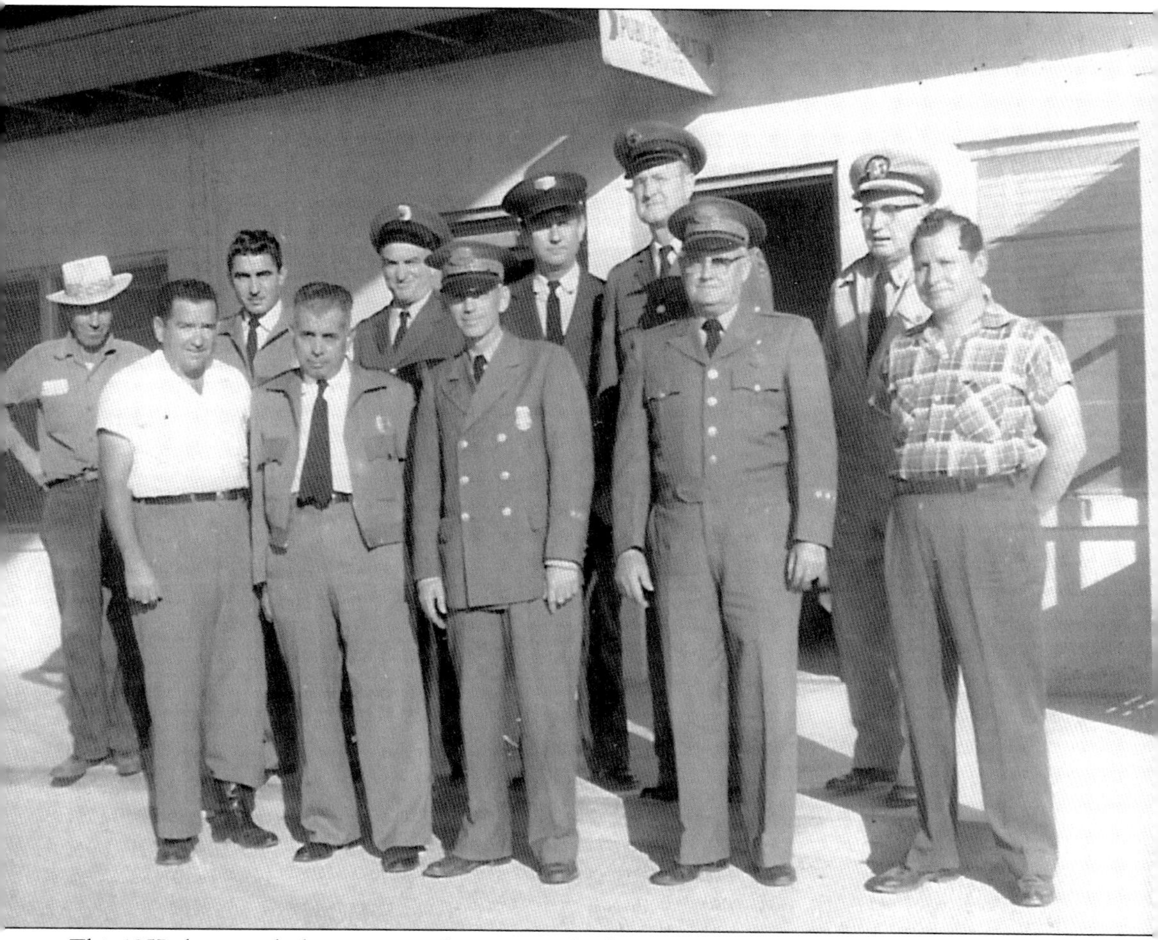

This 1957 photograph shows a team of customs and toll station workers at the Progreso International Bridge. They are, from left to right, Gene Foley, Silverio Hinojosa, Omer Lee Hix, an unidentified immigration officer, Charlie De La Rosa, and other unidentified customs and immigration workers. (Courtesy William C. Cain family.)

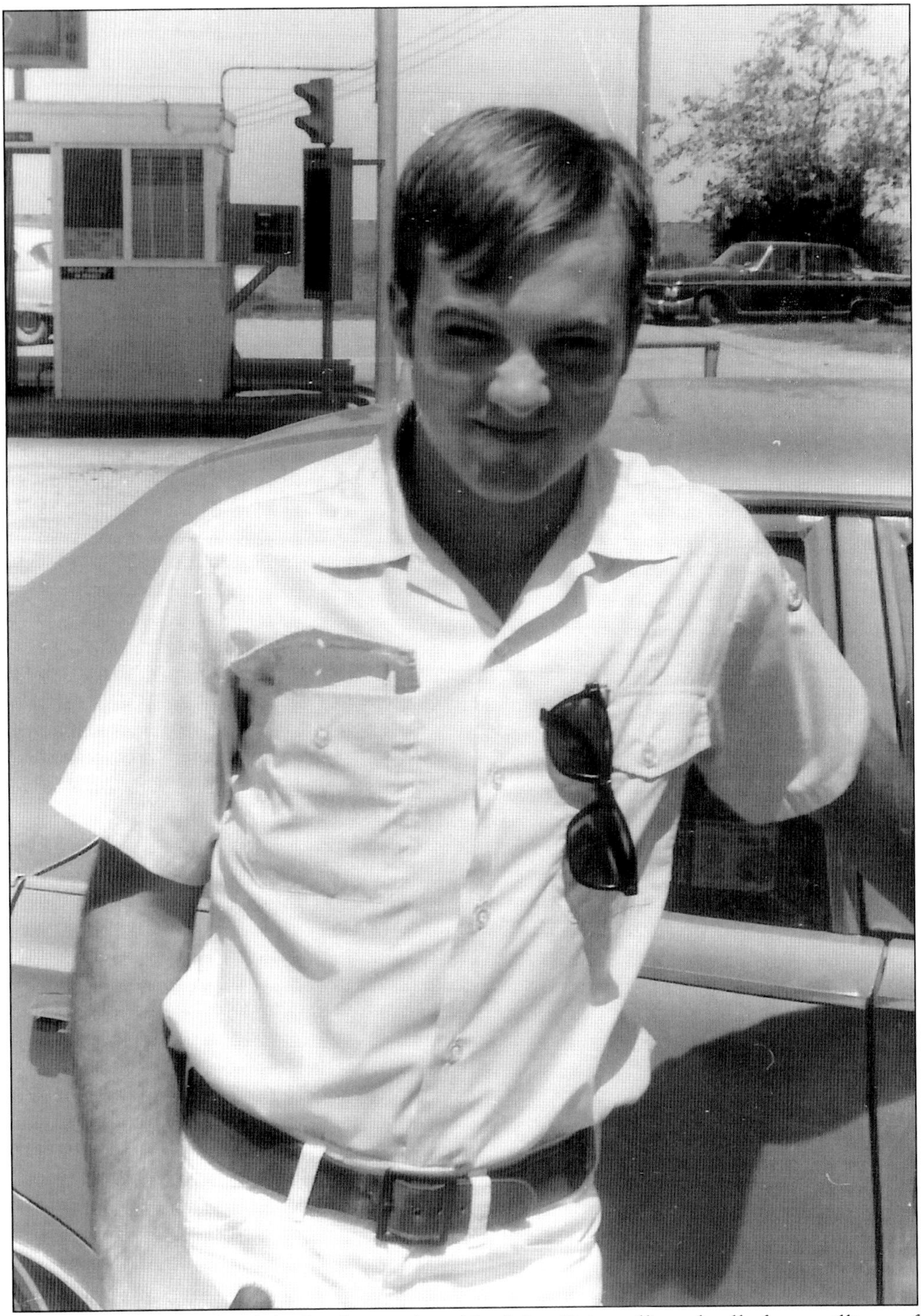

On the American side of the border, workers like John Cain collected tolls from millions of tourists, who over the years have made their way through Progreso. The Progreso International Bridge opened in 1953 and was expanded in the 1980s to make much-needed room for customs authorities. (Courtesy William C. Cain family.)

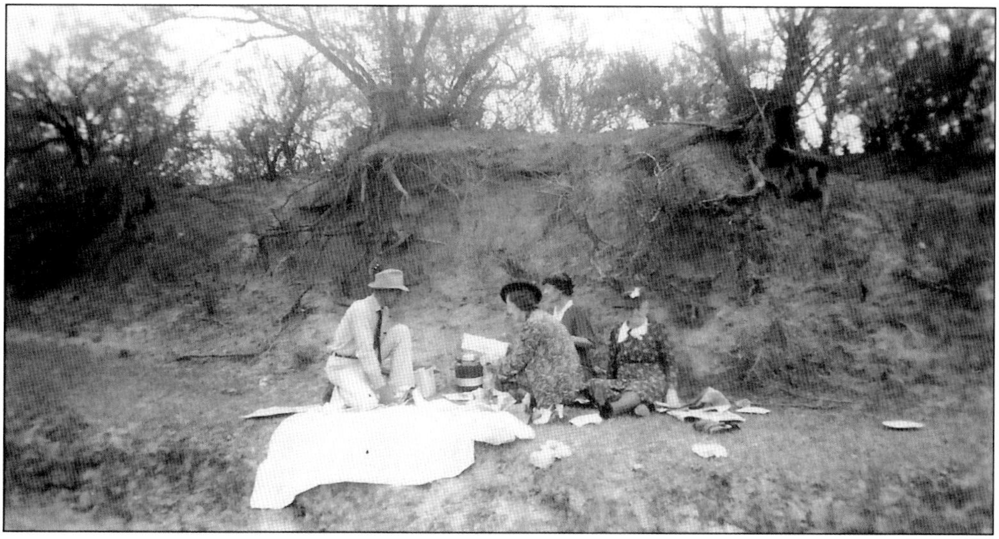

The roots of the families who make up Progreso's history run deep. This photograph, taken along the banks of the Rio Grande, shows how families used their surroundings to dine and entertain guests. (Courtesy William C. Cain family.)

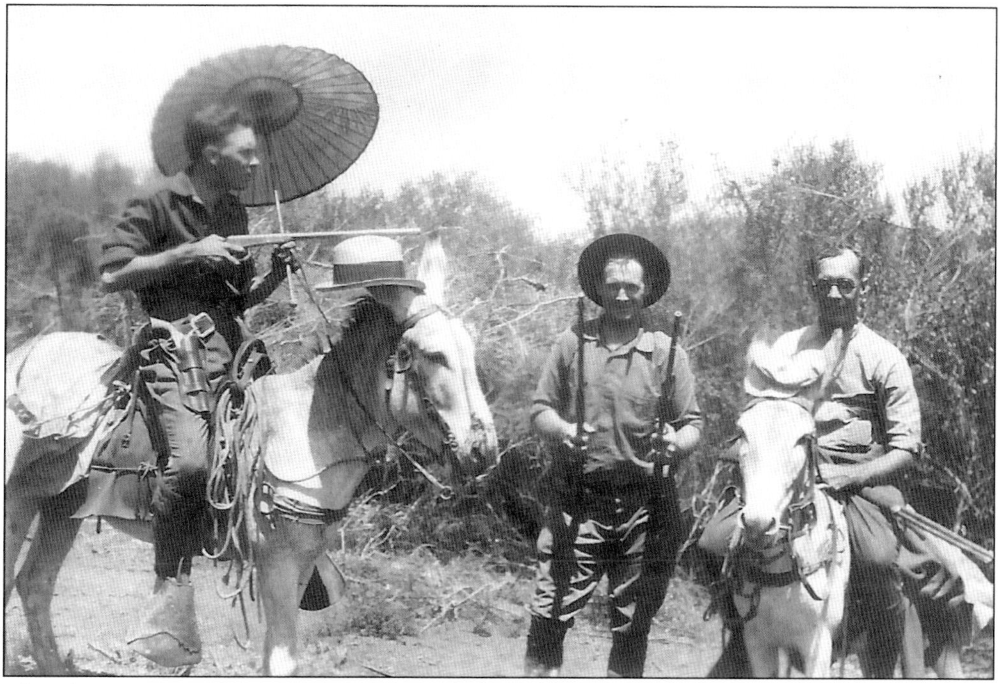

This photograph captures the international flavor and character of the people who have called Progreso home for generations. But most importantly, it introduces a man who helped shape the history of the town. According to William C. Cain family records, Al Cain (right) built the first international bridge in the area, connecting Rio Rico, Mexico, to Thayer, Texas. When the tragic flood of 1941 wiped out the Rio Rico bridge, Cain went upstream to the village of Progreso and convinced local investors to support his idea to build a bridge just west of Toluca Ranch. The present-day Progreso International Bridge attracts hundreds of thousands of tourists every year. (Courtesy William C. Cain family.)

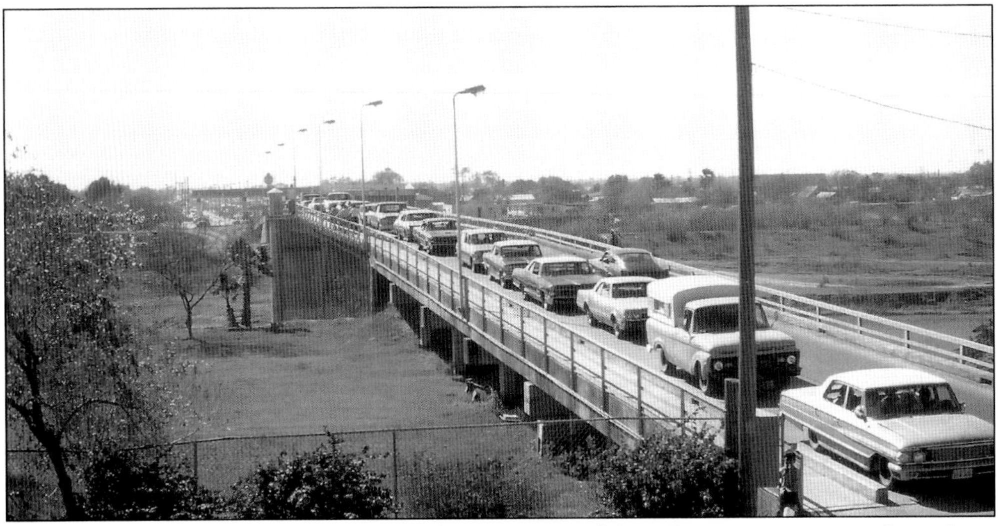

Hundreds of thousands of tourists make their way to and from Progreso every year. Long lines of cars typically wait their turn to cross to Mexico at the Progreso International Bridge. Some visitors enjoy eating good Mexican food, while others prefer sipping on a Mexican margarita during happy hour, but everyone who crosses the border likes shopping for good deals. (Courtesy William C. Cain family.)

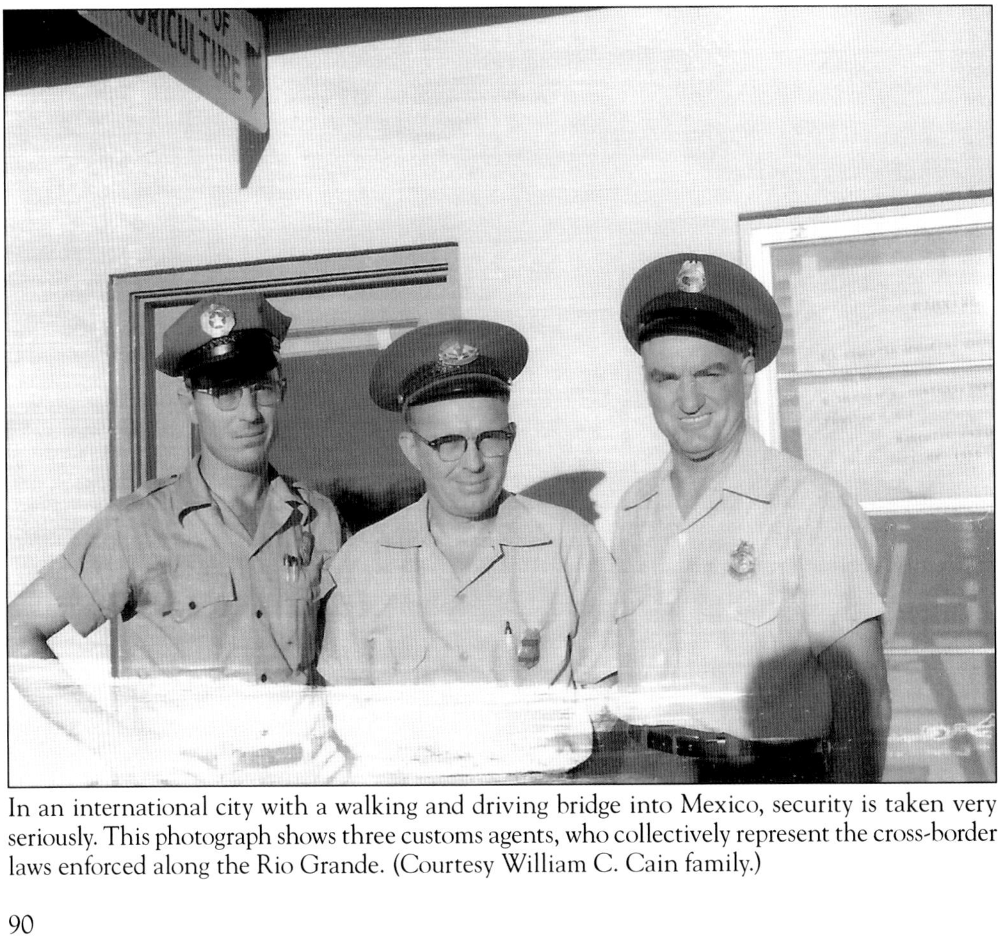

In an international city with a walking and driving bridge into Mexico, security is taken very seriously. This photograph shows three customs agents, who collectively represent the cross-border laws enforced along the Rio Grande. (Courtesy William C. Cain family.)

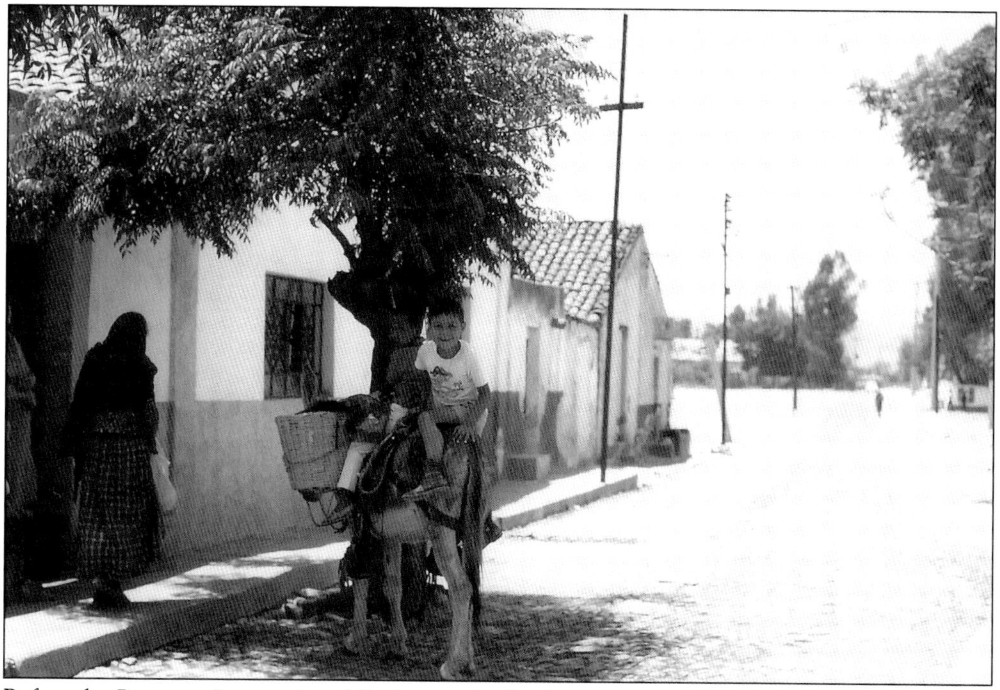

Before the Progreso International Bridge was built, the area across the Rio Grande was an open field. That all changed in the early 1950s when the B and P Bridge Company built the bridge and helped transform an area of Mexico with very few people into the city of Nuevo Progreso. This photograph shows some of the early Nuevo Progreso homes and two children on a donkey. (Courtesy William C. Cain family.)

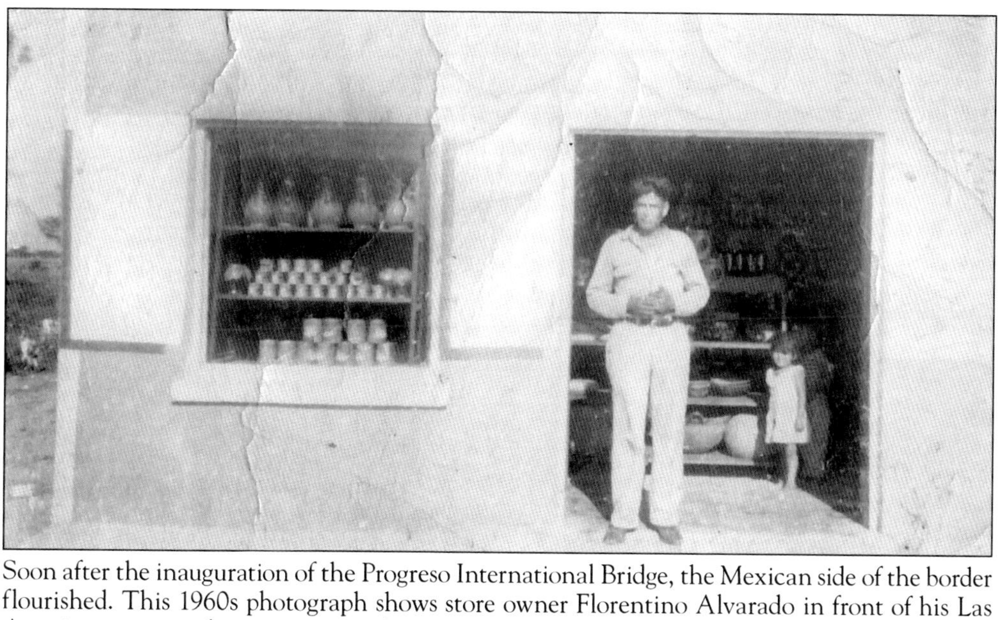

Soon after the inauguration of the Progreso International Bridge, the Mexican side of the border flourished. This 1960s photograph shows store owner Florentino Alvarado in front of his Las Americas store on the main street of Nuevo Progreso, Mexico. Alvarado sold wine, dishes, and souvenirs. (Courtesy Olga Galvan.)

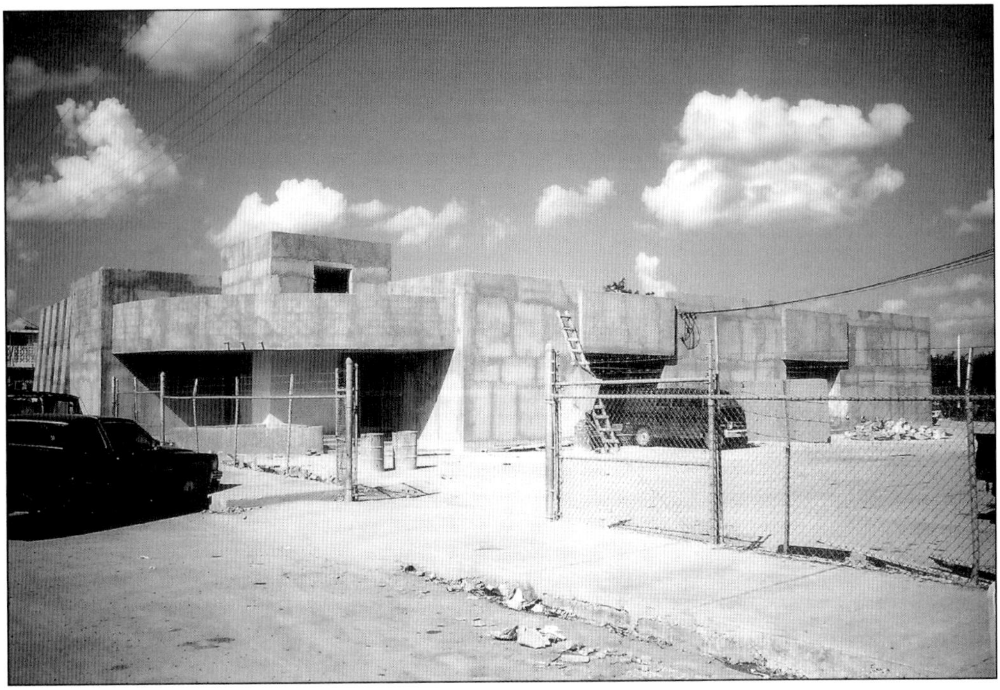

When the Progreso International Bridge first connected the United States to Mexico, Nuevo Progreso did not exist; it did not have a single business. That all changed when Arturo Arredondo built Arturo's Restaurant. Other businesses soon flourished, and the area became known as Las Flores, Spanish for "The Flowers." Later Arturo's Restaurant burned down; these photographs show the rebuilding process. (Both, courtesy William C. Cain family.)

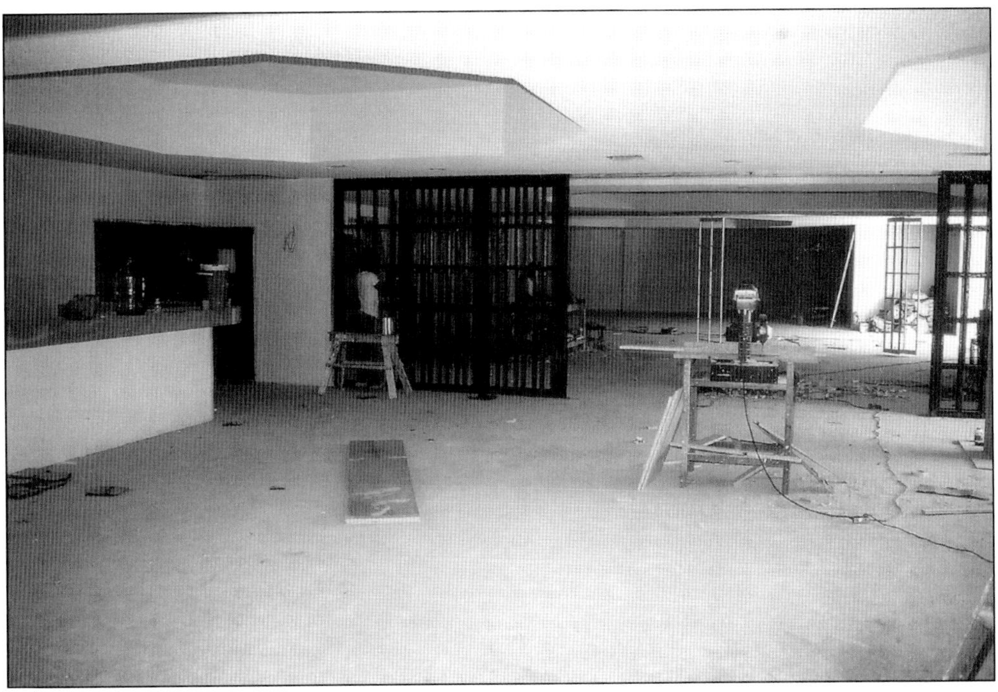

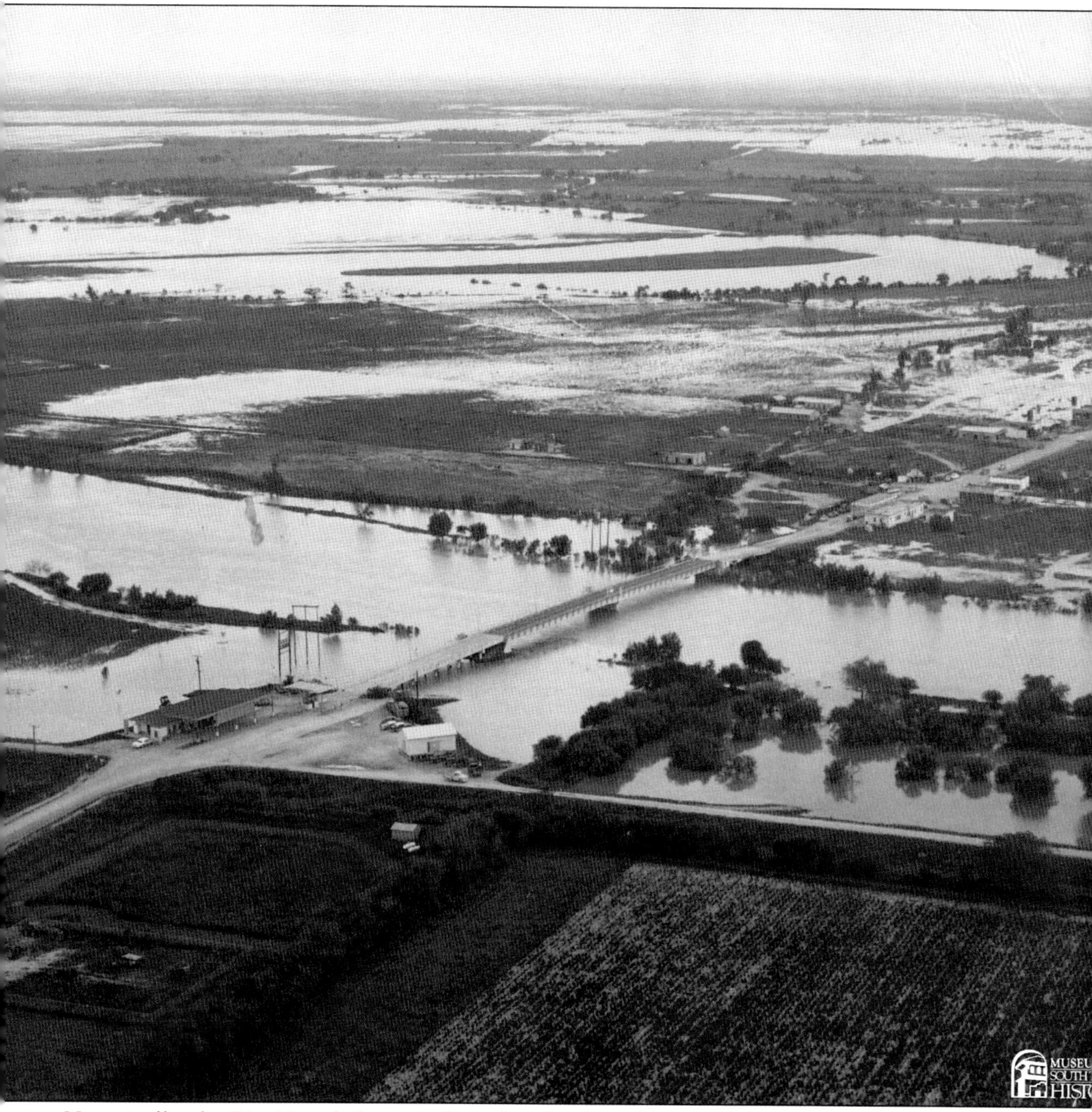

Historically, the Rio Grande has overflowed its bank at the site of the Progreso International Bridge. This photograph was taken from the U.S. side of the border and shows the river spilled over its banks on both the American and Mexican sides. Dealing with dangerous flooding waters has been a challenge for both residents and local farmers throughout history. (Courtesy Museum of South Texas History.)

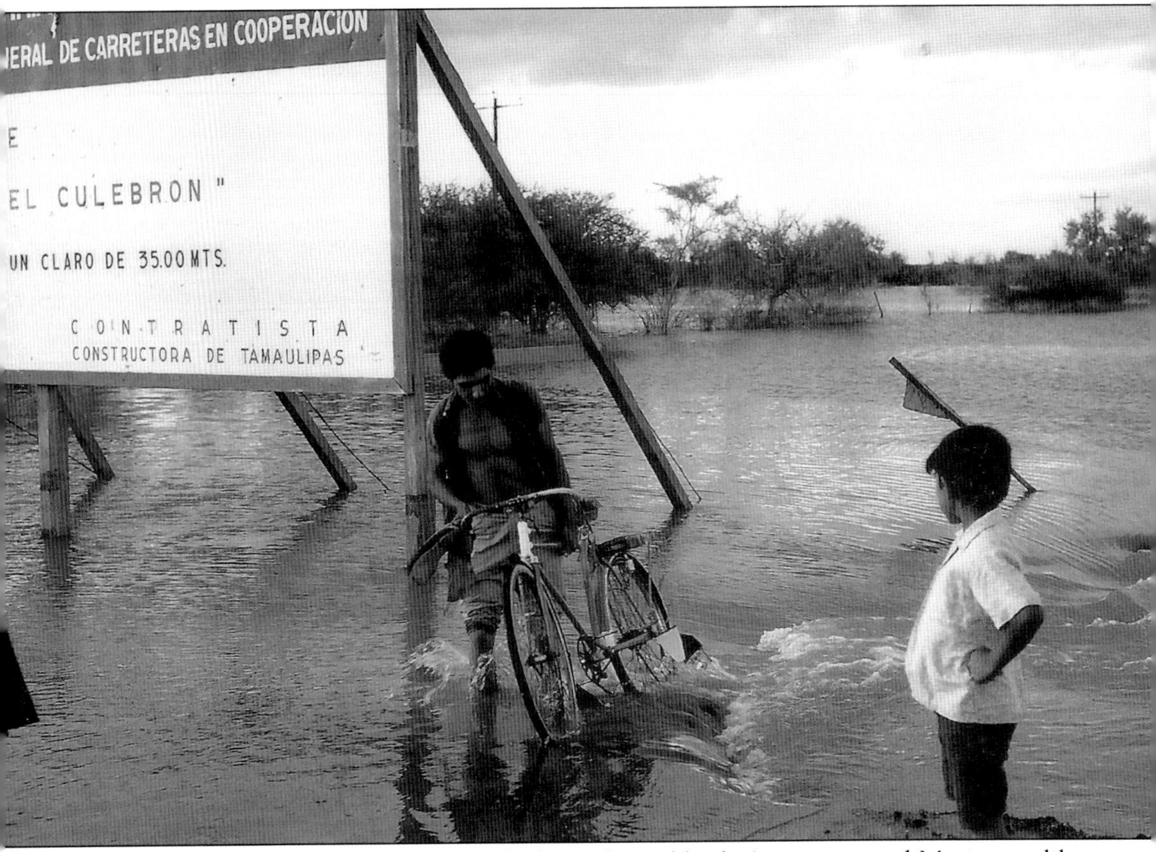


The flooding waters of the Rio Grande have plagued both Americans and Mexicans alike, especially during rainy and hurricane seasons. These children, who perhaps lost their school to the flood, are waiting for the water to recede. (Courtesy William C. Cain family.)

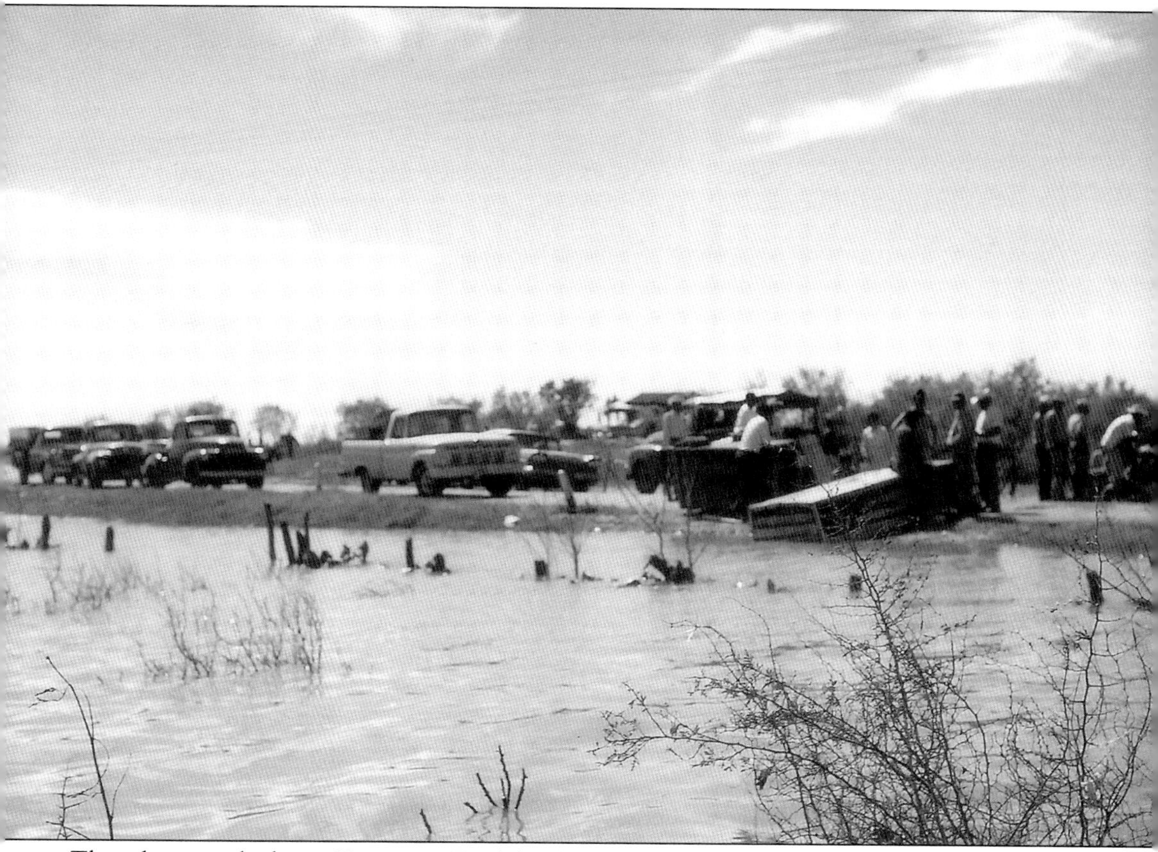

This photograph shows Hurricane Beulah's destruction on the Mexican side of the border. (Courtesy William C. Cain family.)

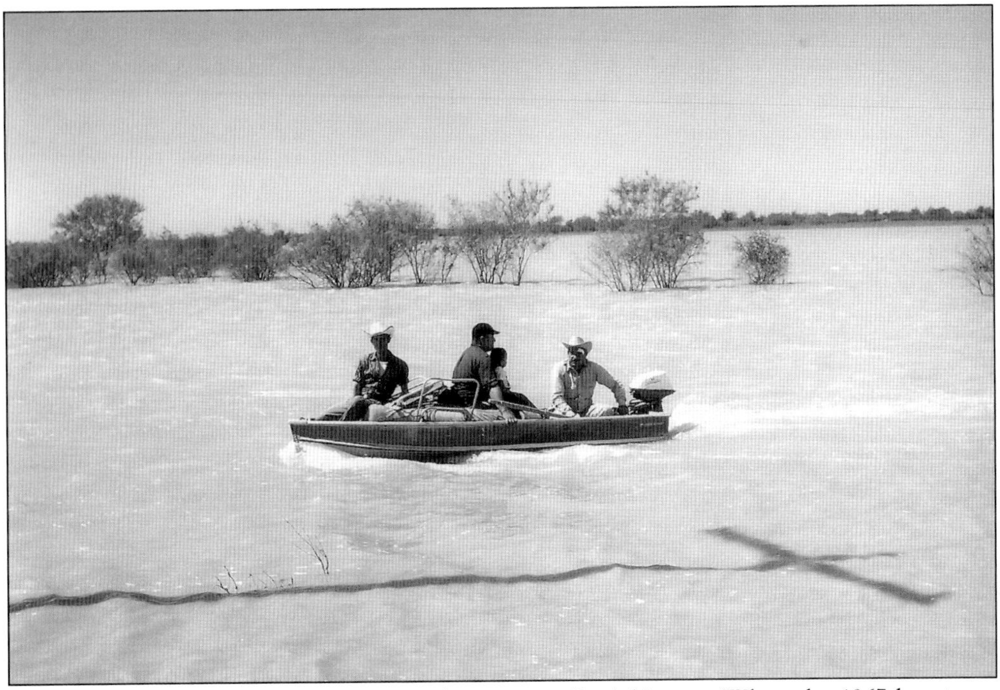

This photograph shows the destruction of Hurricane Beulah's rage. When the 1967 hurricane hit, Progreso area workers and their families used boats to escape the rising waters. (Courtesy William C. Cain family.)

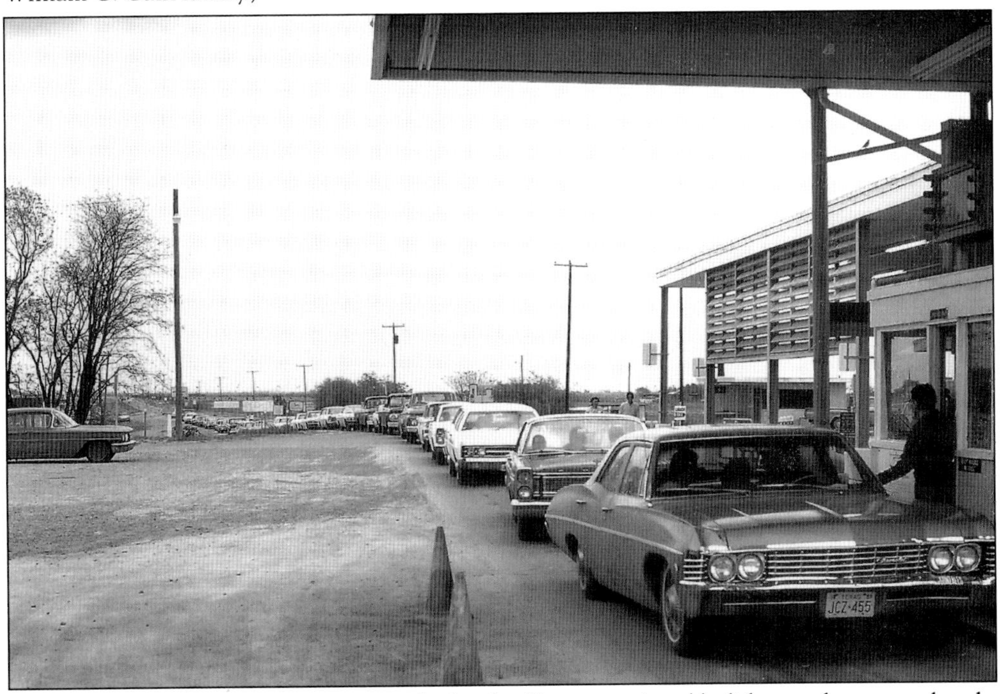

Cars filled with passengers wait to cross the border. During national holidays and some weekends, the line of cars waiting to go to Mexico can be more than 2 miles long. (Courtesy William C. Cain family.)

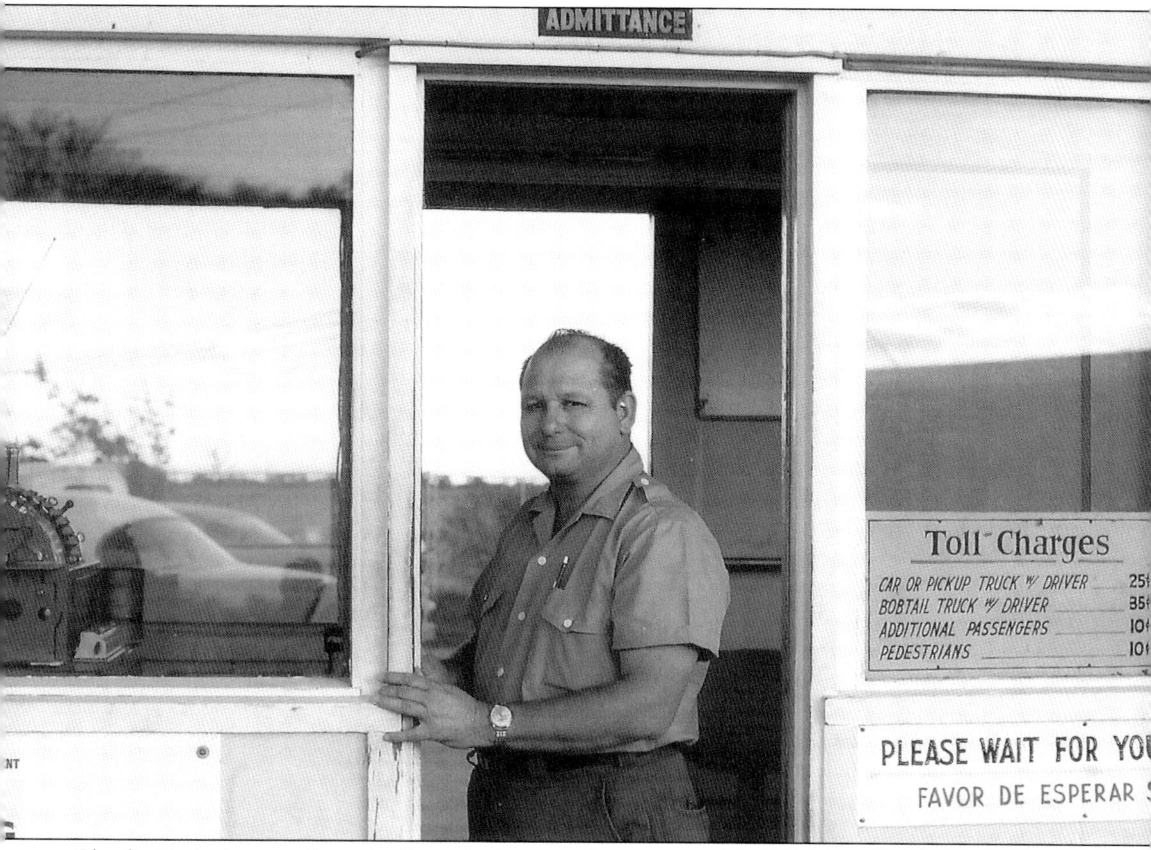


Charlie De La Rosa collected tolls at the Progreso International Bridge. The sign on the booth is a flashback to the good old days, when crossing the border cost only 25¢. The De La Rosa family kept close ties with the Cain family, founders of the Progreso International Bridge, and even baked tamales for the Cains every Christmas. (Courtesy William C. Cain family.)

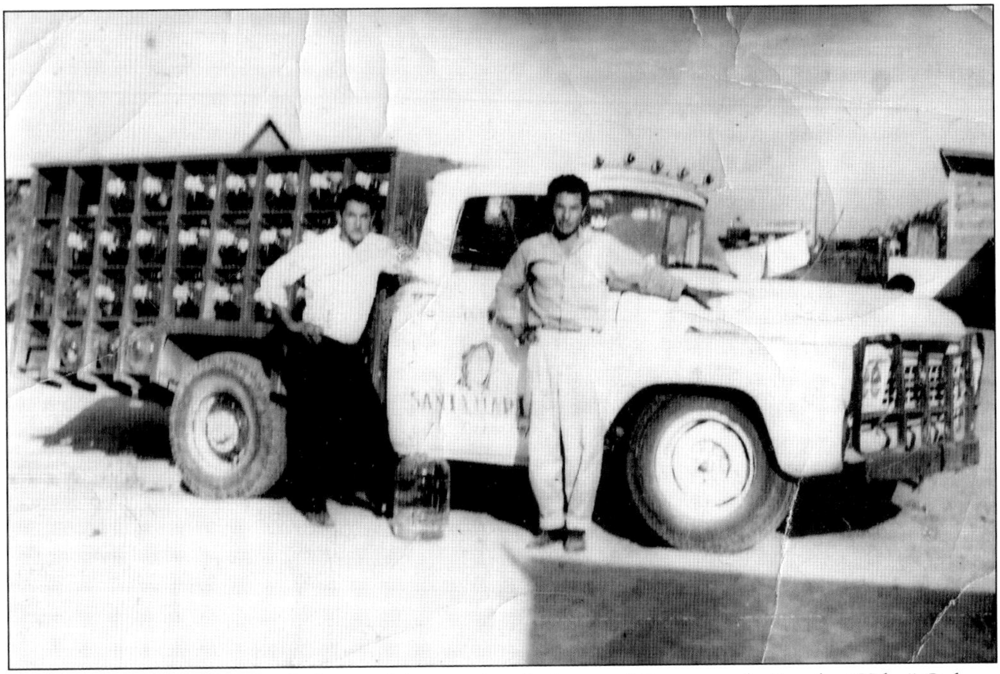

This 1963 or 1964 photograph shows a Mexican bottled water delivery truck. Pancho "Kiko" Galvan (right) and an unidentified man delivered water to businesses and homes in Nuevo Progreso for several years. (Courtesy Olga Galvan.)

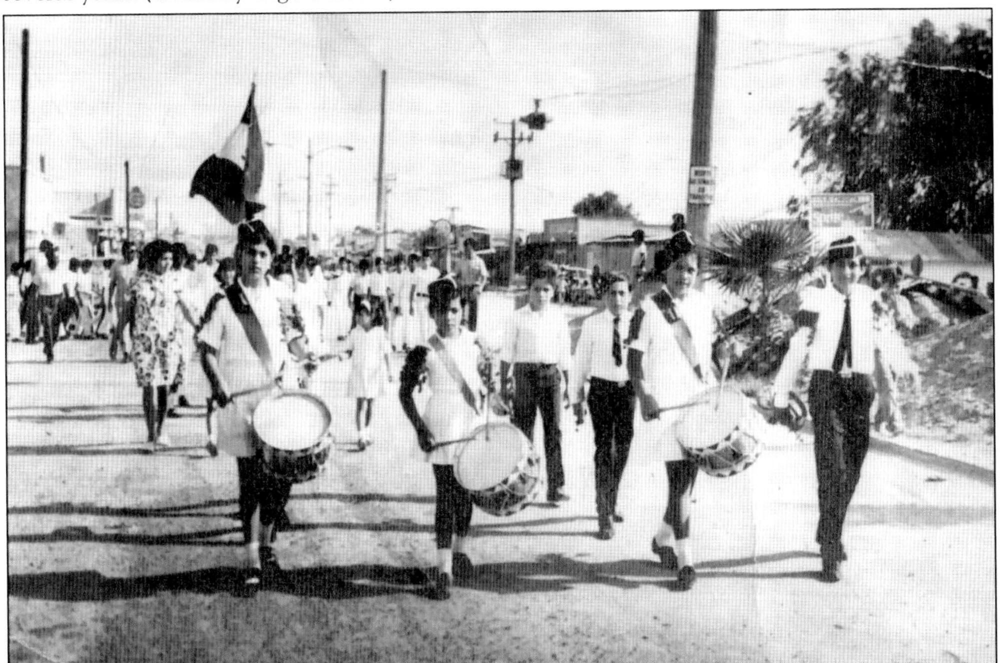

Mexico celebrates Mexican Revolution Day on November 20. Schools, civic societies, political leaders, and business owners participate in the celebration of this national holiday. The unidentified children in this 1954 photograph are from a local school. (Courtesy Olga Galvan.)

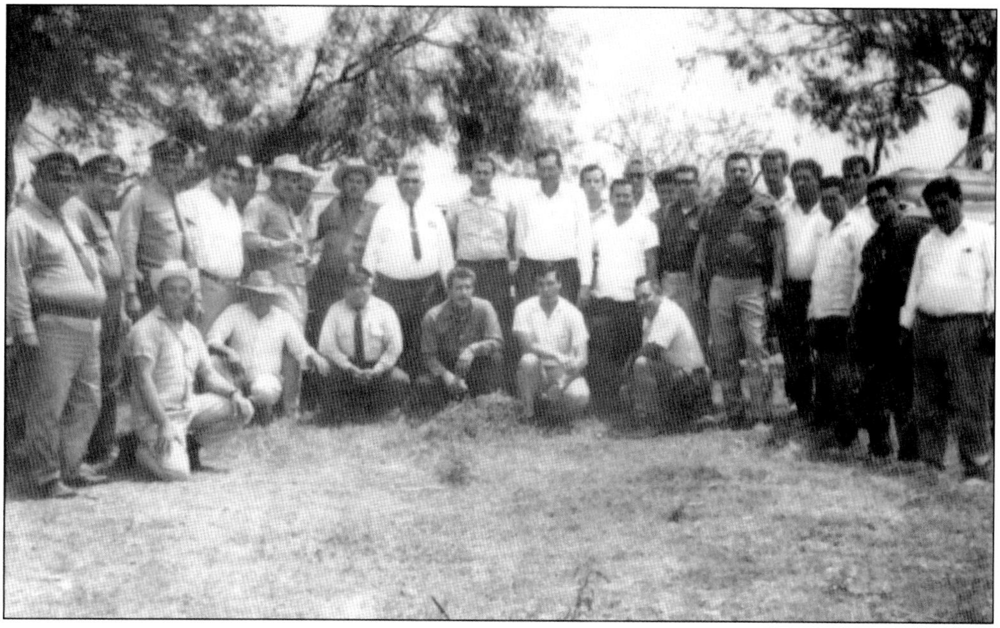

These two 1960s photographs show police officers (above) and city leaders (below) meeting in Nuevo Progreso. From both photographs, it is easy to see that outdoor meetings were well attended. When the Progreso International Bridge was built in 1953, the city of Nuevo Progreso did not exist; by the 1960s, residents had risen to posts of service and leadership. (Both, courtesy Olga Galvan.)

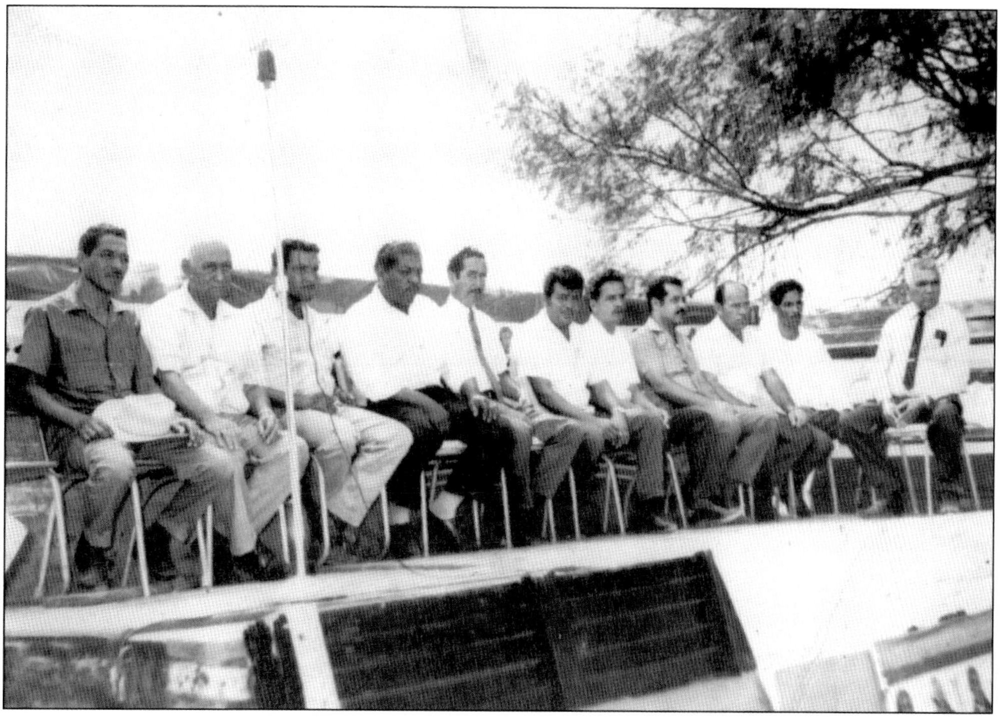

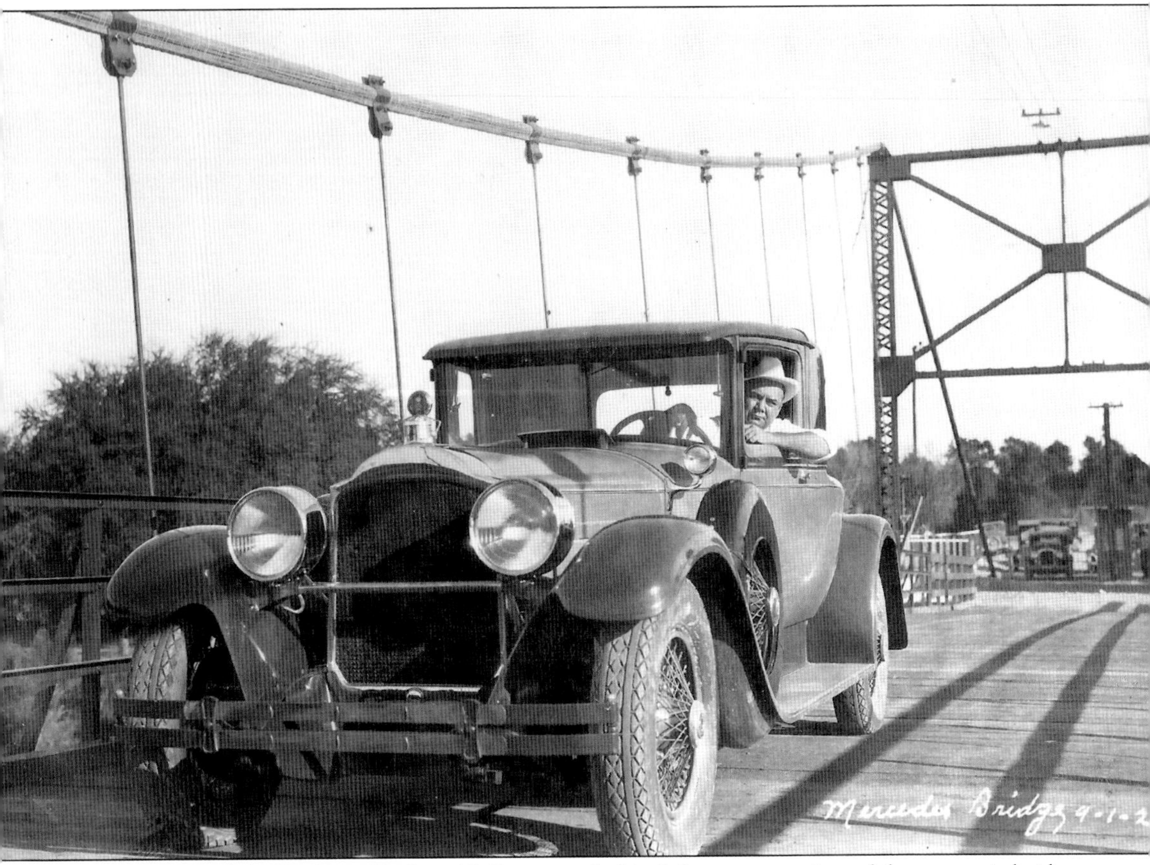


The owner of the Rio Rico Bridge, Al Cain, was behind the construction of the strategic bridge. Cain's vision facilitated river crossings in the lower Rio Grande, and he is shown here crossing the Rio Rico suspension bridge. The bridge connected Thayer, south of Mercedes, and Rio Rico, Mexico, from 1928 to 1941. (Courtesy William C. Cain family.)

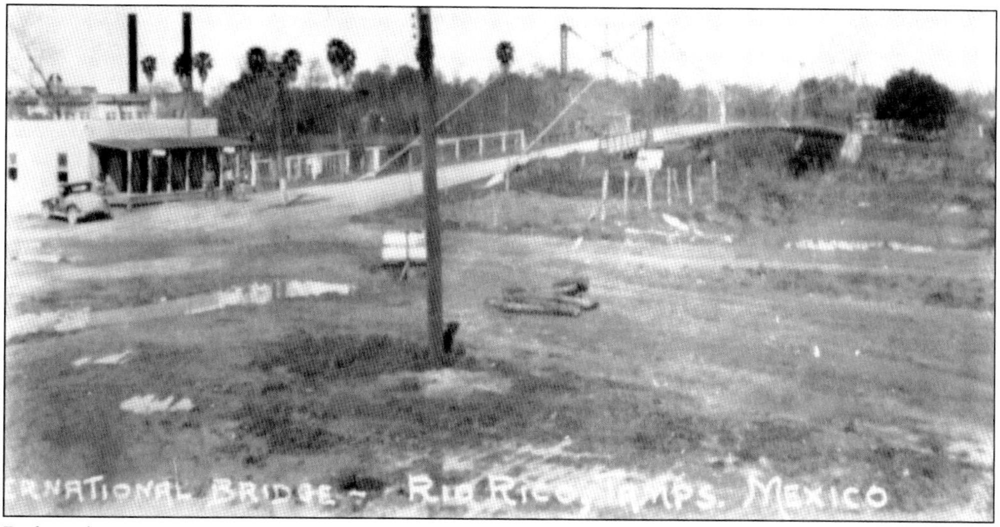


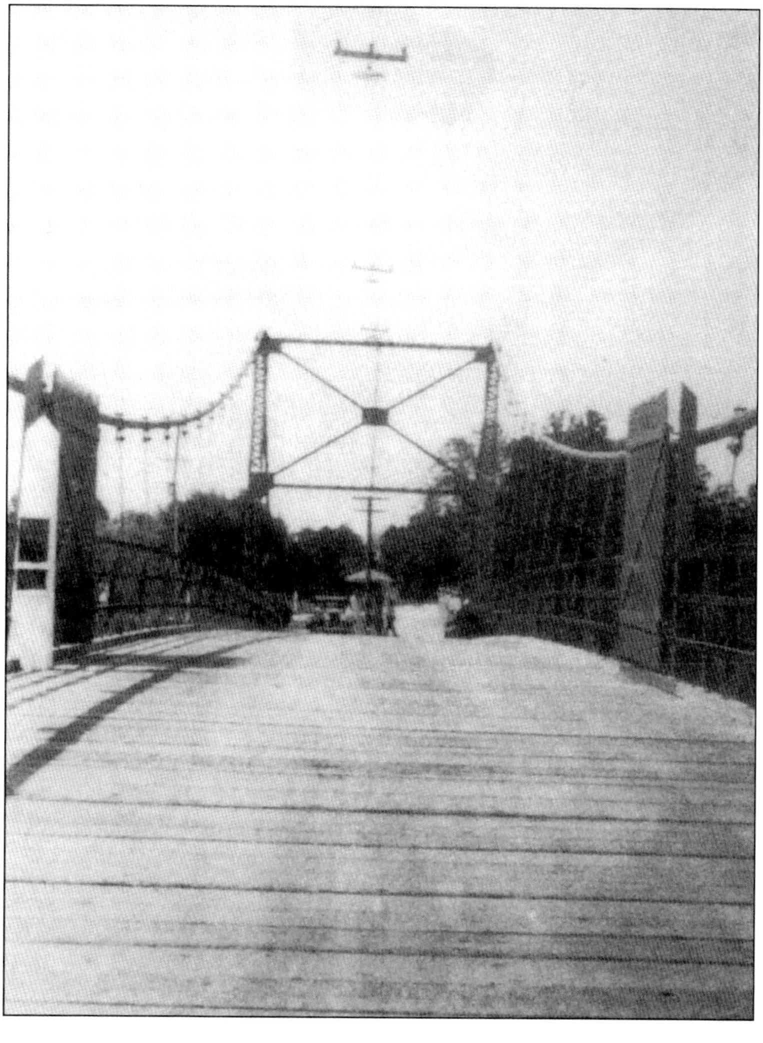

Before the Progreso International Bridge was established, the Rio Rico International Bridge was the closest passageway to Mexico in the immediate area. It connected Rio Rico to Thayer, Texas. These two photographs show the bridge from different angles. The suspension bridge was made of wood and steel. A set of gates, found at the center of the bridge, was locked at midnight to keep people from crossing overnight. The bridge created a successful business haven on each side of the border. (Both, courtesy Weslaco Museum.)

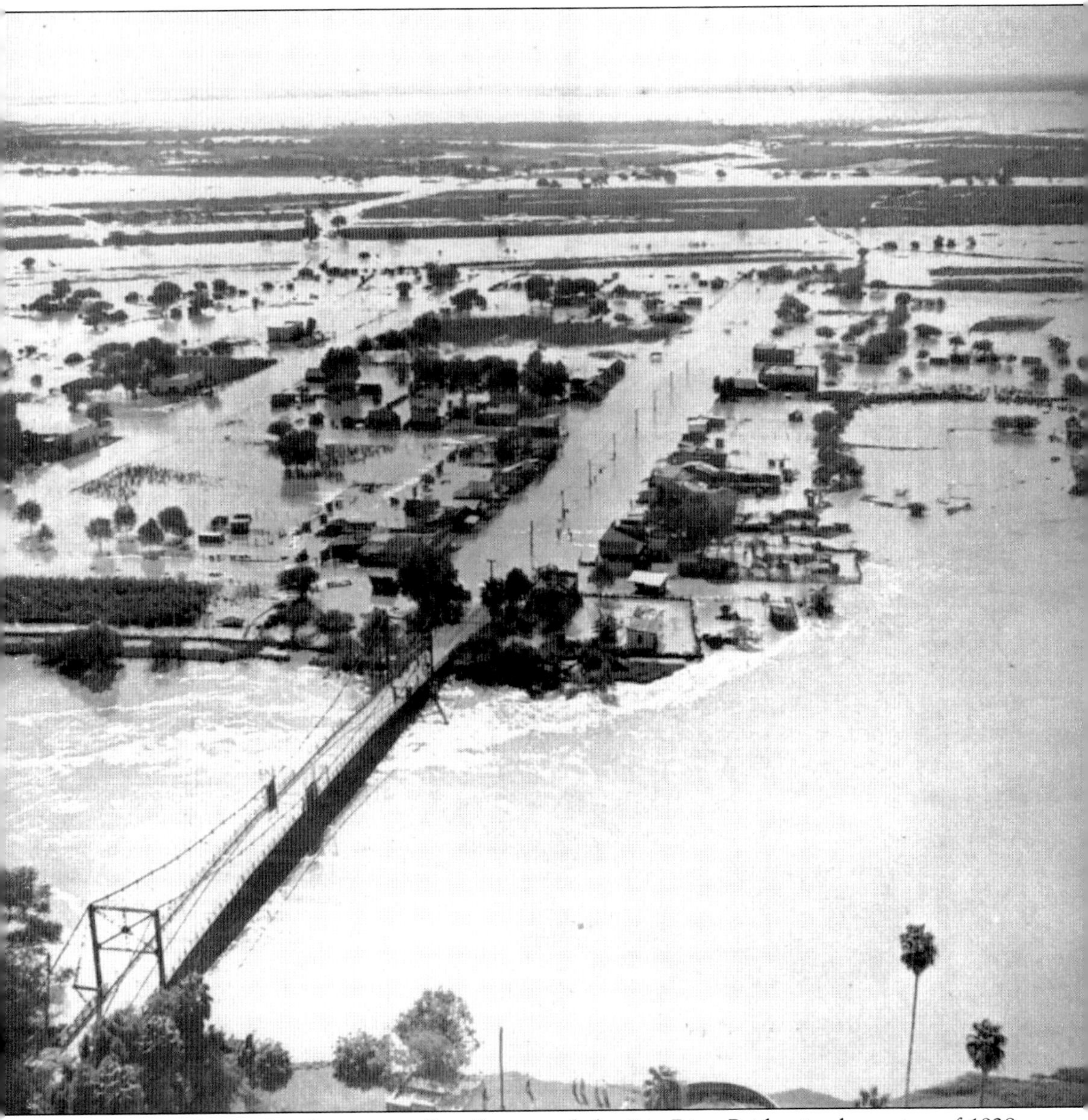

The B and P Bridge Company officially opened the Rio Rico Bridge in the spring of 1928. Newspaper reports show that locals inaugurated the bridge with a barbecue party. The Rio Grande spilled over its banks during hurricane season, but it was the great flood of October 19, 1941, that eventually washed away the entire structure. (Courtesy Weslaco Museum.)

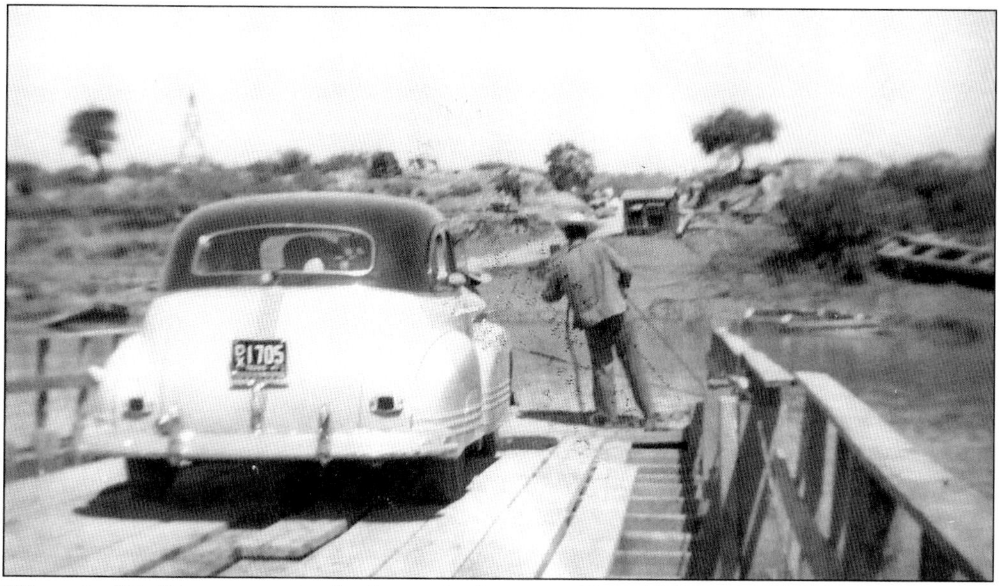

When the Rio Rico suspension bridge washed away in 1941, Al Cain established a ferry service at the same location. Cain used rowboats and later pontoon boats to cross people and their cars to the Mexican side. Adults paid 10¢, and children rode for free. Eventually this area of the Rio Grande eroded to such a degree that rebuilding the Rio Rico Bridge became nearly impossible. (Courtesy William C. Cain family.)

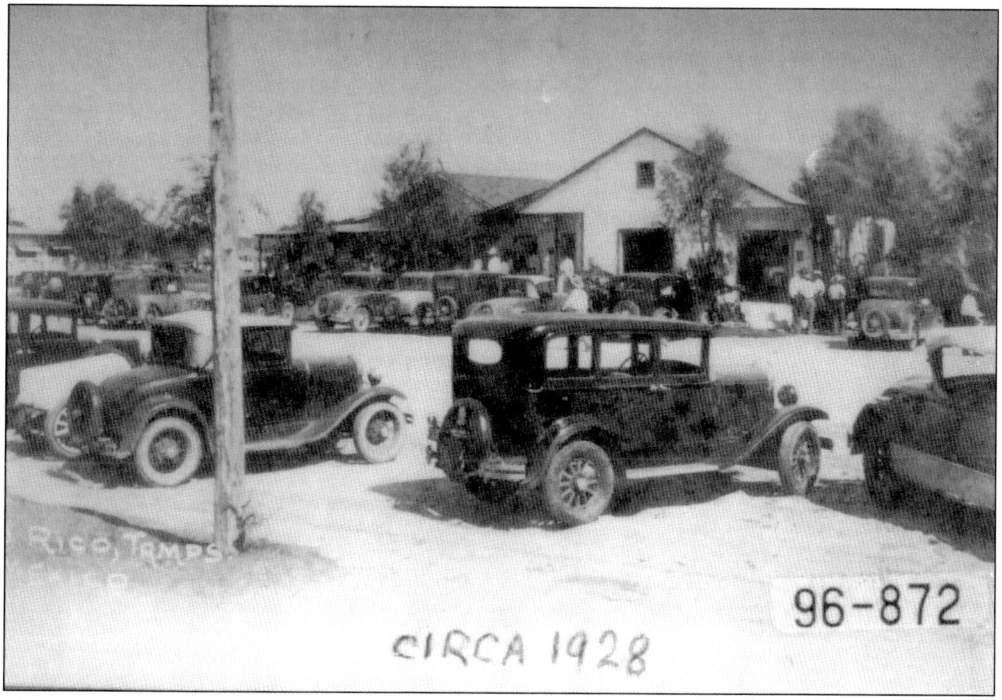


Historical documents show that the Rio Rico Bridge connected Thayer, south of Mercedes, to Rio Rico, Mexico. This photograph shows the main street of Thayer and the toll station at the Rio Rico Bridge. The toll station was next to the Mercedes pumping plant. (Courtesy Weslaco Museum.)

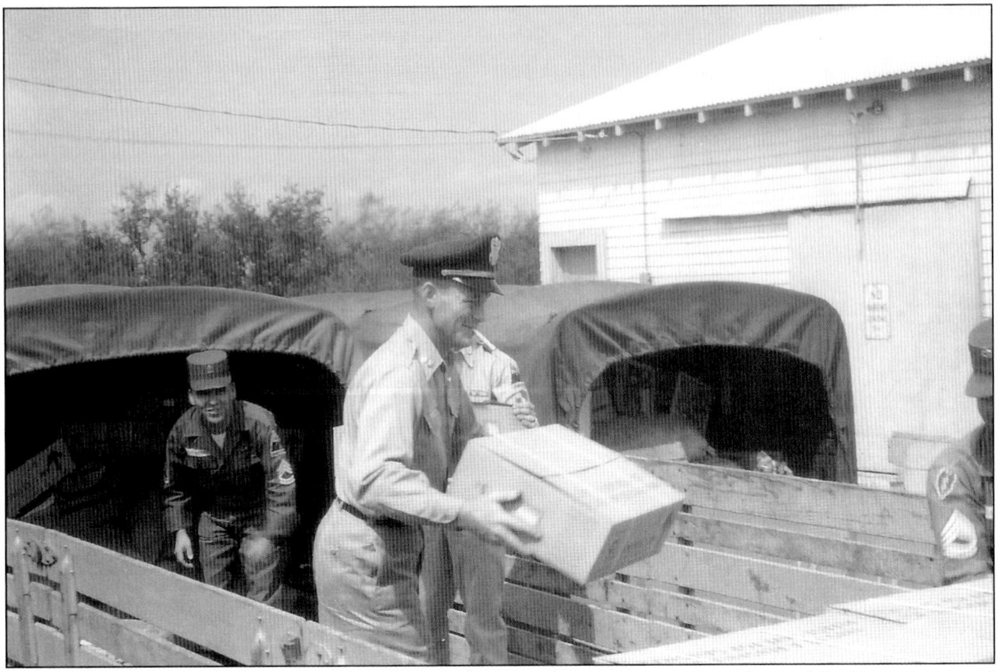

Securing its border is one of the biggest challenges for an international city like Progreso, and dealing with natural disasters is perhaps the second biggest difficulty. Because the Rio Grande has historically overflowed its banks during hurricane season, aid was periodically sent to the Progreso area. Army National Guard trucks from the Headquarters Company 4-1-144 Infantry 49th Armored Division are shown here unloading supplies after Hurricane Beulah. (Both, courtesy William C. Cain family.)

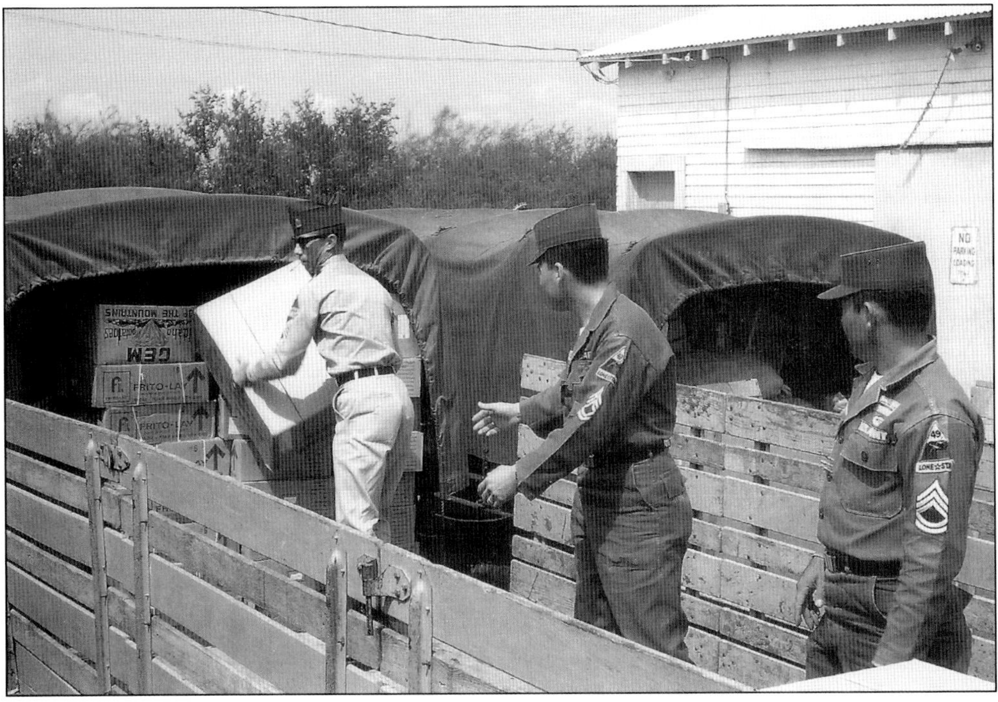

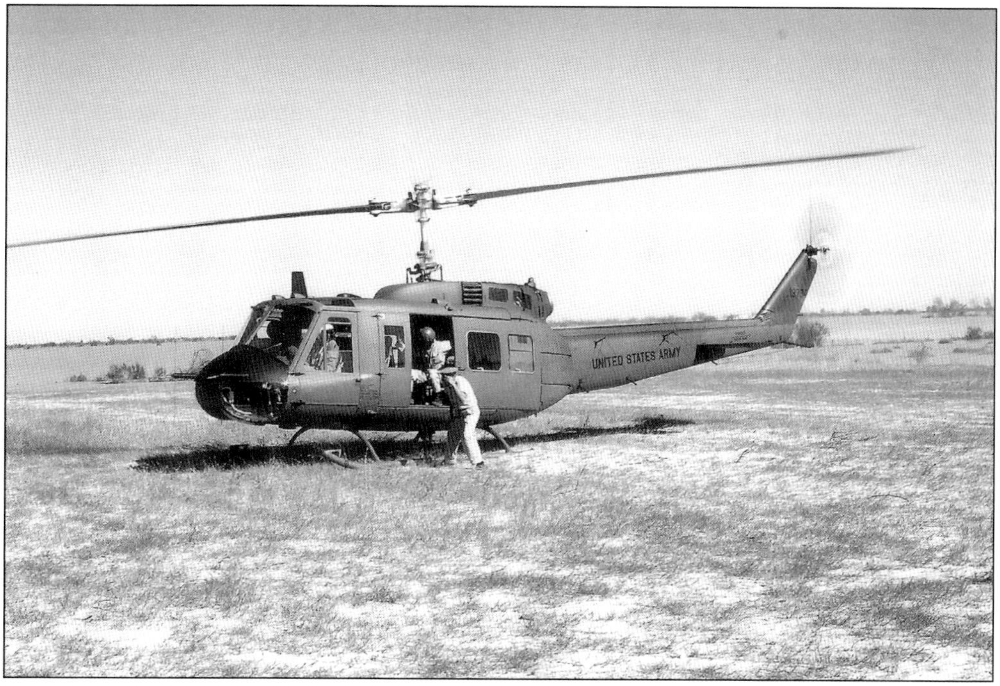


Progreso received national aid after Hurricane Beulah hit in 1967. The storm caused the river to spill over its banks and flood parts of the greater Rio Grande Valley, including Progreso. Rogelio Becerra, a Progreso International Bridge worker, is shown here getting off an army helicopter after assessing the flood situation. National Guard trucks are shown below loaded with supplies. (Both, courtesy William C. Cain family.)

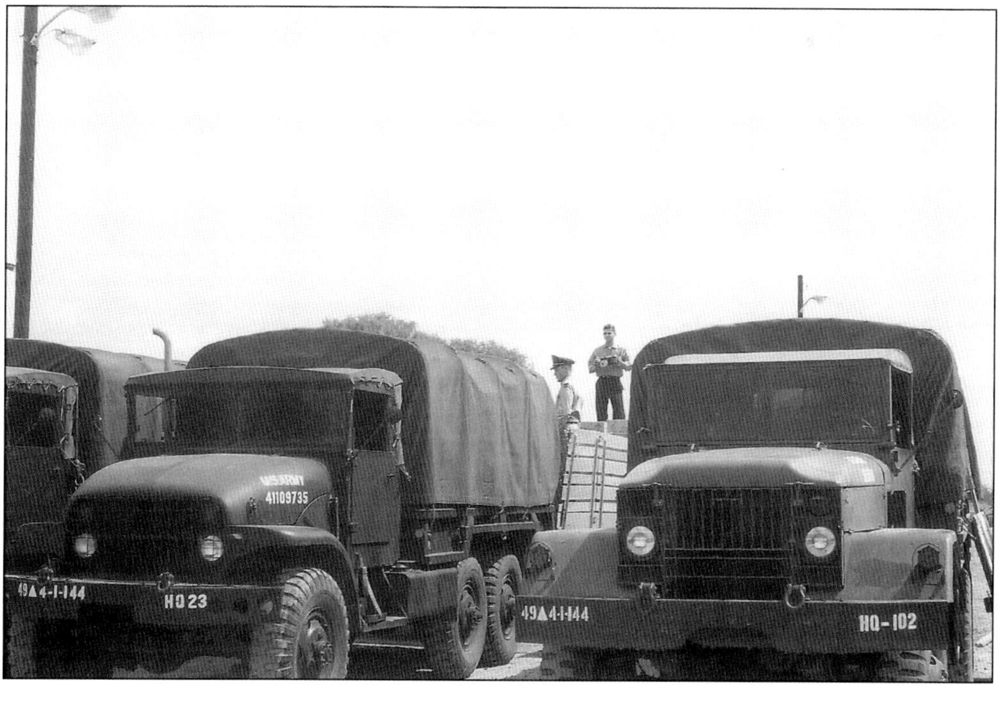

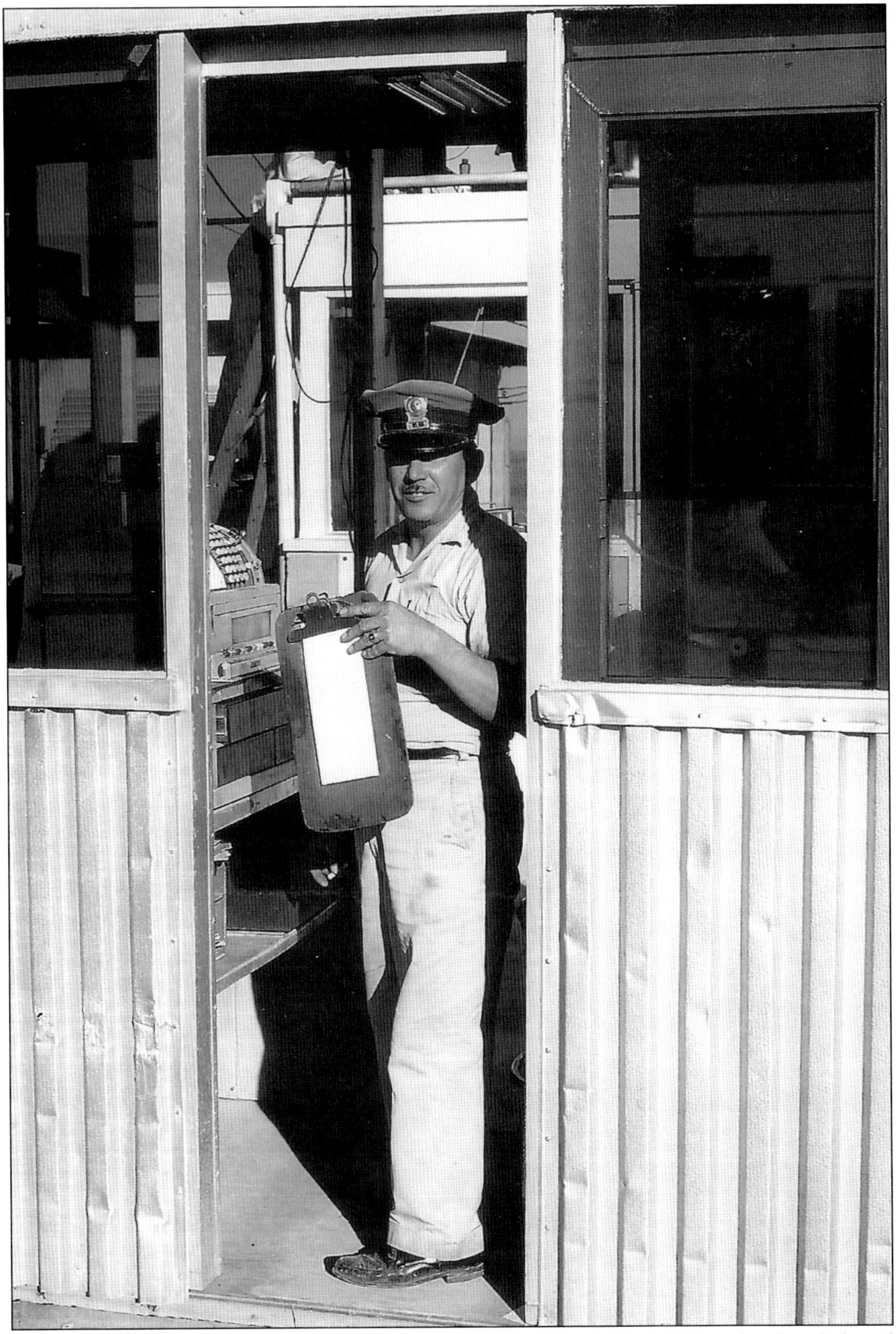

Rogelio Becerra, a tollbooth operator, is shown here standing by a cash register and with a clipboard in hand at the Progreso International Bridge. (Courtesy William C. Cain family.)

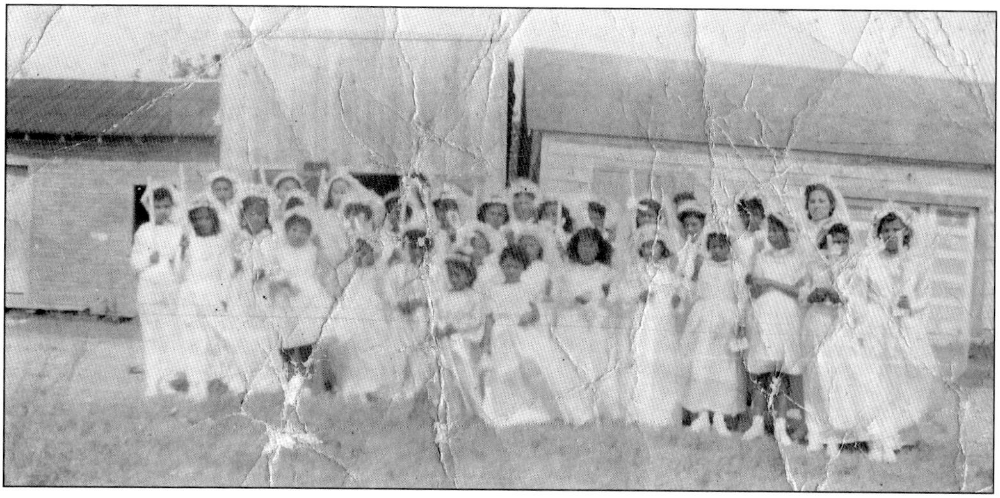

These two photographs show the everyday life of Rio Ricans, or Rio Rico residents. The photographs were taken between 1954 and 1955. The photograph above shows more than two dozen girls celebrating their first communion. The photograph below shows Olga Galvan (right) and Paula Yañes (left) on horseback; both girls were part of a Mexican Revolution parade on November 20 in Rio Rico. (Both, courtesy Olga Galvan.)

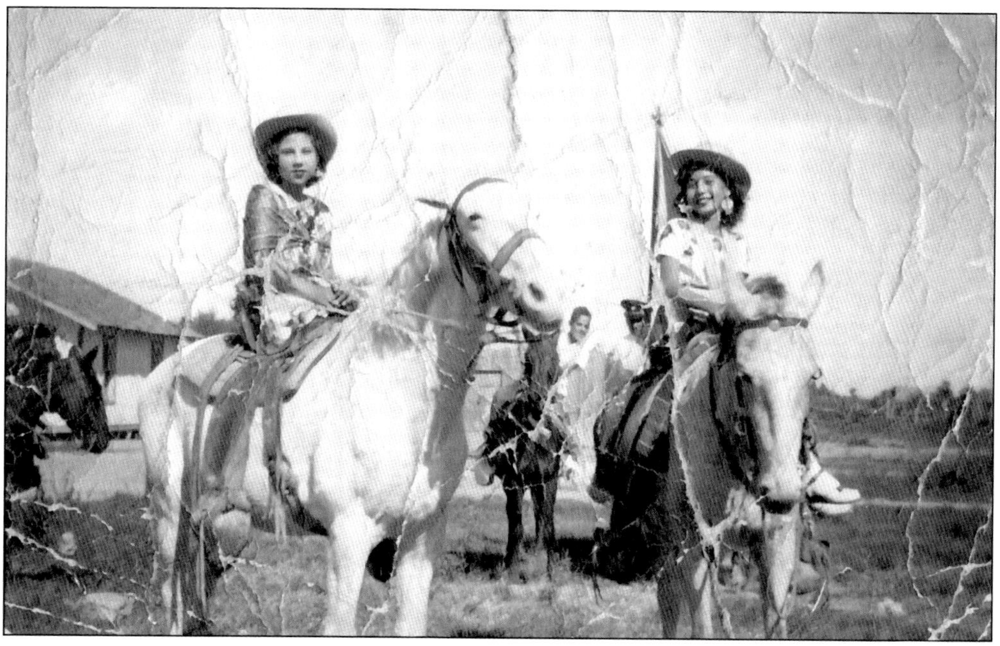

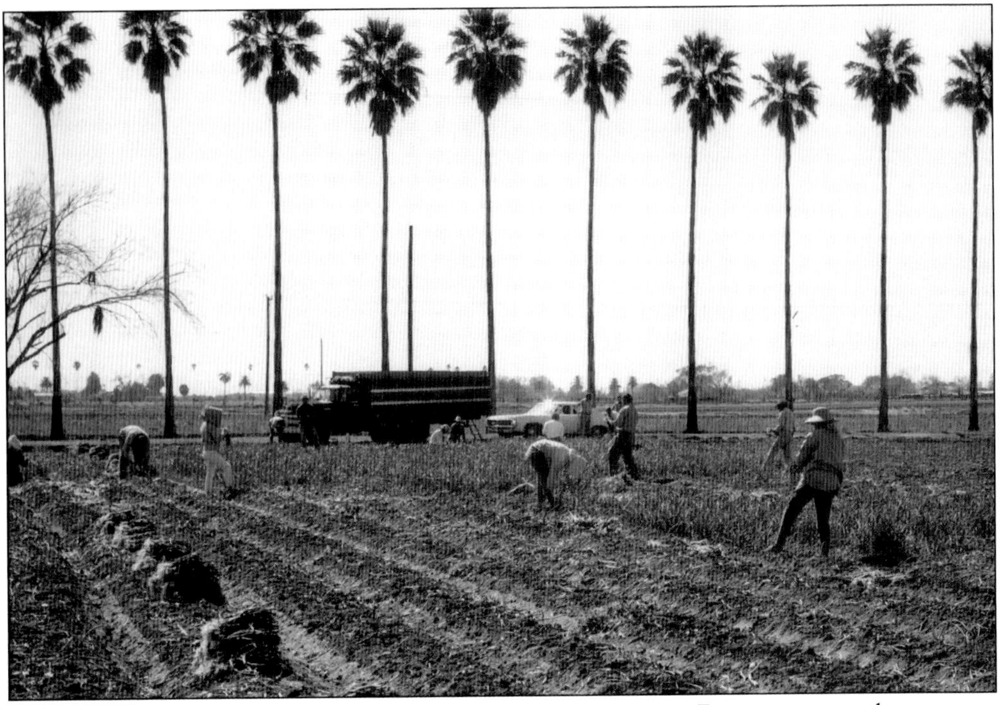

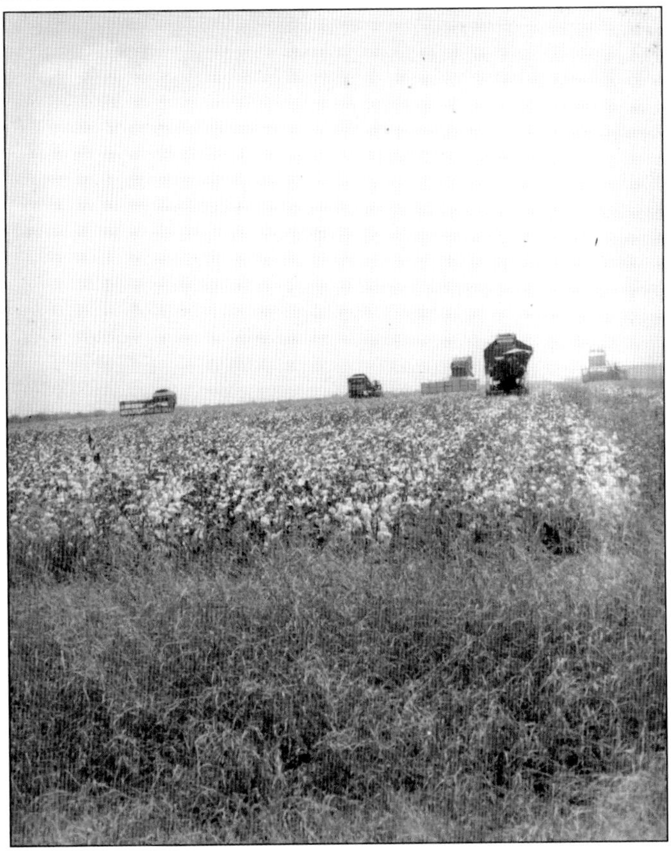

For many years, the agricultural industry flourished on both sides of the Rio Rico Bridge. The photograph above shows Nimitzio Garcia's farm in nearby Mercedes. The unidentified people in the image above are harvesting green onions. At the time, produce was taken by truck to the Weslaco depot and then to major markets in Texas. The photograph at left shows machinery used to pick cotton in the 1960s. During record years, more than 390,000 bales of cotton were harvested in the four-county area of the Rio Grande Valley. (Both, courtesy HCCID No. 9.)

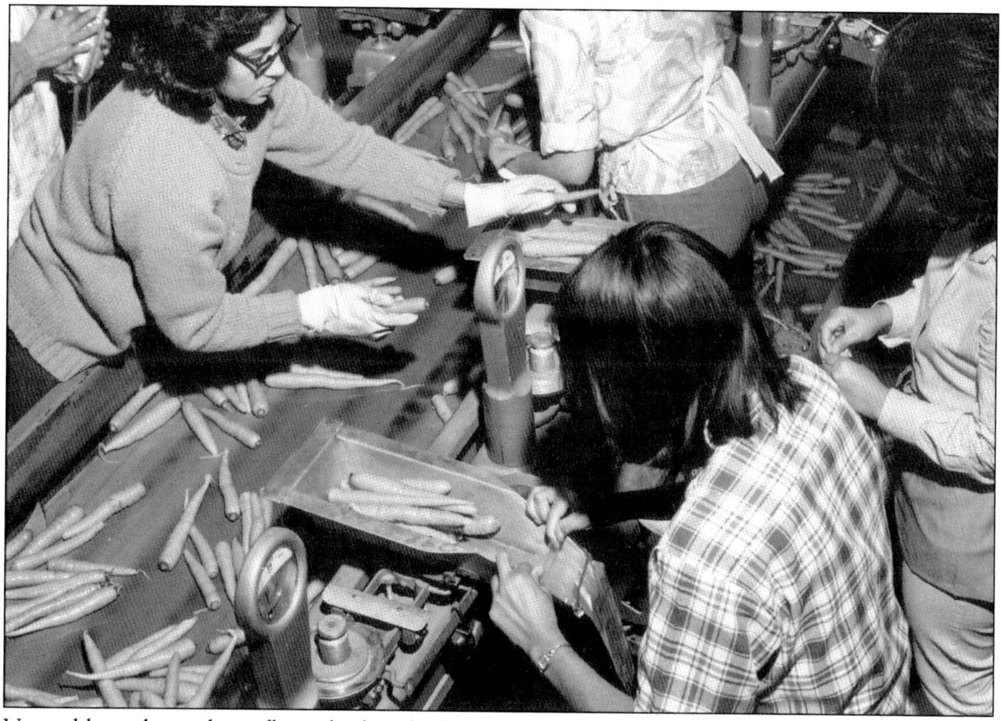

Vegetable packing plants flourished in the lower Rio Grande Valley, especially around towns that had train depots. This photograph shows women packing carrots inside a warehouse in Weslaco. (Courtesy HCCID No. 9.)

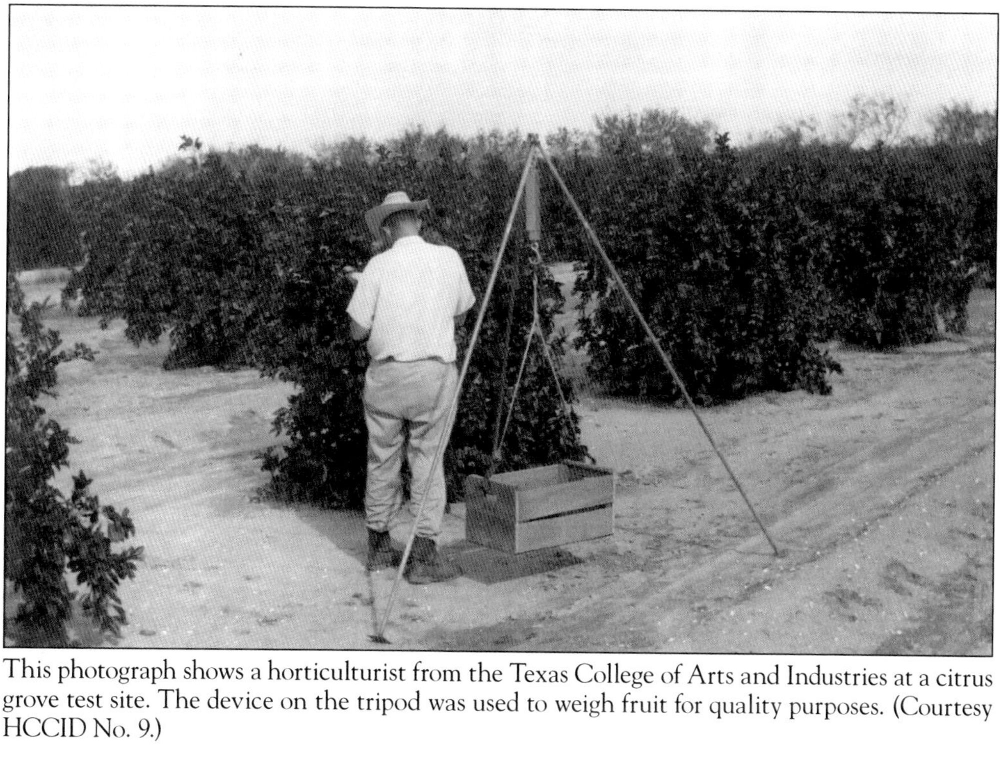

This photograph shows a horticulturist from the Texas College of Arts and Industries at a citrus grove test site. The device on the tripod was used to weigh fruit for quality purposes. (Courtesy HCCID No. 9.)

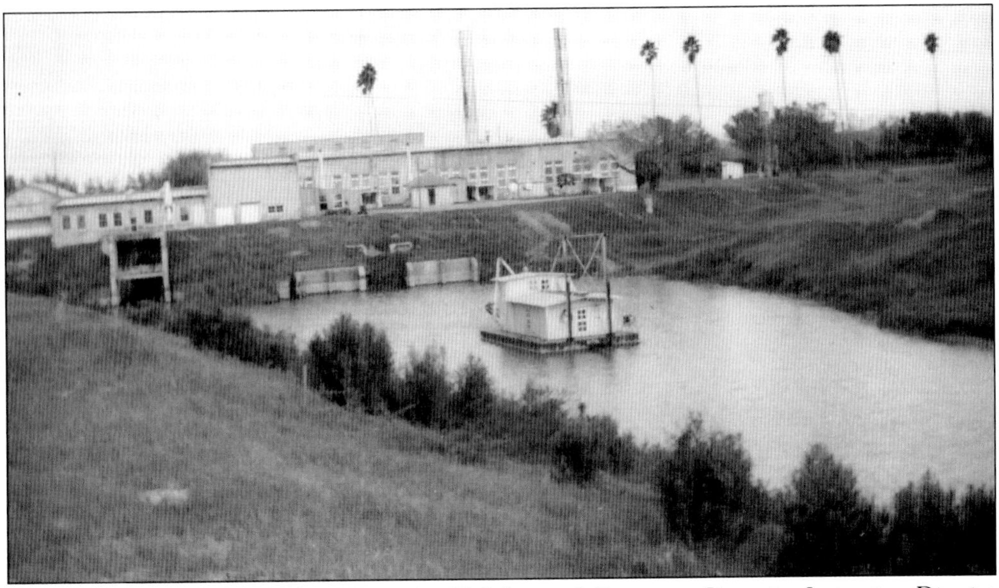

The irrigation system now known as the Hidalgo and Cameron Counties Irrigation District No. 9 was created in 1906. B. F. Yoakum led the formation of the American Rio Grande Land and Irrigation Company. The company knowingly changed the course of the Rio Grande and of the international boundary when it added a canal connecting two points of the river. Company records show that after the canal was created the company sent its attorneys to a U.S. court to plead guilty to tampering with an international boundary. The photograph above shows the pumping station that was established at Thayer, south of Mercedes. The photograph below shows pumps placed inside the building. (Both, courtesy HCCID No. 9.)

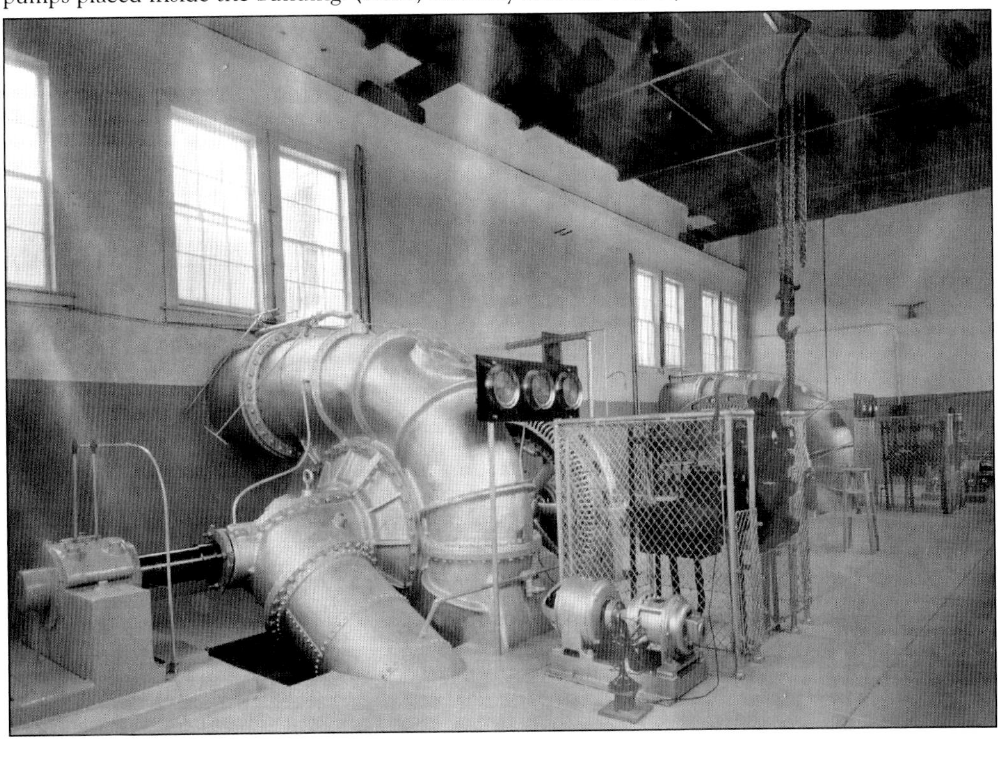

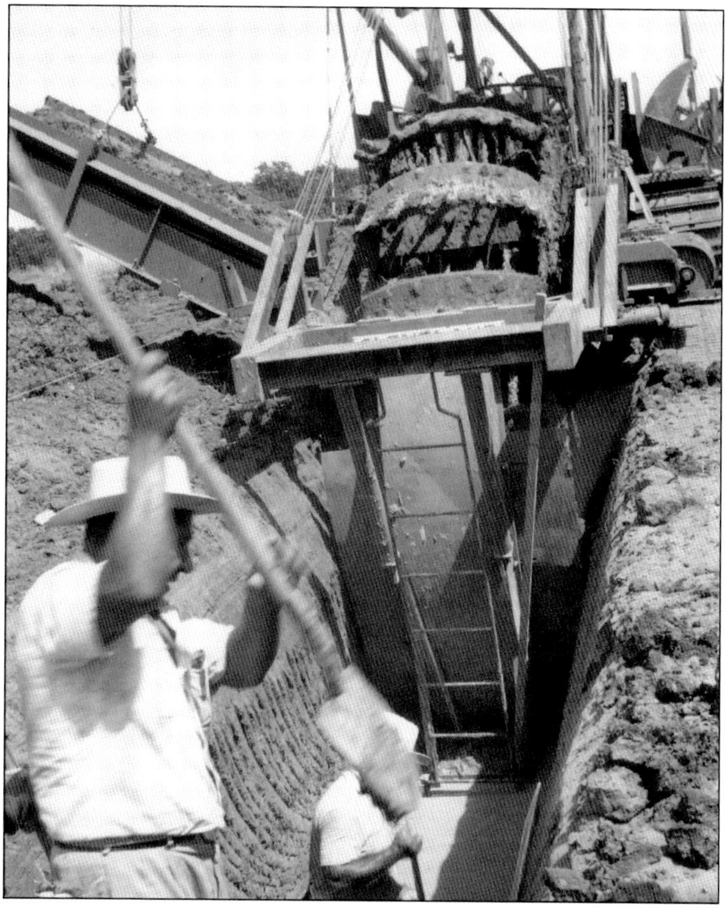

The machinery shown here was used by the Hidalgo and Cameron Counties Irrigation District No. 9 to make the trenches and the concrete pipes used to create gate wells in the 1960s. But the district started installing a series of irrigation pipelines as early as 1906. (Both, courtesy HCCID No. 9.)

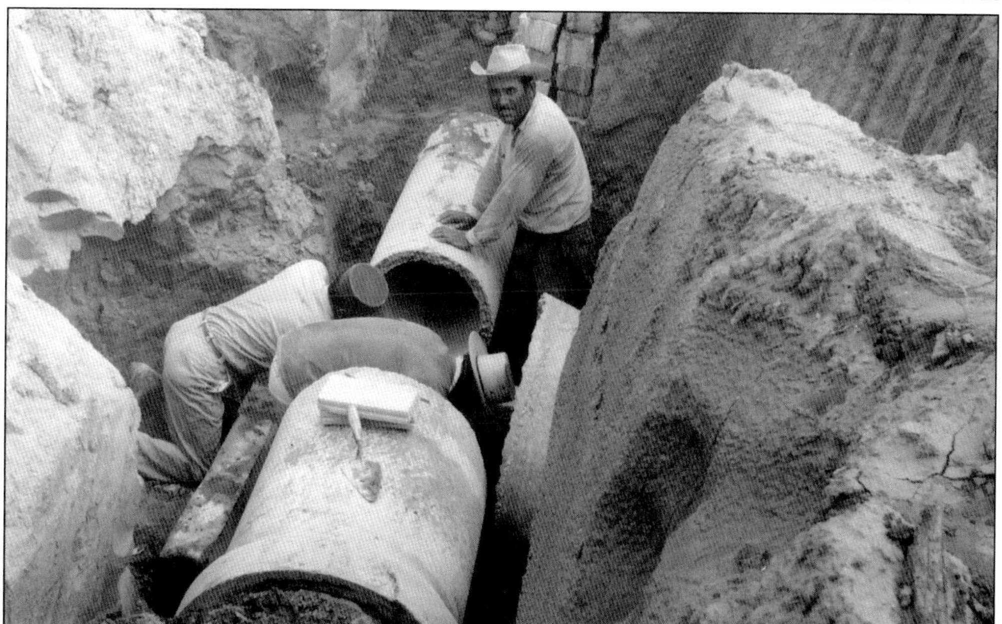

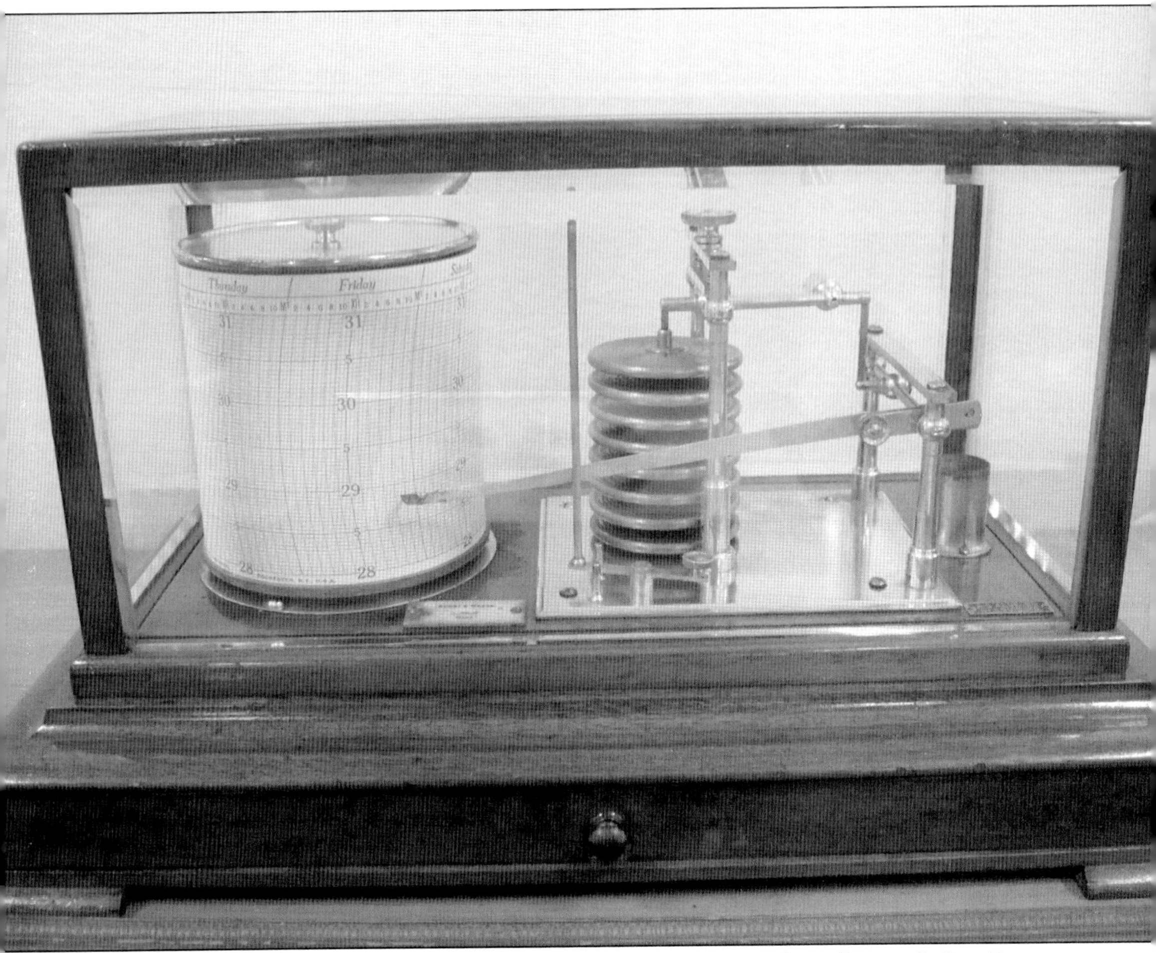

The devastating hurricane of 1933 ravaged through the Rio Grande Valley, including Progreso. The barometer in this photograph was used by the Hidalgo and Cameron Counties Irrigation District No. 9 to measure the strength of the storm. (Courtesy HCCID No. 9.)

The badges in this photograph were salvaged from the original offices of the American Rio Grande Land and Irrigation Company. Each number represented an employee; so at one point, the company had at least 222 employees. (Courtesy HCCID No. 9.)

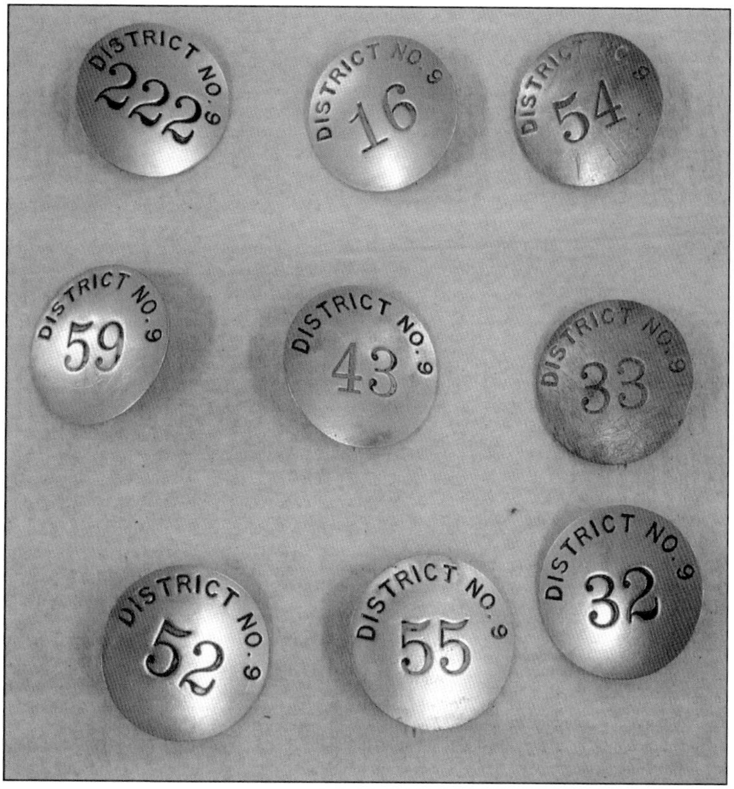


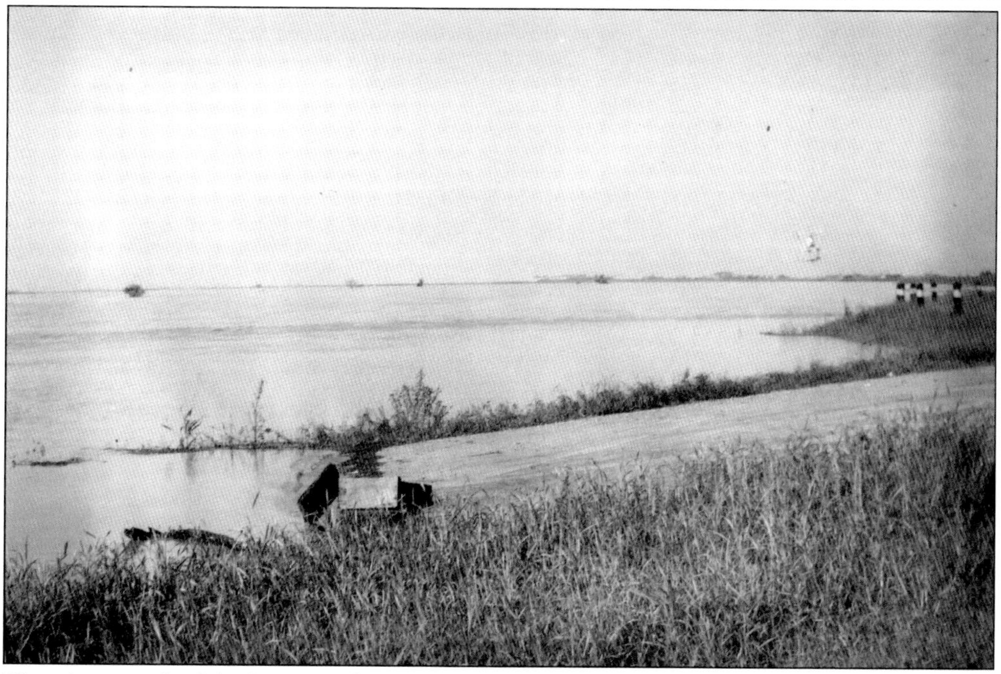

This photograph of the Rio Grande at Rio Rico shows the aftermath of Hurricane Beulah, which made landfall in 1967. The man in the aircraft in the upper right-hand corner is measuring the water levels at Arroyo Colorado and Base Line Road. (Courtesy HCCID No. 9.)

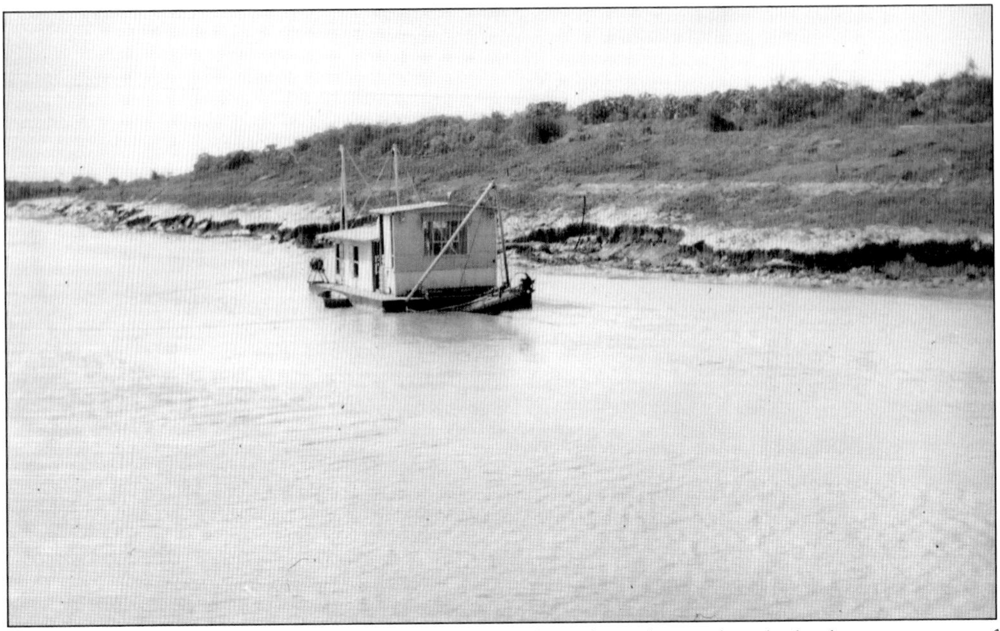

This 1966 photograph shows the dredge boats used to clear the mud and silt along a system of irrigation channels in the lower Rio Grande Valley. Hurricanes routinely fill the irrigation channels with debris and are considered especially destructive. (Courtesy HCCID No. 9.)

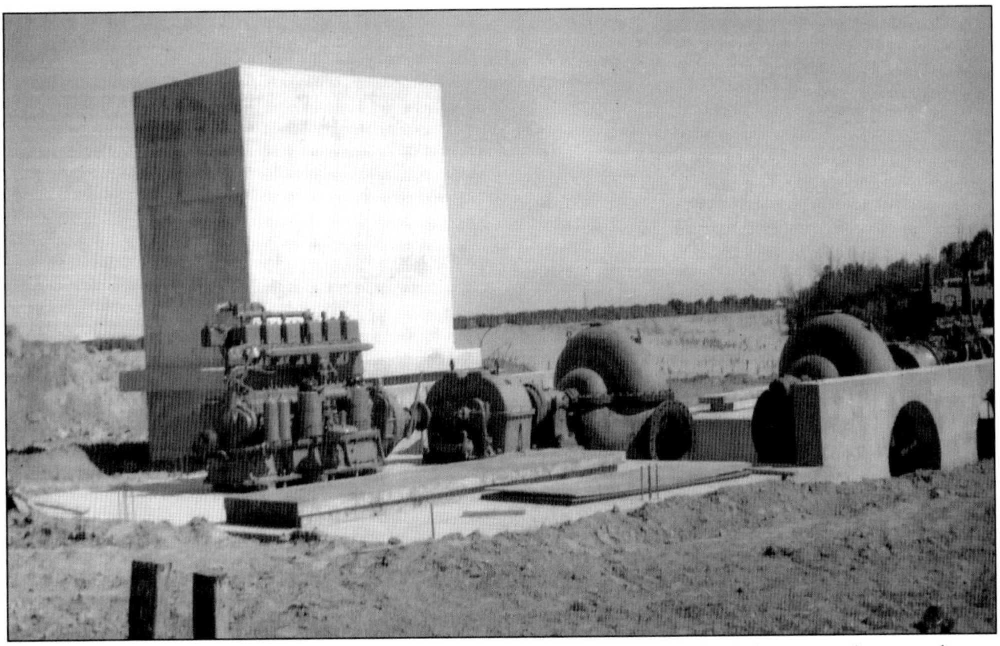

Irrigation systems and pumping plants were pivotal to the survival of the agriculture industry along the Rio Grande. This photograph shows the Donna pumping station, west of present-day Progreso. (Courtesy HCCID No. 9.)

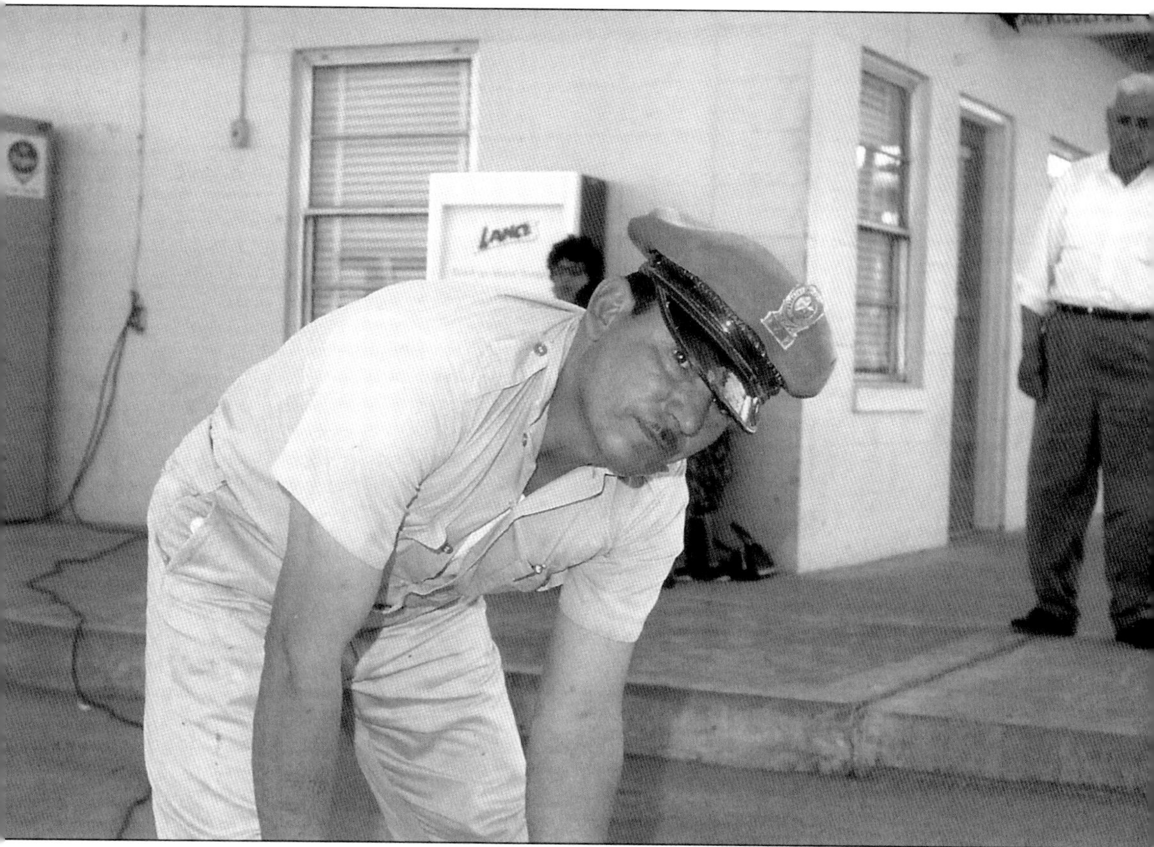

The Progreso and Rio Rico Bridges have been gateways into and out of the United States since 1928. Hardworking people like Rogelio Becerra have always been there to support the vision of the founding Cains, the family behind the first Progreso-Mexico Bridge. (Courtesy William C. Cain family.)

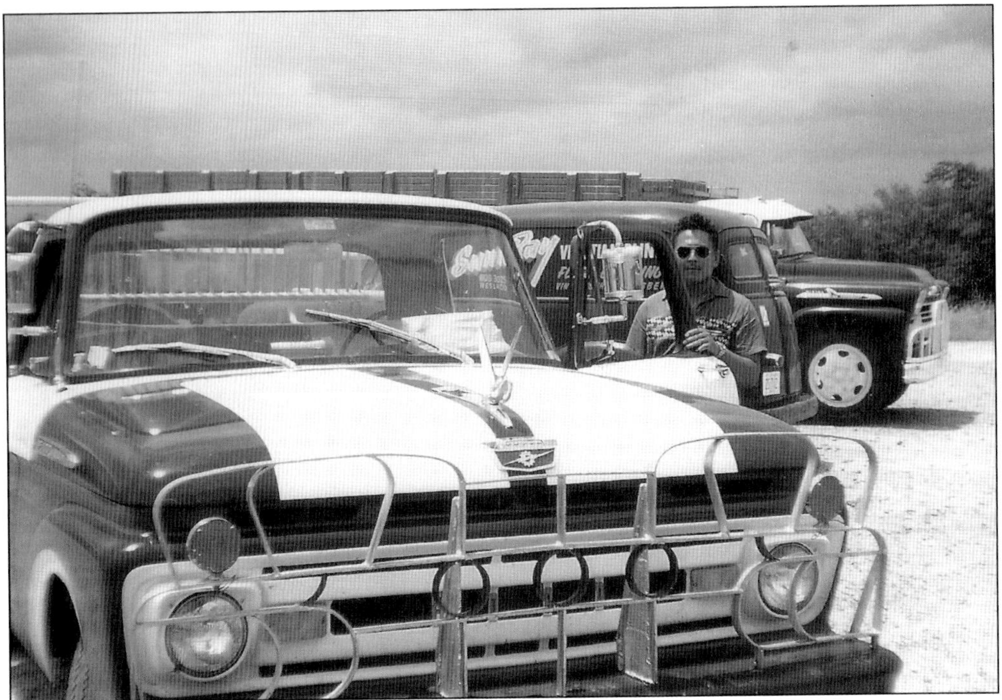

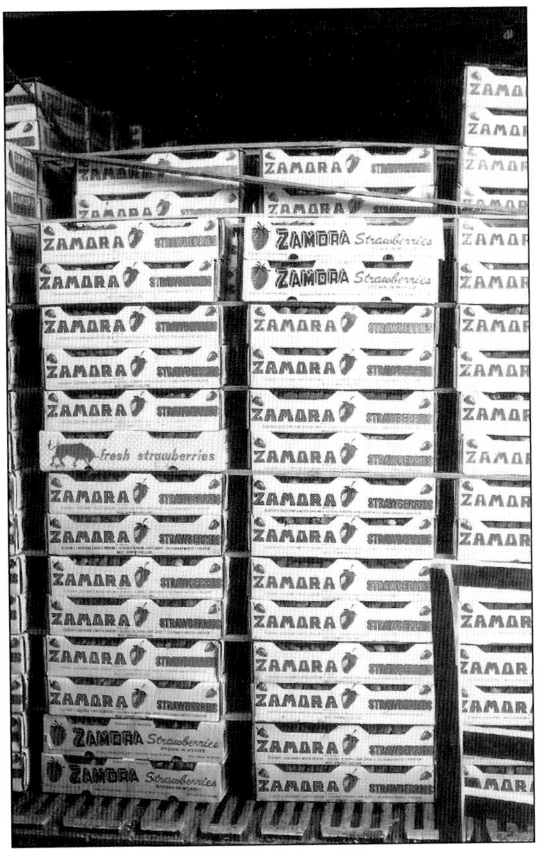


From produce to trinkets, the Progreso International Bridge has been a pipeline of goods on both sides of the border. These two photographs show both the trucks (above) and the products (left) that regularly cross to and from Mexico. (Both, courtesy William C. Cain family.)

*Five*

# The Mighty Red Ants

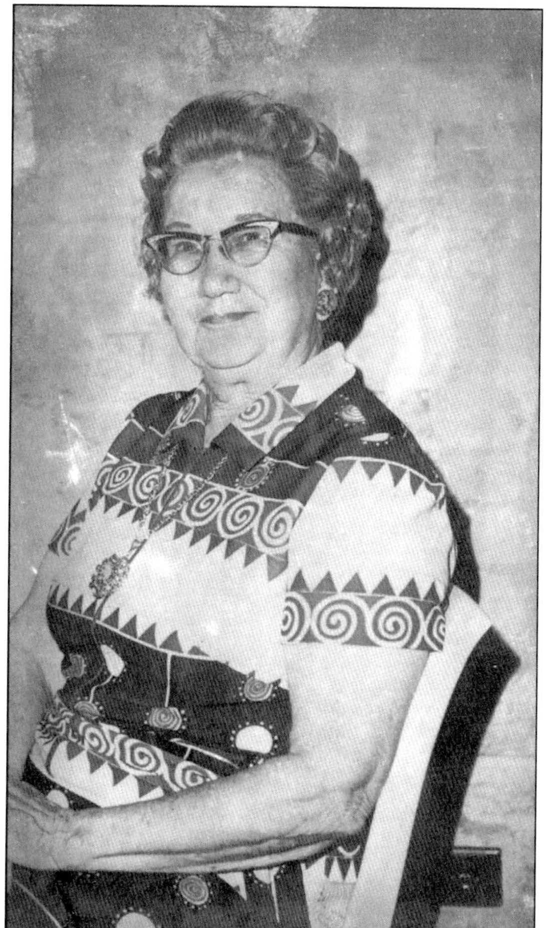

A leader and a visionary at heart, Dorothy Thompson was teacher, boys' and girls' coach, and superintendent at Progreso Schools for about 30 years. First she taught every subject at the Bonnie G. Kramer Elementary School and then at the Progreso School. While coaching the boys' softball team, she gave Progreso its mascot, the Mighty Red Ants. The trophy cases at Progreso High School are full of trophies earned by her teams. Before moving to Progreso, Thompson taught for three years in nearby Relampago and at a school in South Dakota. (Courtesy Soledad G. Rodriguez.)

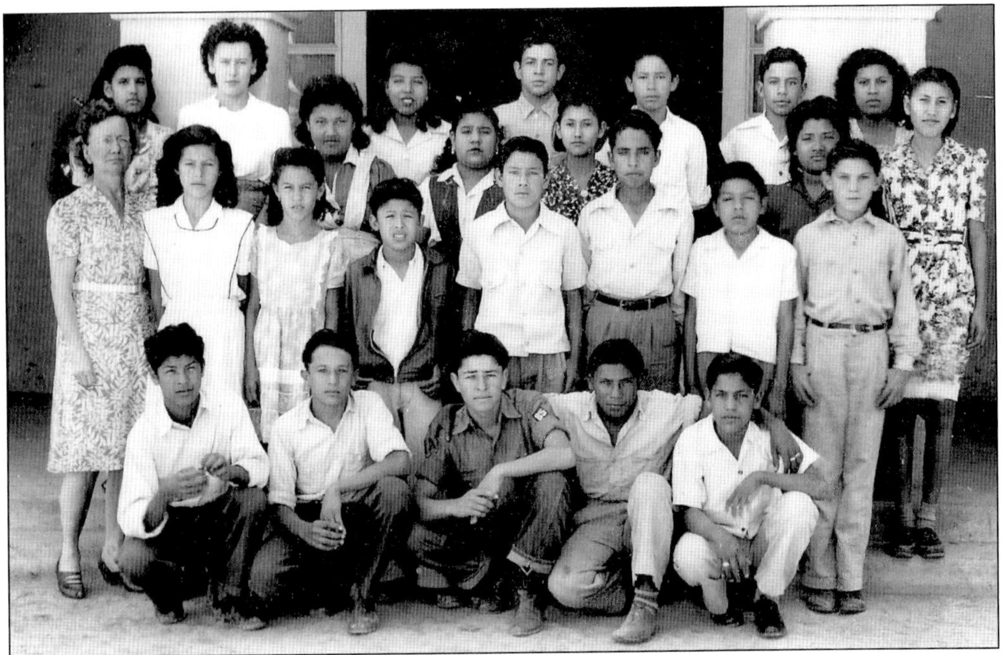

This 1946 class is outside the first school building in the village of Progreso. The wooden structure was located in an area called La Diez y Seis, Spanish for "The Sixteen," named after the 16 houses that were located on present-day Johnny Vela Street. The school was known as the Bonnie G. Kramer Elementary School, named after one of three schoolteachers. (Courtesy Soledad G. Rodriguez.)

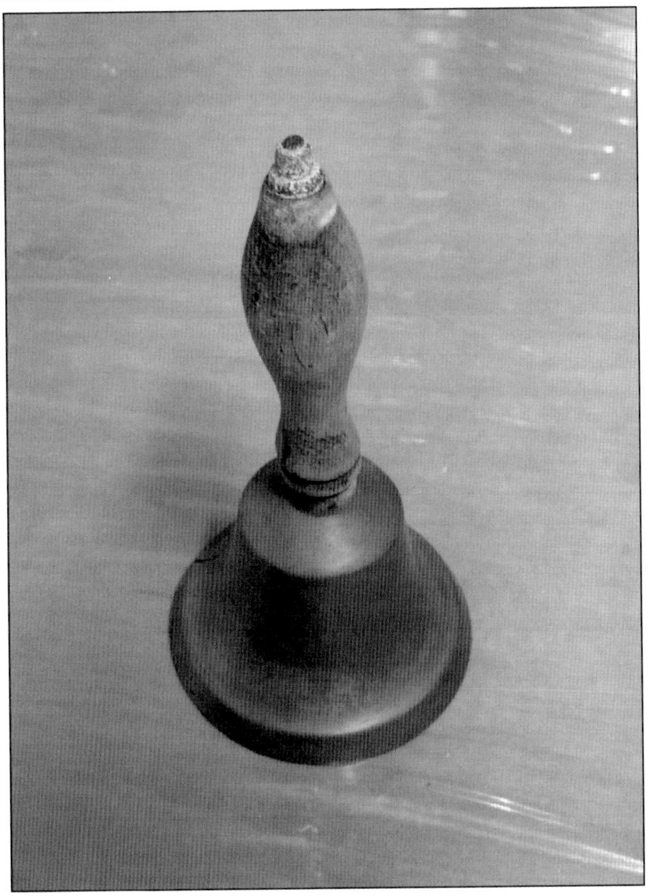

Dorothy Thompson stood by the door of the Bonnie G. Kramer Elementary School and rang this hand-held school bell for years. Before her death, Thompson gave the bell to Soledad Garza Rodriguez for safekeeping. (Courtesy Soledad G. Rodriguez.)

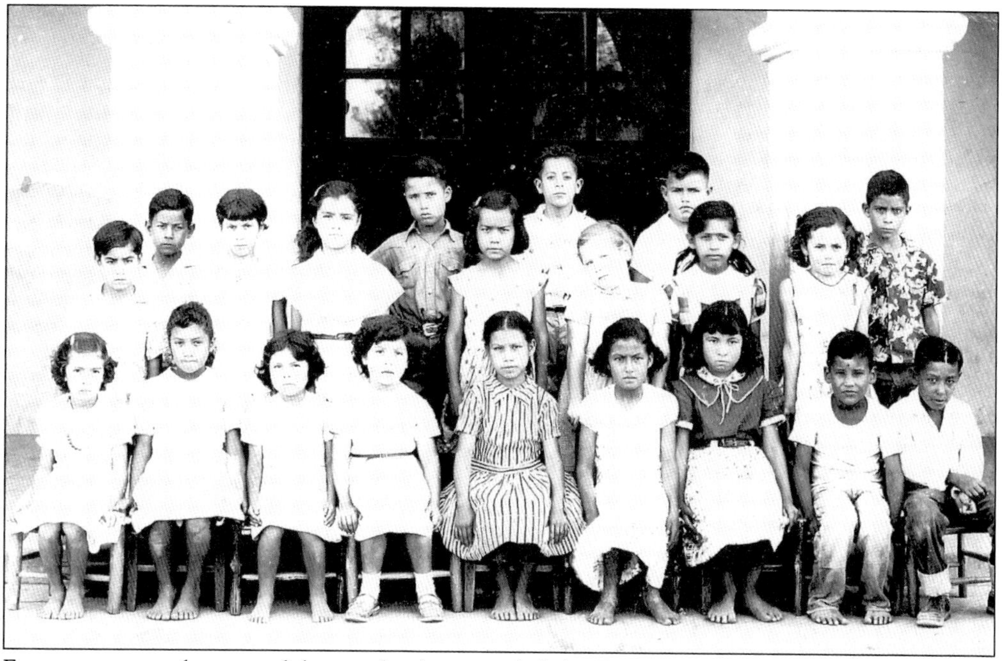

For many years, the ages of the pupils who attended the Bonnie G. Kramer Elementary School varied significantly because the school supported the education of students from kindergarten through eighth grade. (Courtesy Soledad G. Rodriguez.)

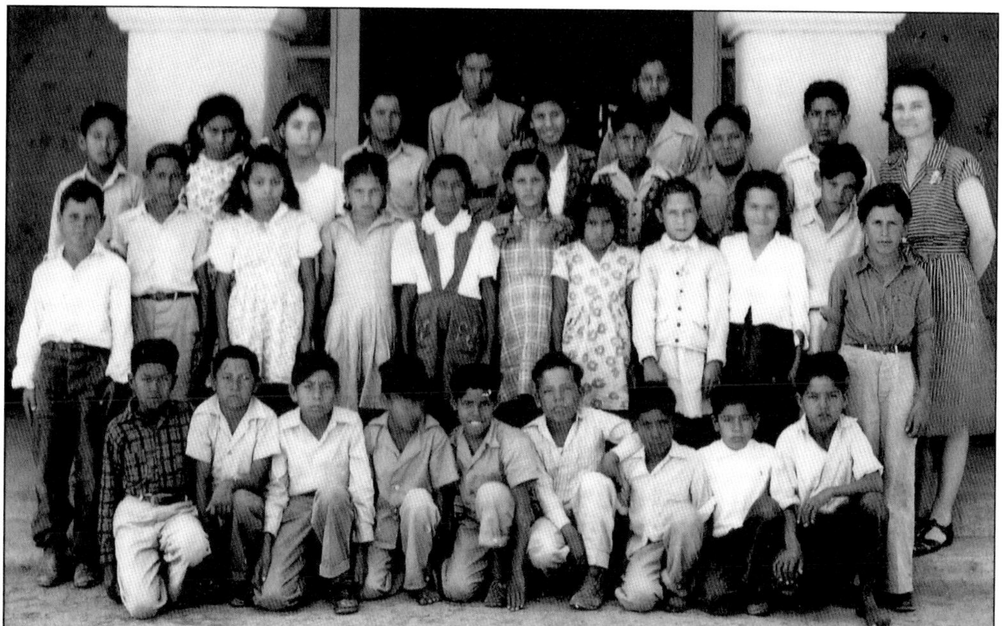

After completing the eighth grade at Progreso School, students attended high school in the nearby cities of Weslaco and Mercedes. This 1945 photograph shows the students of the Bonnie G. Kramer Elementary School with an unidentified teacher. (Courtesy Soledad G. Rodriguez.)

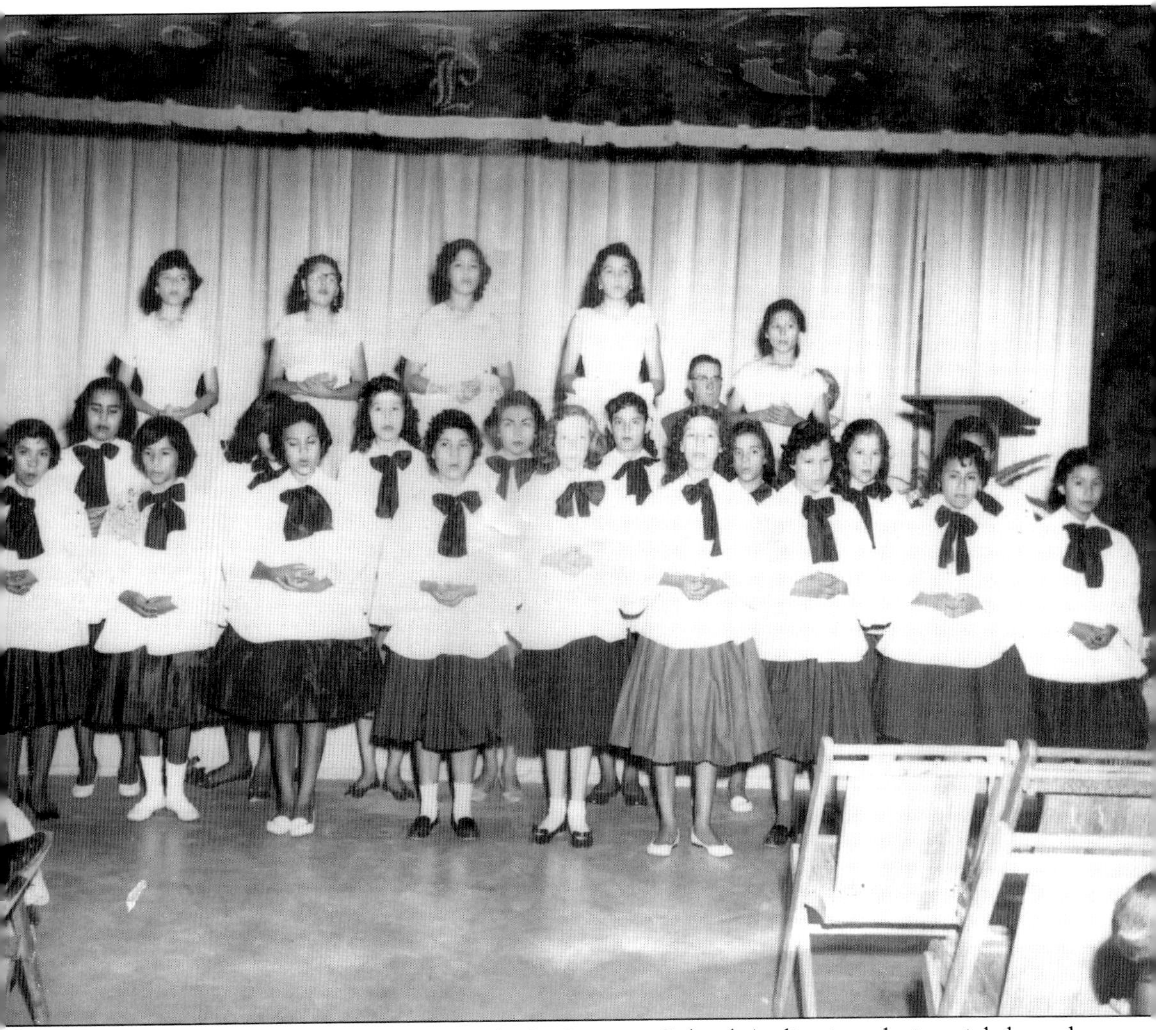

This 1959 photograph was taken inside the Progreso School Auditorium during eighth grade graduation. Students are, from left to right, (first row) Otilia Treviño, Catherine Treviño, Francis Salinas, Gloria Mena, June Meyers, Maria Gonzales, Rosa Mena, Rachel Cano, and Tomitia Ybarra; (second row) Otilia Garcia, unidentified, Olivia Gonzales, Julia Rodríguez, Maria Gonzales, Victoria Villarreal, Oralia Krummel, and unidentified; (third row) Gloria Champion, Herminia Casares, Matilde Salinas, Matilde Cavazos, and Alicia Marquez. (Courtesy Soledad G. Rodriguez.)

For the first few years of her job, Bonnie G. Kramer commuted to Progreso from the nearby city of Mercedes by horse and buggy. She was one of three teachers who founded the Progreso education system and eventually dedicated 28 years of her life to teaching its students. Later the school building was named Bonnie G. Kramer Elementary in her honor. (Courtesy Soledad G. Rodriguez.)

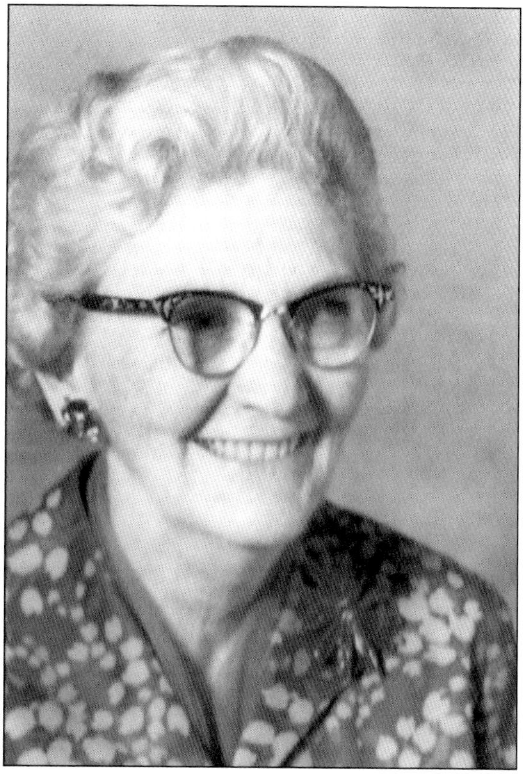

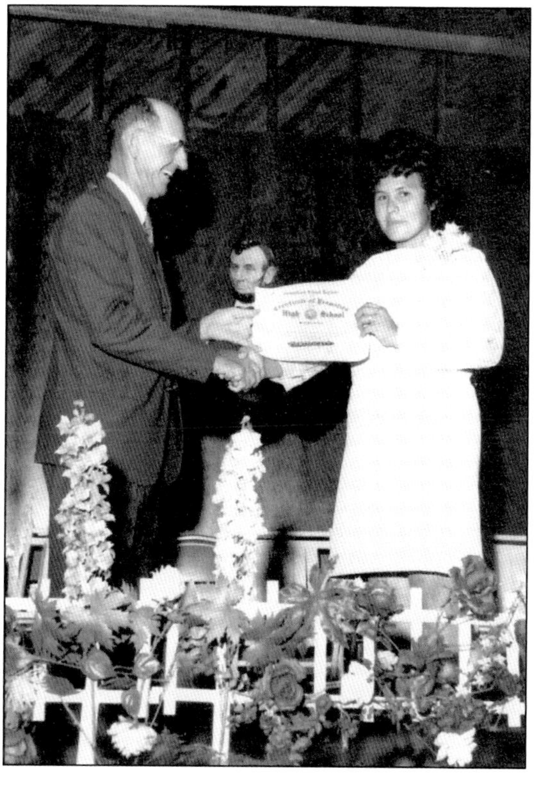

This 1967 photograph shows school board member E. B. Fuller presenting Molly Rodriguez with her eighth grade certificate of completion. After graduating from Progreso School, students attended high schools in the nearby cities of Weslaco and Mercedes. (Courtesy Soledad G. Rodriguez.)

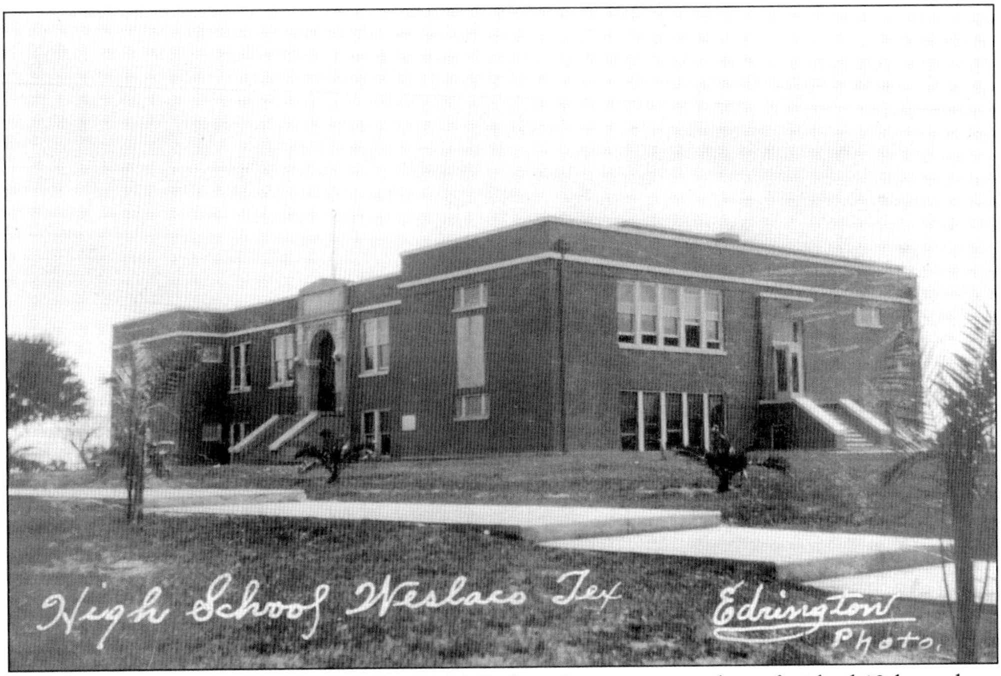


Progreso's first senior class graduated in 1986. Before then, many students finished 12th grade at nearby Weslaco High School. It is not clear when this photograph was taken, but it shows the original Weslaco school building, built in 1923. (Courtesy Weslaco Museum.)

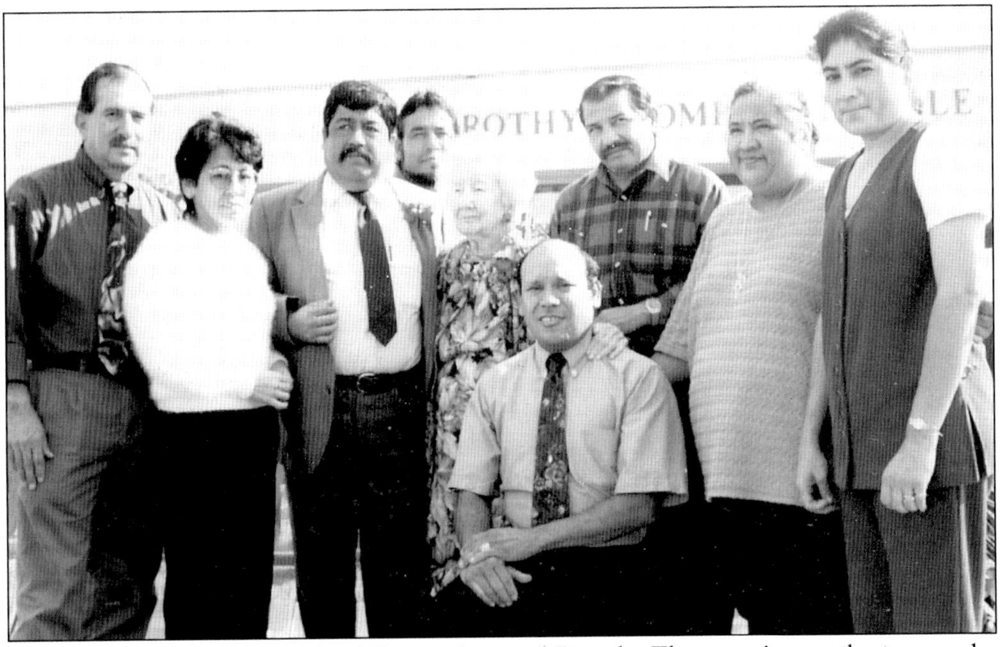

The Progreso Independent School District honored Dorothy Thompson's contributions to the Progreso education system when it named its middle school after her. Before teaching in Progreso for more than three decades, Thompson taught at schools in Relampago and in South Dakota. (Courtesy Martha E. Ramos.)

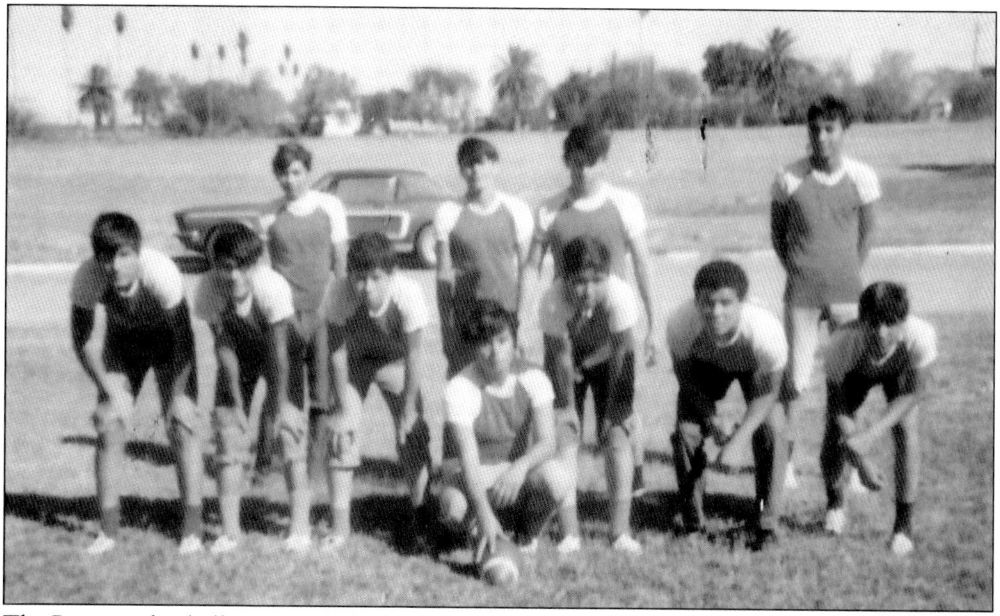

The Progreso football team took the district championship in 1975. This 1971 photograph shows some of the members of the winning team. The group's mascot, the Mighty Red Ants, was chosen by pioneer teacher and coach Dorothy Thompson during a softball game. (Courtesy Soledad G. Rodriguez.)

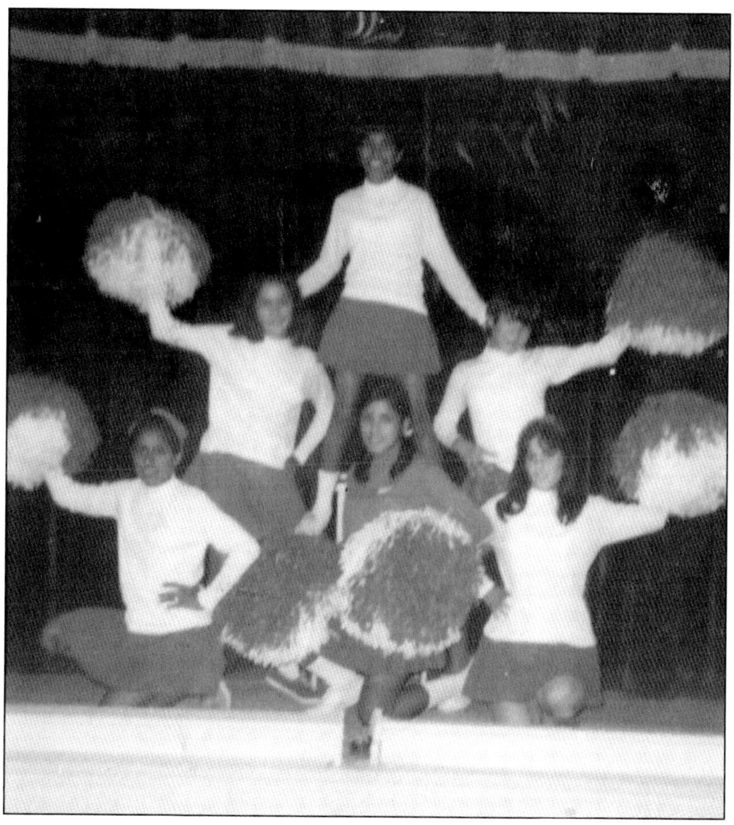

This 1969 or 1970 photograph shows six cheerleaders, five with pompoms, inside Progreso School. (Courtesy Soledad G. Rodriguez.)

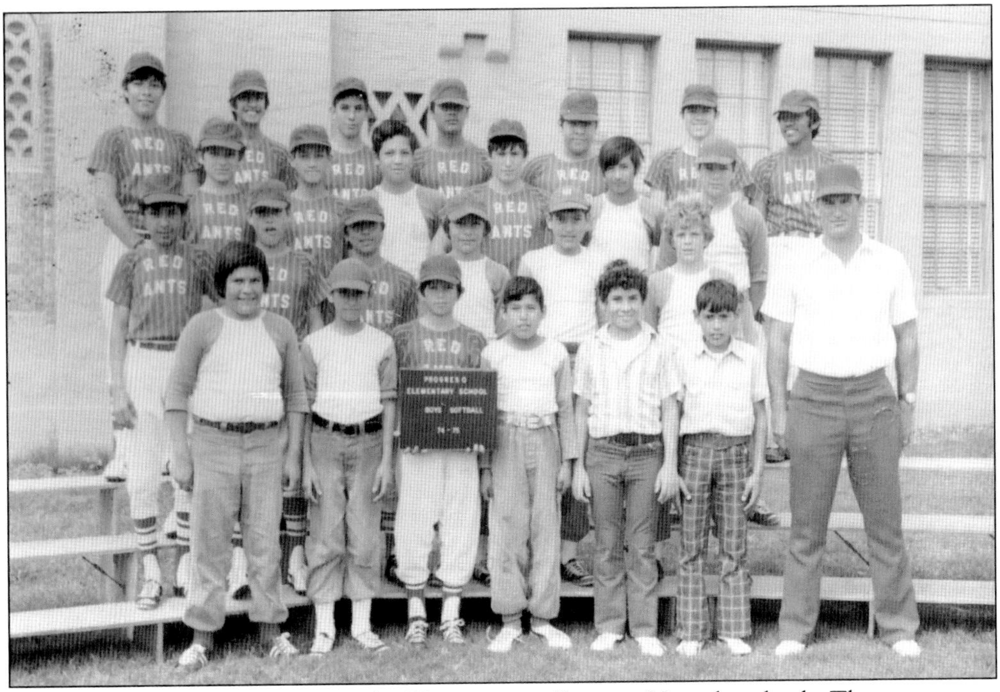


These images are part of the Dorothy Thompson collection. Upon her death, Thompson gave her collection of photographs to Soledad Garza Rodriguez for safekeeping. The photograph above shows the 1974–1975 boys softball team. The photograph below was taken in 1975 and includes members of the Lady Red Ants, the team that took the Softball Border League Championship in 1973. (Both, courtesy Soledad G. Rodriguez.)

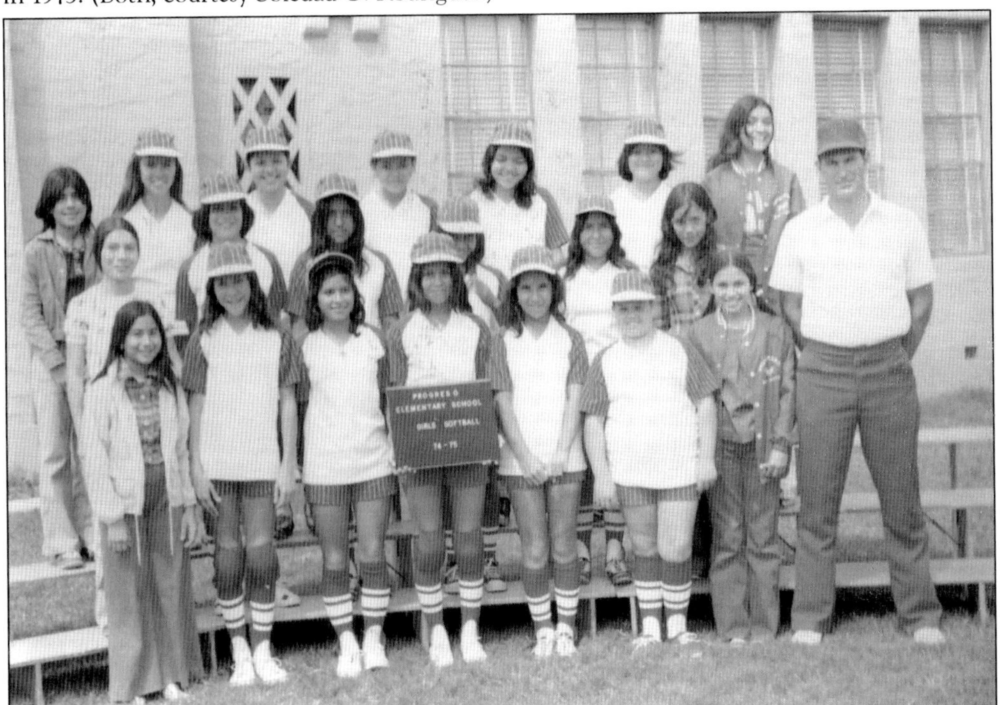

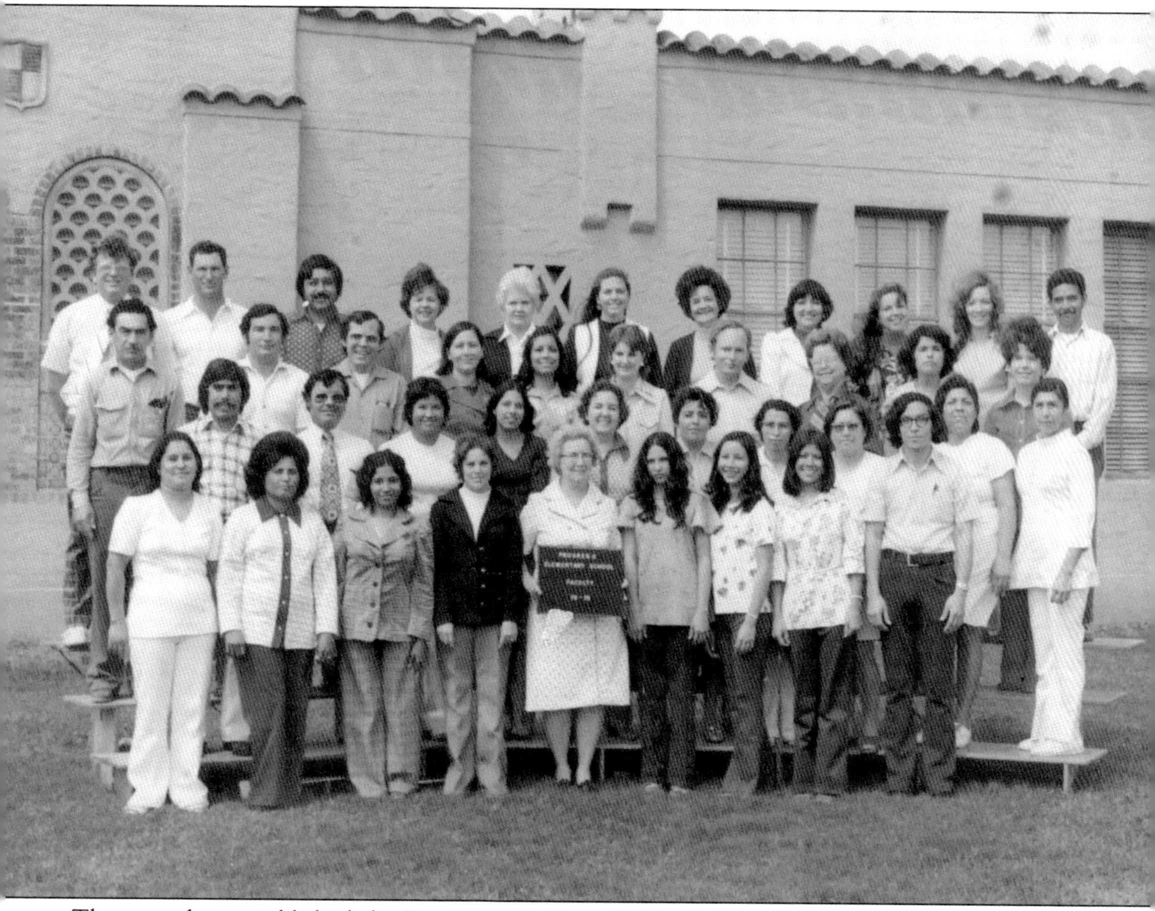

Three teachers established the Progreso school system in the late 1920s, but by the 1970s the number of staff was significantly larger. This photograph shows employees including teachers, cafeteria and office support staffs, and the superintendent. (Courtesy Soledad G. Rodriguez.)

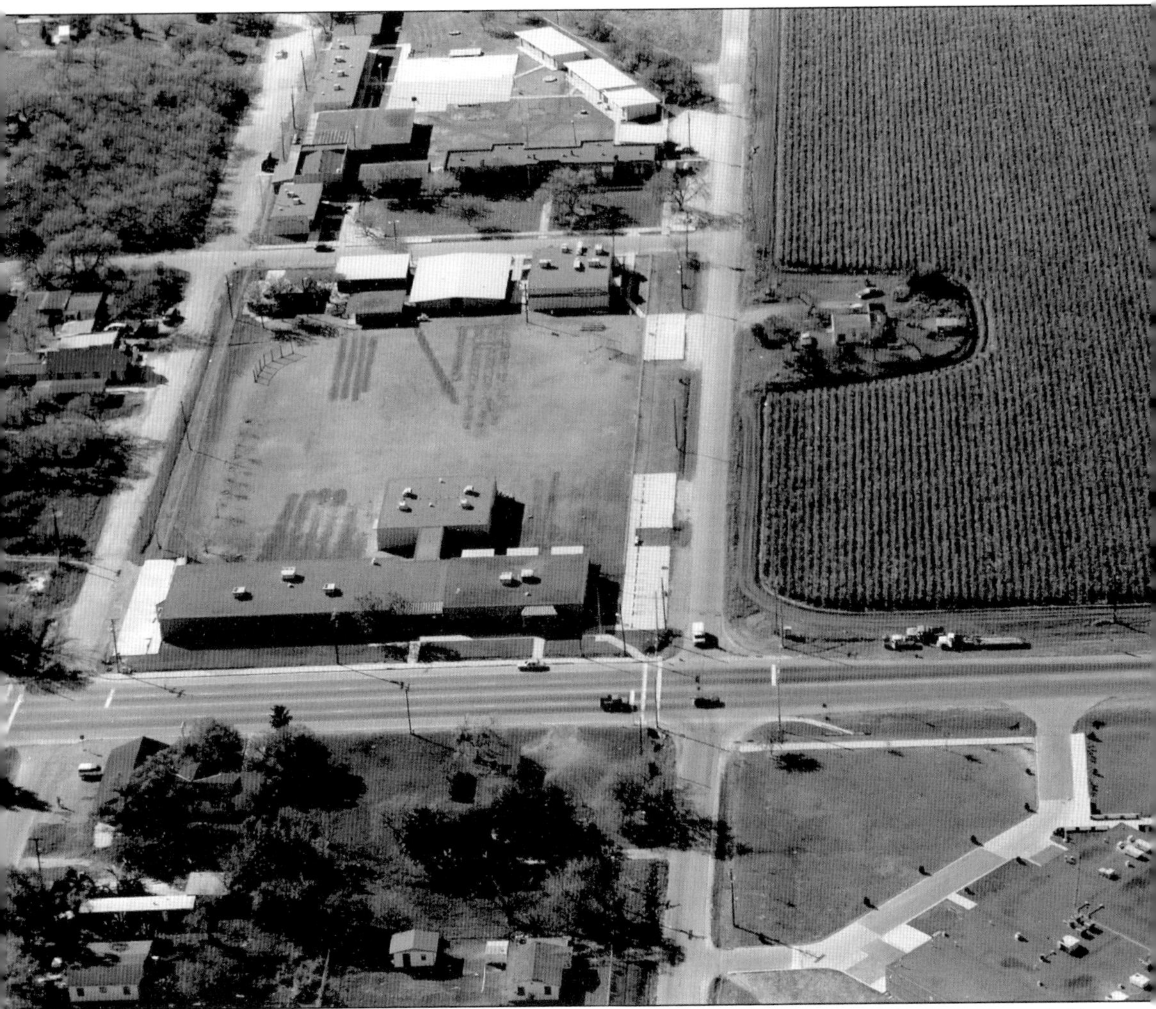

This 1989 aerial photograph shows Progreso High School (lower right corner), a sugarcane field (upper right corner), the original Progreso School building (top center), the original Progreso Middle School (center), and other outdoor classroom buildings. (Courtesy Soledad G. Rodriguez.)

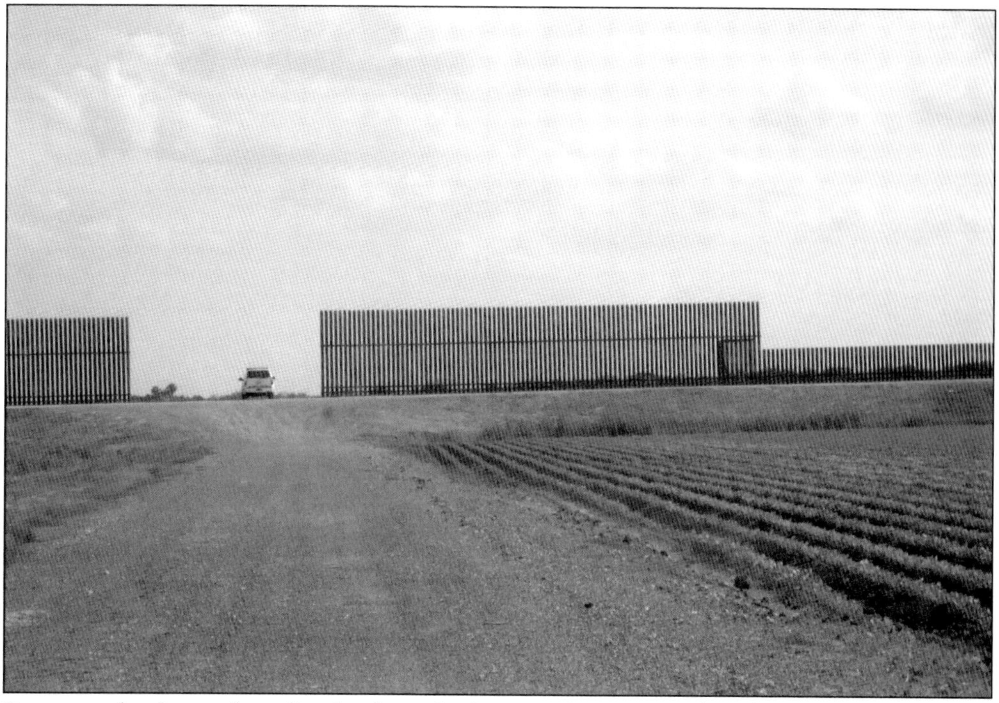

Progreso schools are about 2 miles from the Progreso International Bridge and the border that divides the United States and Mexico. For many years, the boundary between the two countries changed frequently, many times as a consequence of the shifting path of the Rio Grande. Today a wall guarded by the U.S. Border Patrol separates the two countries. This photograph was taken just east of the Progreso International Bridge. (Courtesy author's collection.)

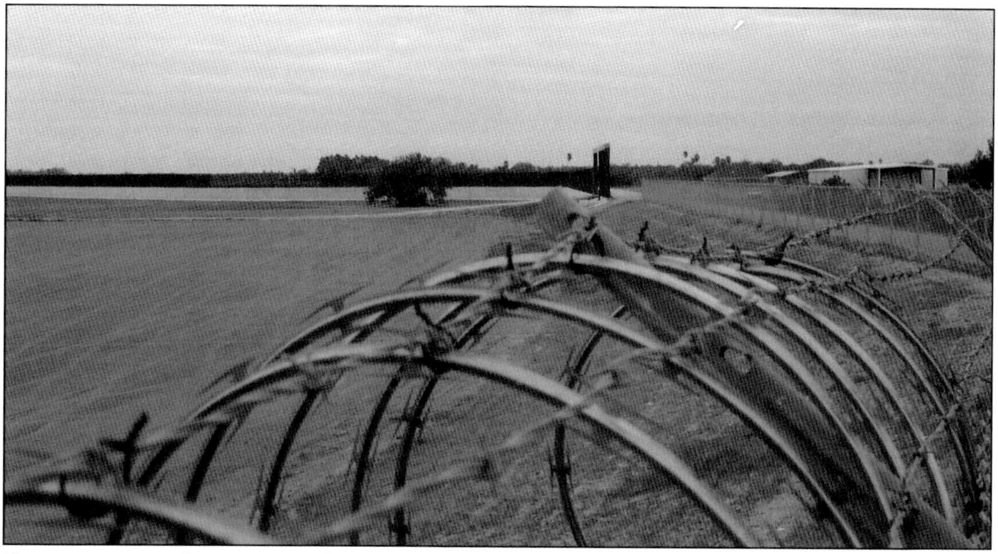

For many years, the Rio Grande was the only barrier between the United States and Mexico, but the Secure Fence Act of 2006 changed that. This law authorized 700 miles of fence between the two countries, including the area in modern-day Progreso. This photograph was taken west of the Progreso International Bridge, which is just south of Progreso schools. (Courtesy author's collection.)